Picasa for Seniors

Studio Visual Steps

Picasa
for Seniors

Get Acquainted with Picasa: Free, Easy-to-Use Photo Editing Software

www.visualsteps.com

This book has been written using the Visual Steps™ method.
Cover design by Studio Willemien Haagsma bNO

© 2011 Visual Steps
Edited by Jolanda Ligthart, Mara Kok and Rilana Groot
Translated by Chris Hollingsworth, *1ˢᵗ Resources* and Irene Venditti, *i-write* translation services.
Editor in chief: Ria Beentjes

Third printing: February 2011
ISBN 978 90 5905 246 8

Do you have questions or suggestions?
E-mail: info@visualsteps.com

Would you like more information?
www.visualsteps.com

Website for this book:
www.visualsteps.com/picasa
Here you can register your book.

Register your book
We will keep you aware of any important changes that are necessary to you as a user of the book. You can also take advantage of our periodic newsletter informing you of our product releases, company news, tips & tricks, special offers, free guides, etcetera.

Table of Contents

Foreword

Dear readers,

Picasa is a remarkable and free software application for organizing and editing your digital photo collection. You can add tags to your photos, such as the names of people or places to help you find them more easily later on. You can also create albums, and play slide shows.

Furthermore, the program offers you a variety of options for basic photo editing. You can fine tune your photos manually by applying special effects or use the terrific *One-click* fix that *Picasa* provides to correct your photos automatically. For instance, you can alter or enhance colors or correct red eyes that may occur when using the flash, with just one mouse click.

In *Picasa* it is very easy to share your pictures with others. Not only can you print your photos, but you can easily burn the photos to CD or DVD. And you can use the program to create a web album and publish your photos to your blog.

In this book you will learn all the basic functions of the *Picasa* program by reading the step-by-step instructions and looking at the practice photos. It is recommended to create a new *Windows* user account before you start using this book. While you are practicing with *Picasa*, you will use the practice photos, so your own photo collection remains untouched. Afterwards you can use your knowledge to start working with your own photos.

At the end of this book you will find a separate chapter, which contains an action plan for importing and enhancing your own photo collection in *Picasa*.

Have lots of fun with this book!

Henk Mol

P.S.
Feel free to send us your questions and suggestions.
The e-mail address is: info@visualsteps.com

Visual Steps Newsletter

All Visual Steps books follow the same methodology. Clear and concise step-by-step instructions with screen shots to demonstrate each task.
A complete list of all our books can be found on our website **www.visualsteps.com**
You can also sign up to receive our **free Visual Steps Newsletter**.

In this Newsletter you will receive periodic information by e-mail regarding:
- the latest titles and previously released books;
- special offers, supplemental chapters, tips and free informative booklets.

Also, our Newsletter subscribers may download any of the documents listed on the web pages **www.visualsteps.com/info_downloads** and **www.visualsteps.com/tips**

When you subscribe to our Newsletter you can be assured that we will never use your e-mail address for any purpose other than sending you the information as previously described. We will not share this address with any third-party. Each Newsletter also contains a one-click link to unsubscribe.

Introduction to Visual Steps™

The Visual Steps handbooks and manuals are the best instructional materials available for learning how to work with computers and computer programs. Nowhere else you will find better support for getting to know the computer, the Internet, *Windows* or related software.

Properties of the Visual Steps books:
- **Comprehensible contents**
  Addresses the needs of the beginner or intermediate computer user for a manual written in simple, straight-forward English.
- **Clear structure**
  Precise, easy to follow instructions. The material is broken down into small enough segments to allow for easy absorption.
- **Screen shots of every step**
  Quickly compare what you see on your own computer screen with the screen shots in the book. Pointers and tips guide you when new windows are opened so you always know what to do next.
- **Get started right away**
  All you have to do is switch on your computer, place the book next to your keyboard, and begin at once.

In short, I believe these manuals will be excellent guides for you.

dr. H. van der Meij
Faculty of Applied Education, Department of Instruction Technology, University of Twente, the Netherlands

What You Will Need

In order to work through this book, you will need a number of things on your computer:

The most important requirement for using this book is that you have the English version of the *Picasa 3* program installed on your computer. The program undergoes frequent changes. If you notice something different on your computer screen, be sure to check the news page from the website by this book to see if any recent articles have been posted:
www.visualsteps.com/picasa
If you do not have this program installed yet, see *Chapter 1 Installing Picasa*. There you can read about the system requirements and how to install *Picasa*.

Apart from that, your computer should run the English version of **Windows 7**, **Windows Vista** (including *Service Pack 1*), or **Windows XP** (including *Service Pack 3*).

The screen shots in this book have been made on a *Windows 7* computer. For using the exercises in this book it does not make any difference whether your computer runs *Windows 7*, *Windows Vista* or *Windows XP*. Any possible differences between the *Windows* editions will be clearly indicated in the text.

In order to download *Picasa* you will need an active Internet connection.

You will need a printer for printing the photos. If you do not have a printer, you can skip the printing exercises.

You do not really need to have all the other equipment, such as a digital photo camera or a scanner.
In this book you will learn how to use the program by watching the practice photos. You can download these practice photos from the website that goes with this book. In *section 1.2 Downloading Practice Files* you can read how to do that.

How to Use This Book

This book has been written using the Visual Steps™ method. You can work through this book independently at your own pace.

In this Visual Steps™ book, you will see various icons. This is what they mean:

Techniques
These icons indicate an action to be carried out:

 The mouse icon means you should do something with the mouse.

 The keyboard icon means you should type something on the keyboard.

 The hand icon means you should do something else, for example insert a CD-ROM in the computer. It is also used to remind you of something you have learned before.

In addition to these icons, in some areas of this book extra assistance is provided to help you successfully work through each chapter.

Help
These icons indicate that extra help is available:

 The arrow icon warns you about something.

 The bandage icon will help you if something has gone wrong.

 Have you forgotten how to do something? The number next to the footsteps tells you where to look it up at the end of the book in the appendix *How Do I Do That Again?*

In separate boxes you will find tips or additional, background information.

Extra information
Information boxes are denoted by these icons:

 The book icon gives you extra background information that you can read at your convenience. This extra information is not necessary for working through the book.

 The light bulb icon indicates an extra tip for using the program.

Prior Computer Experience

If you want to use this book, you will need some basic computer skills. If you do not have these skills, it is a good idea to read one of the following books first:

 **Windows 7 for SENIORS**
Studio Visual Steps
ISBN 978 90 5905 126 3

 **Windows Vista for SENIORS**
Studio Visual Steps
ISBN 978 90 5905 274 1

 **Windows XP for SENIORS**
Addo Stuur
ISBN 978 90 5905 044 0

Website

On the website that accompanies this book, **www.visualsteps.com/picasa**, you will find practice files and more information about the book. This website will also keep you informed of any errata, recent updates or other changes you need to be aware of, as a user of the book.
Please, also take a look at our website **www.visualsteps.com** from time to time to read about new books and other handy information such as informative tips and booklets.

The Screen Shots

The screen shots in this book were made on a computer running *Windows 7 Ultimate*. The screen shots used in this book indicate which button, folder, file or hyperlink you need to click on your computer screen. In the instruction text (in **bold** letters) you will see a small image of the item you need to click. The black line will point you to the right place on your screen.

The small screen shots that are printed in this book are not meant to be completely legible all the time. This is not necessary, as you will see these images on your own computer screen in real size and fully legible.

Here you see an example of an instruction text and a screen shot. The black line indicates where to find this item on your own computer screen:

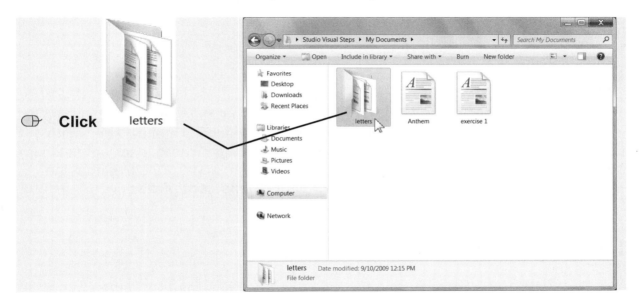

Sometimes the screen shot shows only a portion of a window. Here is an example:

It really will **not be necessary** for you to read all the information in the screen shots in this book. Always use the screen shots in combination with the image you see on your own computer screen.

Test Your Knowledge

Have you finished reading this book? Then test your knowledge with the *Picasa* test.
Visit the website: **www.ccforseniors.com**

This multiple-choice test will tell you how good
your knowledge of *Picasa* is. If you pass the test,
you will receive your *free Computer Certificate* by
e-mail.

For Teachers

This book is designed as a self-study guide. It is also well suited for use in a group or
a classroom setting. For this purpose, we offer a free teacher's manual containing
information about how to prepare for the course (including didactic teaching methods)
and testing materials. You can download this teacher's manual (PDF file) from the
website which accompanies this book: **www.visualsteps.com/picasa**

Register Your Book

You can register your book. We will keep you informed of any important changes that
you need to know of, as a user of the book. You can also take advantage of our
periodic Newsletter informing you of our product releases, company news, tips &
tricks, special offers, etcetera.

1. Installing Picasa

In recent years, *Picasa*, the free software application from *Google* for organizing and editing digital photos, has become enormously popular. Not only is the software free to download, it offers many numerous features, has an easy-to-use interface and is safe to use. You never need to worry about losing an original photo when using the editing tools because *Picasa* always leaves your original files in tact.

In this book you will learn step-by-step all of the basic operations for managing, editing and sharing your digital photos. First, you will learn how to install the program and the practice files.

In this chapter you will learn:

- about the system requirements for *Picasa*;
- how to download the practice files;
- how to download and install *Picasa*.

 Please note:

In order to download the program and the practice files, you will need an active Internet connection.

 Please note:

Download the files in the same order as is described in this chapter. First, you need to download the practice files. Afterwards you can install the program.

1.1 Preparation

If you want to install *Picasa*, you will need an Internet connection. The system requirements for running *Picasa* are as follows:

- A computer with a 300 MHz Pentium-processor and MMX-technology;
- At least 256 MB free internal (RAM) memory;
- 100 MB free disk space on your hard disk drive (recommended);
- A screen resolution of at least 800 x 600 pixels and 16-bits colors;
- *Windows XP*, *Windows Vista* or *Windows 7* operating system;
- *Microsoft Internet Explorer 6.0* or higher;
- *Microsoft DirectX 8.1* or higher;
- Optional: an Internet connection with a speed of 56K (or higher) is needed to access online services.

 Tip

New user account
After *Picasa* has been installed, the program will automatically search for all the images of the current user. Your computer may contain thousands of photos and other images, so this may take a while. This is why we have decided to create a new user account for the purpose of this book. We recommend that you create a new user account while you work through this book. This means your account will only contain the sample pictures and you will see the same windows as in the book. As soon as you open *Picasa* from your regular user account, the program will automatically add all your own pictures. In *Appendix D Creating a New User Account*, at the end of this book, you will find a step-by-step explanation of how to create a new user account.

☞ **Create a new user account and log in to this account while working through this book**

1.2 Downloading Practice Files

If you want to use the exercises in this book, you will need to download the practice files first. Here is how to do that:

☞ **Open** *Internet Explorer* ¹

☞ **Open the www.visualsteps.com/picasa web page** 🦶²

Now you will see the relevant website for this book. On the *Practice files* page you can download the practice files:

On the left-hand side of the window:

⊕ **Click** Practice files

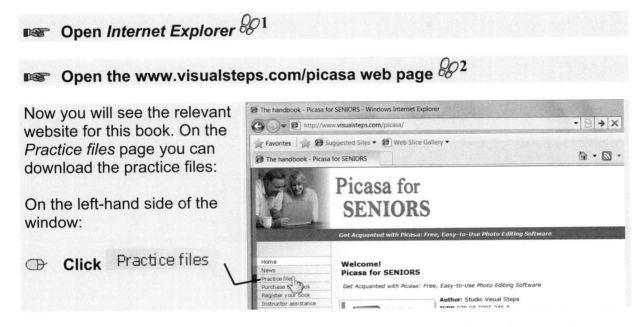

Now you will see a compressed folder containing the practice files. You need to copy this folder to the (*My*) *Pictures* folder:

➥ Please note:

In *Windows 7* and *Windows XP* this folder is called *My Pictures*. In *Windows Vista* the folder is called *Pictures*.

⊕ **Right-click**
[Practice-files-Picasa.zip

Now you will see this menu:

⊕ **Click** Save Target As...

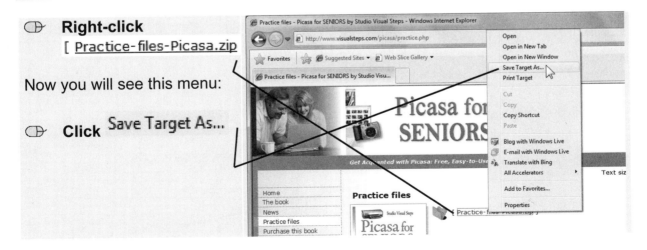

The *Practice-files-Picasa* folder is a compressed folder. First, you need to save this folder to the (*My*) *Pictures* folder.

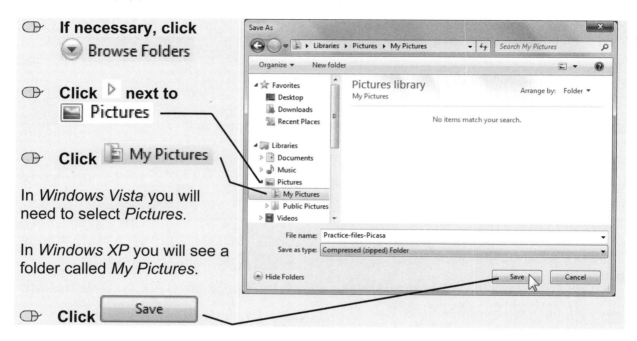

☞ **If necessary, click**
  ▼ **Browse Folders**

☞ **Click** ▷ **next to**
  🖼 **Pictures**

☞ **Click** 🖼 **My Pictures**

In *Windows Vista* you will need to select *Pictures*.

In *Windows XP* you will see a folder called *My Pictures*.

☞ **Click** [Save]

🐦 Please note:

If your computer is using the *Windows XP* operating system, you will see a different window. But you can simply go ahead with all the actions that are described in this section.

☞ **Execute all the actions as described above and below**

☞ **Click** [Save]

When the file has been fully downloaded, you will see this window:

☞ **Click** [Open Folder]

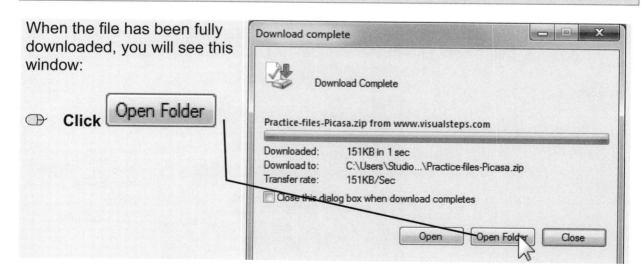

☞ **Right-click**

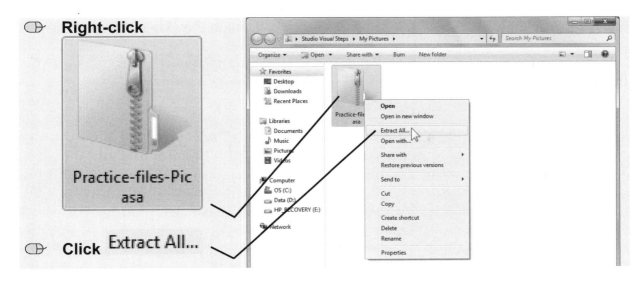

          **Practice-files-Pic
                asa**

☞ **Click** Extract All...

If you are using *Windows XP*, the *Extract files* wizard will now open. In this case, just follow the instructions in the various windows and then click ⬚ Next > ⬚ twice.

Now the files will be extracted:

☞ **Uncheck the box** ☑
     next to
     Show extracted files when comp

At the bottom of the window:

☞ **Click** ⬚ Extract ⬚

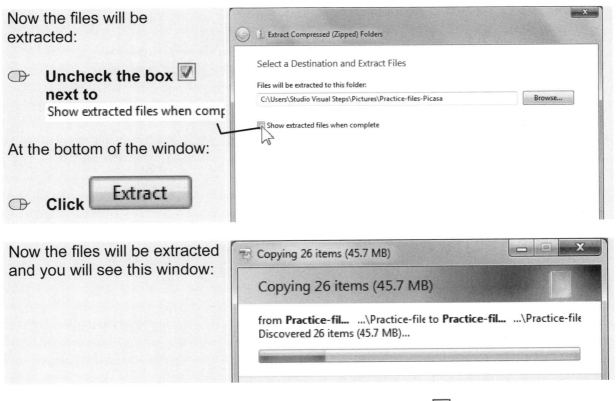

Now the files will be extracted and you will see this window:

If you are using *Windows XP*, you need to uncheck the box ☑ next to Show extracted files, in the last window of the *Extract files* wizard, click ⬚ Finish ⬚.

Now the *Practice-files-Picasa* folder has been stored inside the (*My*) *Pictures* folder.

You can delete the compressed folder:

☞ **Right-click**

☞ **Click Delete**

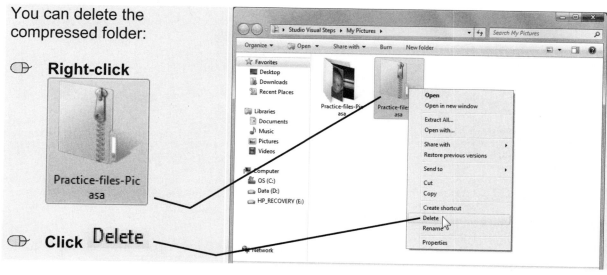

Now you will see the *Delete Folder* window:

☞ **Click** Yes

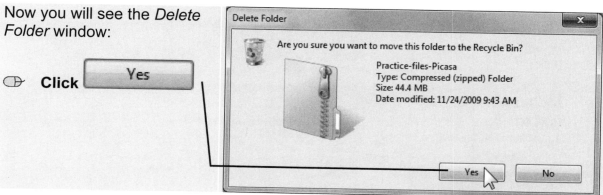

The compressed folder has been deleted:

☞ **Close the (*My*) *Pictures* window** ℰℰ3

1.3 Installation

In order to install *Picasa*, you first need to download the program from the Internet:

☞ **Open the picasa.google.com web page** 👣²

Note: It is not necessary to type the 'www' for this particular web address.

Now you will see a brief introduction to *Picasa*:

🖝 **Click**
Download Picasa 3.6

At the top of the window you will see this warning message:

🖝 **Click**
⬇ To help protect your security, Internet |

🖝 **Click** Download File...

🖝 **Click** Run

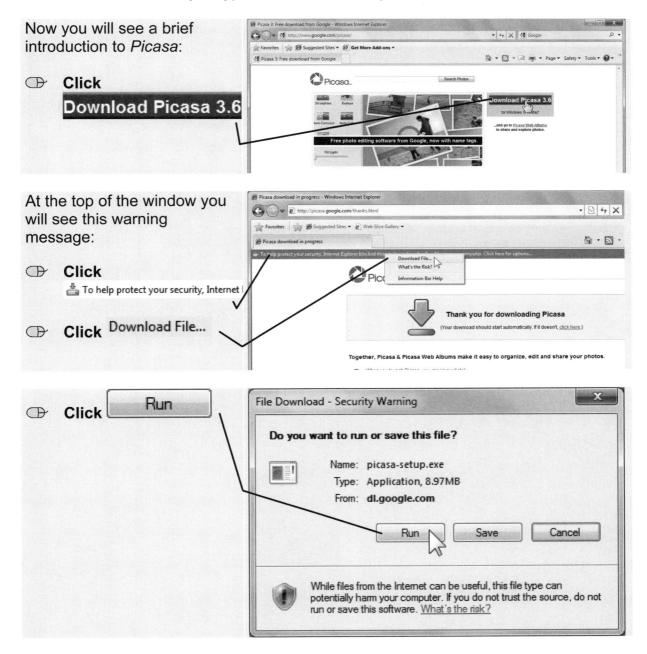

Picasa will now be downloaded:

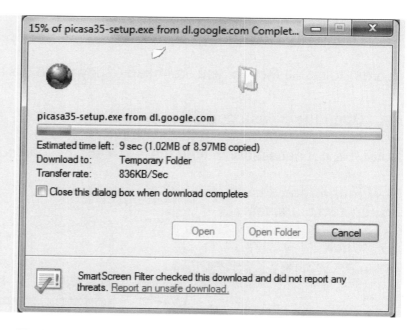

After the file has been downloaded, you will see this window:

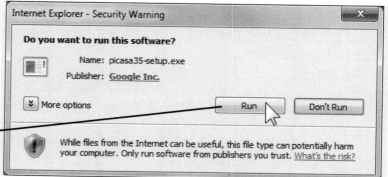

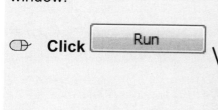 Click

If you are using a *Windows 7* or a *Windows Vista* computer, your screen may turn dark and you will then need to give permission to continue:

In the next window you need to agree to the license terms:

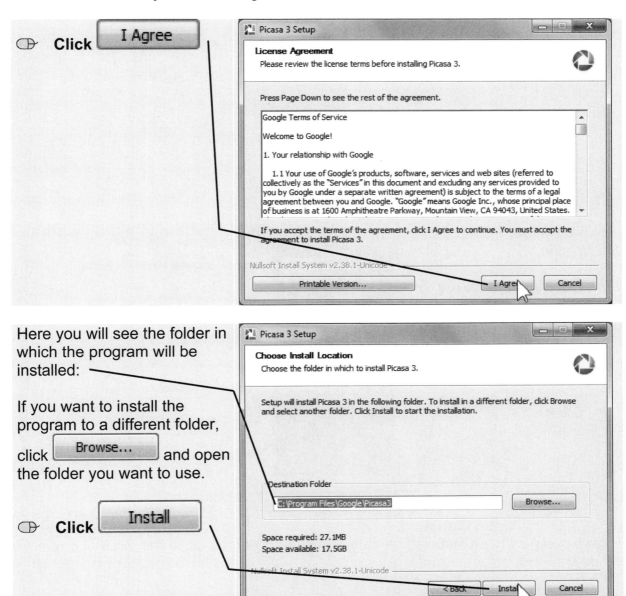

☞ **Click** I Agree

Here you will see the folder in which the program will be installed:

If you want to install the program to a different folder, click Browse... and open the folder you want to use.

☞ **Click** Install

Now *Picasa* will be installed:

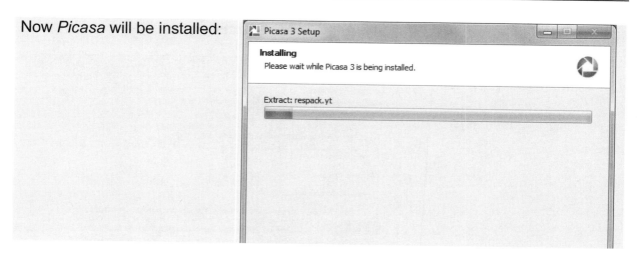

You will see the *Picasa 3 Setup* folder:

☞ **Uncheck the boxes** ☑ **next to**
Set Google as my default search engine in I

Send anonymous usage stats to Goog

and Run Picasa 3

☞ **Click** Finish

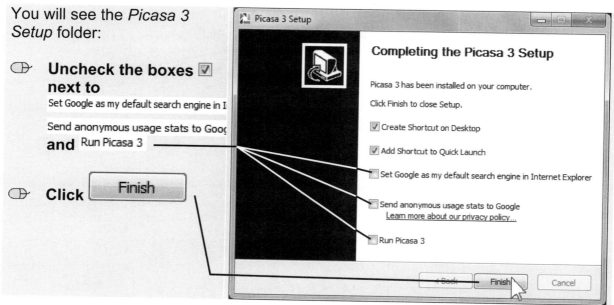

Picasa has now been installed on your computer. You can close the *Internet Explorer* window:

☞ **Close *Internet Explorer*** 𝓔³

On your desktop you will see

the *Picasa* icon :

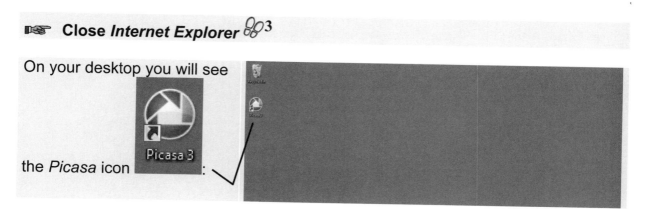

2. The Library

Picasa allows you to manage your entire photo and video collection. When you open Picasa for the first time, the program automatically scans your computer for folders containing pictures and videos. Picasa will ask you which folders to use.

Once the scanning is completed, the pictures or videos are displayed in the Picasa library with the same folder names that appear on your computer's hard drive. The folders that you see in Picasa are the same folders you see in Windows Explorer. Any changes you make to a folder in the Picasa library will affect the matching folder in Windows Explorer. For example, if you delete a picture from a folder in Picasa, you are also deleting it from the folder of the same name in Windows Explorer. Picasa will always prompt you first before any action is carried out.

The Picasa library not only contains folders. It also contains the albums you have made with Picasa. You can create albums that combine pictures and videos taken from different folders. A Picasa album is a virtual collection of photos or videos. This means that a Picasa album is only visible in Picasa itself. You will not be able to display a Picasa album in Windows Explorer. The difference between a Picasa album and a folder is that when you move or delete a photo from an album, the file still remains intact in its original location on your computer's hard drive. Only the virtual connection to the file has been modified.

In this chapter you will learn how to:

- open Picasa;
- use the library and the library window;
- recognize people by using name tags;
- view pictures;
- move pictures;
- find pictures;
- delete pictures;
- create and use an album;
- view the pictures in a slide show;
- use Picasa to scan the folders on your computer's hard drive.

**Please note:**

If you want to use the exercises in this chapter, you need to download the Practice-files-Picasa folder and save it to the (My) Pictures folder on your computer. You can read how to do this in Chapter 1 Installing Picasa.

2.1 Opening Picasa for the First Time

You are now going to open *Picasa*. The easiest way to do this is by using the icon on your desktop:

⊕ **Double-click**

HELP! I do not see the Picasa icon on my desktop.

If you do not see the *Picasa* icon on your desktop:

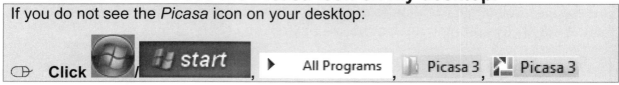

⊕ **Click**   **start** , ▶   All Programs ,   Picasa 3 ,   Picasa 3

It is possible that *Internet Explorer* opens a window showing you some information about *Picasa's* newest features.

☞ **If necessary, close *Internet Explorer*** 🐾³

When you open *Picasa* for the first time, the program will offer to scan your computer for images. You can select the folders you want to scan yourself:

⊕ **Click**

   Only scan My Documents, My Pictu

⊕ **Click**   Continue

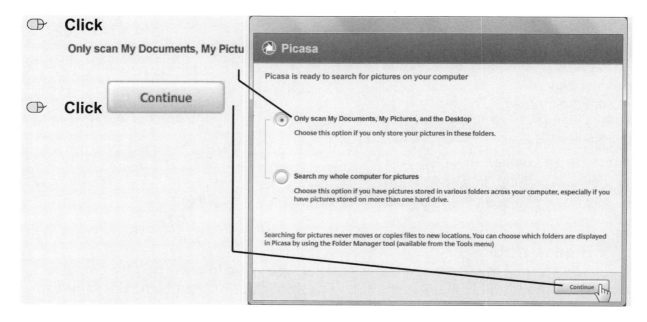

💡 Tip

Which folders should you scan

If you like to store your pictures in the (*My*) *Pictures* or (*My*) *Documents* folders, you

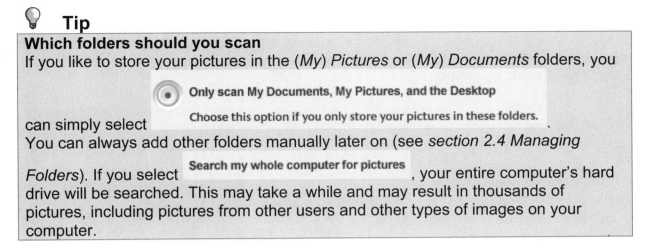

can simply select   .
You can always add other folders manually later on (see *section 2.4 Managing*

Folders). If you select [Search my whole computer for pictures], your entire computer's hard drive will be searched. This may take a while and may result in thousands of pictures, including pictures from other users and other types of images on your computer.

Picasa also contains a photo viewer. When you open *Picasa* for the first time, you can set this viewer as your default photo viewer:

Here, the default viewer option is active:

All file types have been checked:

If the options on your own computer are not yet selected:

☞ **Check the boxes** ☑
next to the file types

☞ **Click**

| Finish |

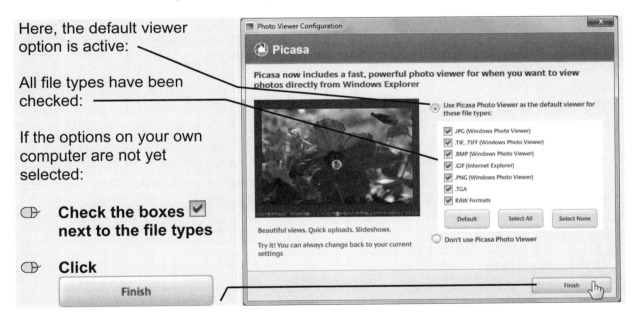

Picasa will now search the selected folders on your computer's hard drive. Folders which contain pictures or videos will be displayed in the *Picasa library*.

2.2 Layout of the Library

After opening *Picasa* you will always see the *library* window first, with the folder list shown on the left-hand side:

  Click the 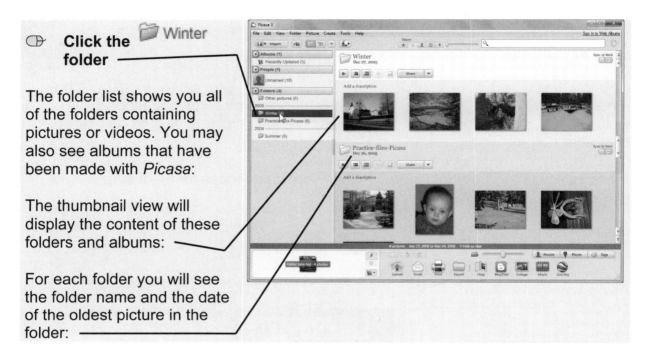 **Winter**
folder

The folder list shows you all of the folders containing pictures or videos. You may also see albums that have been made with *Picasa*:

The thumbnail view will display the content of these folders and albums:

For each folder you will see the folder name and the date of the oldest picture in the folder:

In the *Photo Tray* located at the bottom of the window you can perform various actions on a single picture or on a whole group of pictures that are currently displayed in the tray. You can use the buttons to print, send by e-mail, or move to another folder.

 Please note:

The sequence of the pictures shown in the folders and albums on your computer may be different from the examples shown in this book.

HELP! I see different pictures.

Is your window displaying pictures from a different folder? If that is the case, it does not matter. It will not make any difference in the following exercises.

If you have selected the   Search my whole computer for pictures   option, or have not created a new user account, you will see many more pictures in your window.

You can also delete an album in *Picasa*. Here is how to do that:

In the folder list:

- ☞ **Click the**
  |★ Recently Updated (3)
  album

- ☞ **Click** File

- ☞ **Click**
  Remove from Album

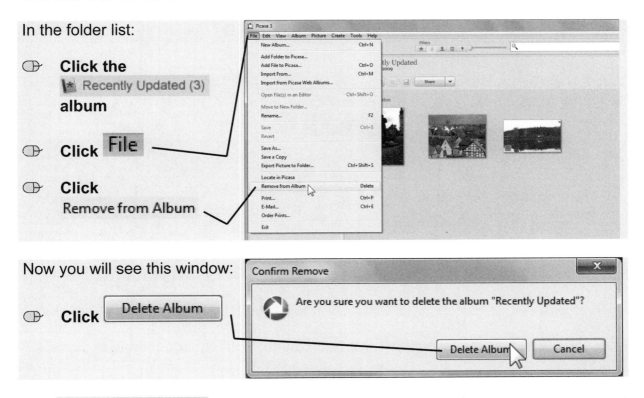

Now you will see this window:

- ☞ **Click** Delete Album

The |★ Recently Updated (3) album has now been removed from the folder list.

2.3 Name Tags

As *Picasa* scans your images it also uses face recognition technology to search for faces. The pictures of these faces will be collected in the People album. If you give a name to these faces, it makes it easier later on to find all of the pictures of the same person:

In the folder list:

- ☞ **Click** Unnamed (18)

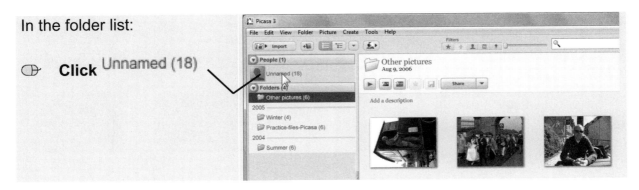

HELP! I do not see the Unnamed (18) **folder.**

> Scanning all the faces may take a while, depending on the number of pictures your computer contains.

You will see some information about name tags:

☞ **Click** Close

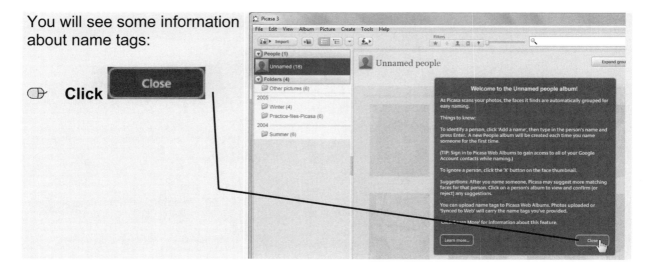

Now you will see all the faces that have been found. You can add names to these faces:

☞ **If necessary, drag the scroll bar downwards**

Under :

☞ **Click** Add a name

⌨ **Type:** Hank

⌨ **Press** Enter ↵

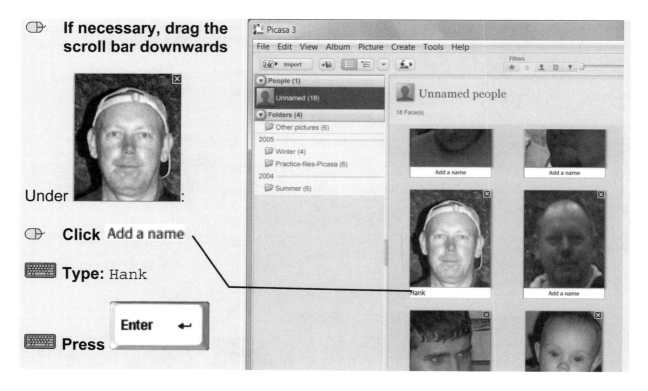

Now you will see a new window, with the person's name:

⊕ **Click** New Person

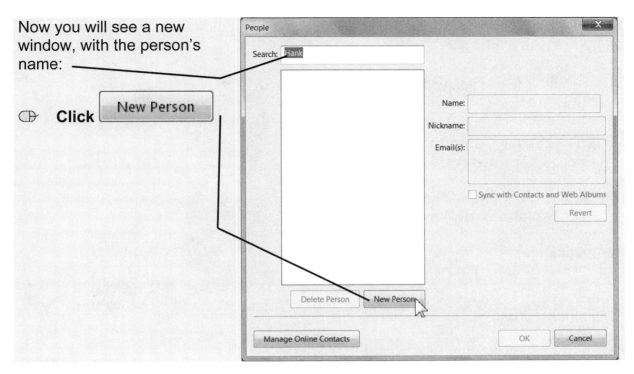

Here you can complete the name, type a nickname, and add an e-mail address:

⊕ **Uncheck the box** ☑
next to
Sync with Contacts and Web

⊕ **Click** OK

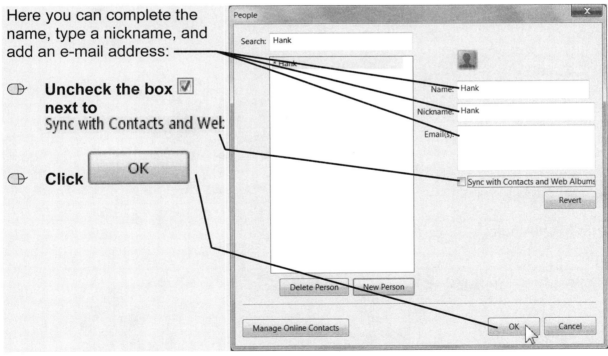

If there are several photos of the same person, you can directly add the person's name to these photos:

In the **People** folder you will see Hank (1):

- ☞ **If necessary, drag the scroll bar downwards**

- ☞ **Right-click one of the other pictures of Hank**

- ☞ **Click** Move to People Album

- ☞ **Click** Hank

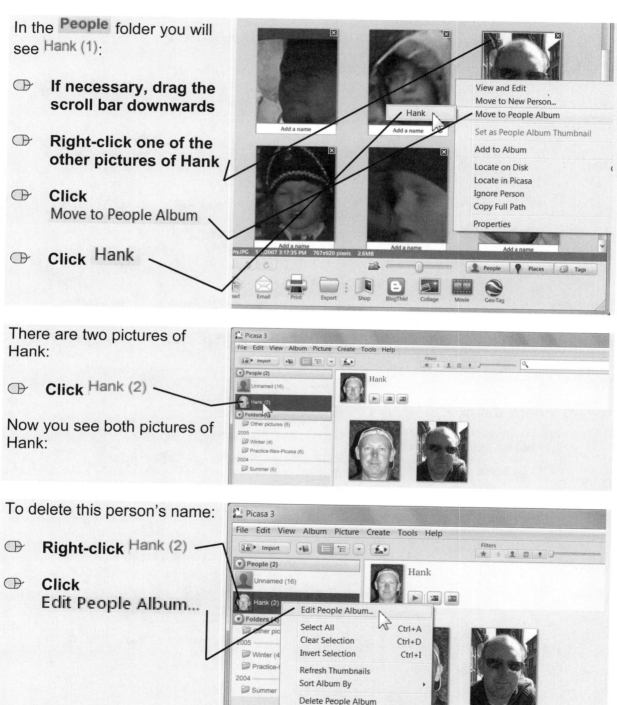

There are two pictures of Hank:

- ☞ **Click** Hank (2)

Now you see both pictures of Hank:

To delete this person's name:

- ☞ **Right-click** Hank (2)

- ☞ **Click** Edit People Album...

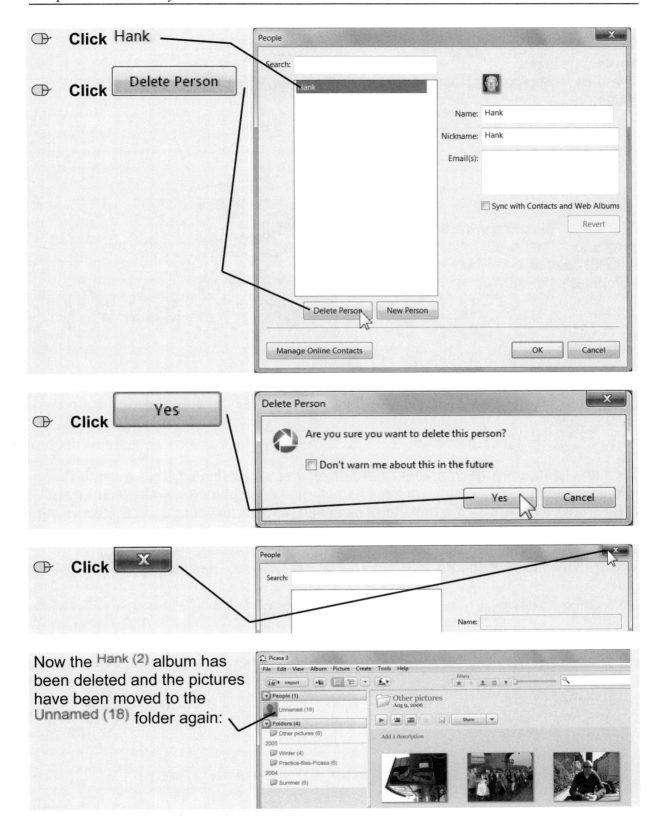

💡 Tip

Unknown faces

If you have photographs of people you do not know, you can remove them from this album:

For each picture you want to remove:

☞ **Click**

The link to this picture will be removed from this album, but it is not deleted from your computer's hard drive.

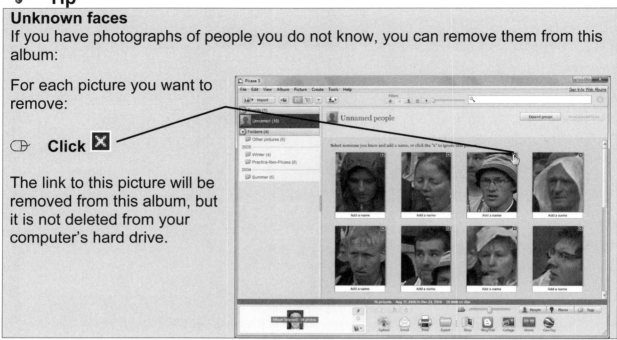

2.4 Managing Folders

For each folder on your computer's hard drive, you can define whether or not it should be scanned by *Picasa*. In this chapter you have set the (*My*) *Documents* and (*My*) *Pictures* folders as the ones to be scanned, as well as your desktop. Depending on the content of your folders, scanning them could mean that dozens of subfolders and thousands of pictures will be scanned. The *Folder Manager* will let you specify exactly which folders should be scanned. Here is how you use this tool:

☞ **Click** Tools

☞ **Click**
   Folder Manager...

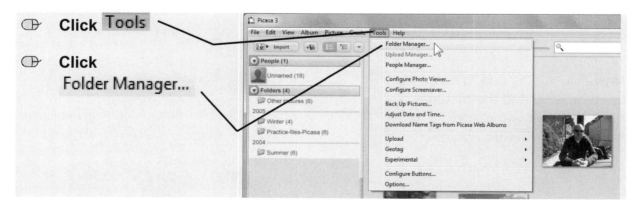

You will see the C icon next to the folders that can be scanned:

☞ **If necessary, click ▷ next to** My Pictures

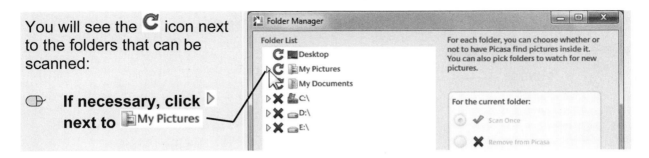

If you do not want *Picasa* to scan a specific folder, you can remove this folder from *Picasa*:

☞ **If necessary, click ▷ next to** C Practice-files-Picasa

☞ **Click** Other pictures

☞ **Click** ✗ Remove from Picasa

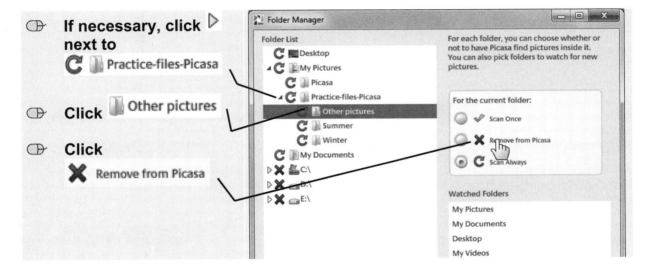

The folder remains stored on your hard disk. Only the link to the folder is removed from the *Picasa* folder list.

☞ **Click** Winter

☞ **Click** ✗ Remove from Picasa

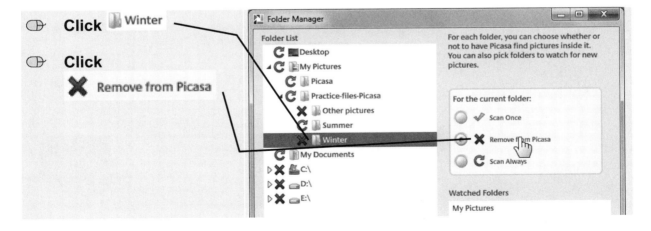

Now you will see an ✖ next to the 📁 Other pictures and 📁 Winter folders: ———

👆 **Click** OK

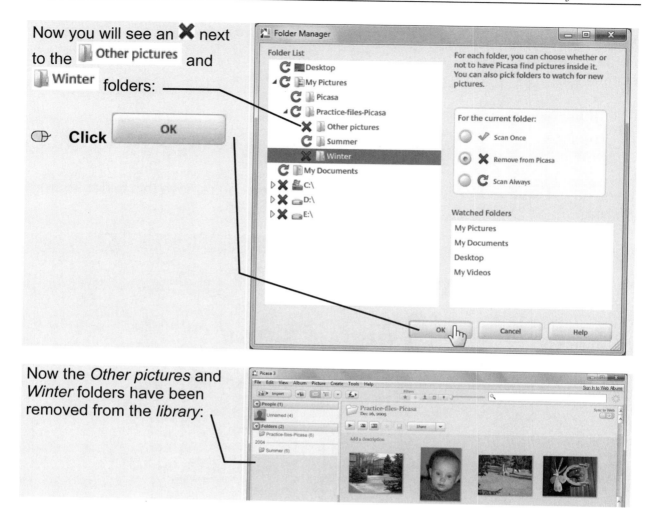

Now the *Other pictures* and *Winter* folders have been removed from the *library*: ⟍

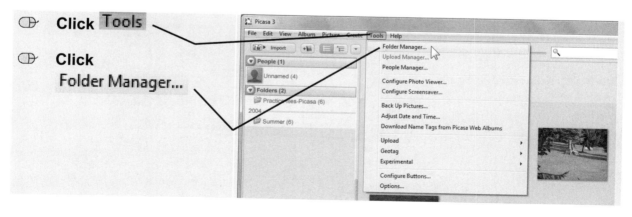

If you let *Picasa* scan these folders again, the pictures will reappear in the *library* once more. The following step will demonstrate this:

👆 **Click** Tools

👆 **Click** Folder Manager...

⊕ **If necessary, click** ▷
next to 🗐My Pictures

⊕ **If necessary, click** ▷
next to
C 📁 **Practice-files-Picasa**

⊕ **Click** 📁 **Winter**

⊕ **Click** **C** **Scan Always**

⊕ **Click** OK

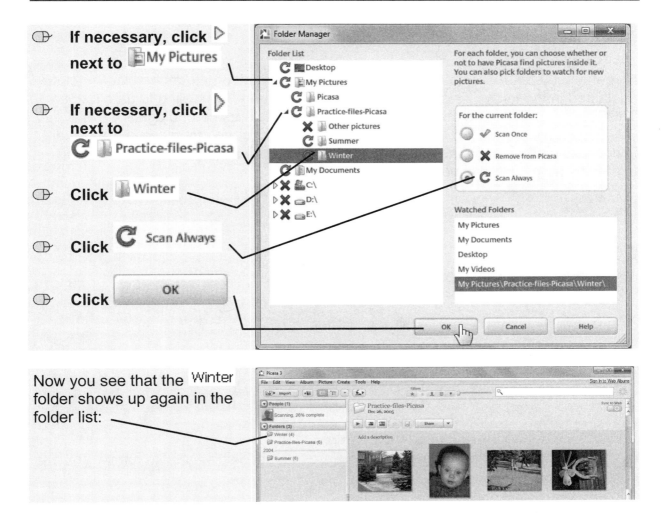

Now you see that the Winter
folder shows up again in the
folder list:

💡 **Tip**

Organize your folders
If you let *Picasa* scan your computer's entire hard drive, *Picasa* will also include
many icons and symbols. When you surf the web with *Internet Explorer*, many
images from the web pages you have viewed are stored on your computer. If you
want to avoid these images from being scanned by *Picasa*, you can use the method
described in the next section.

If you select Scan Always , all modifications in the folders will automatically be
scanned. When you add a new photo or a subfolder, this will immediately be

included in *Picasa*. If you want to scan a folder just once, then select Scan Once .
Next to the folder you will see a ✔ symbol. You can decide to have this folder
scanned again at any time you like.

2.5 Ordering Folders

By default, the folder list in *Picasa* is sorted by the creation date of the oldest picture contained in the folder. This means the folders are sorted according to date (or year). This can be useful if you always want to view your pictures chronologically.
But if you have pictures from different dates (or years) stored together in the same folder, this method might not be so convenient. In this case it is easier to sort the folders by name. Here is how to do that:

Click
📁 Practice-files-Picasa

Click ▾

Click Sort by Name

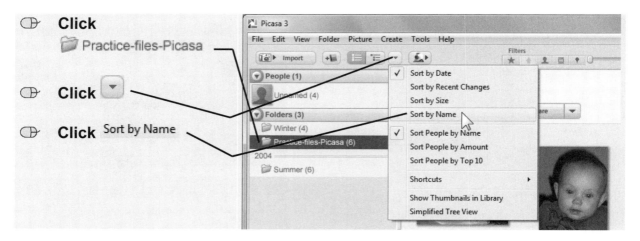

Now the folders will be sorted by their name.
By default, the thumbnail images of the pictures do not display the file name. You can change this setting:

Click View

Click
Thumbnail Caption

Click Filename

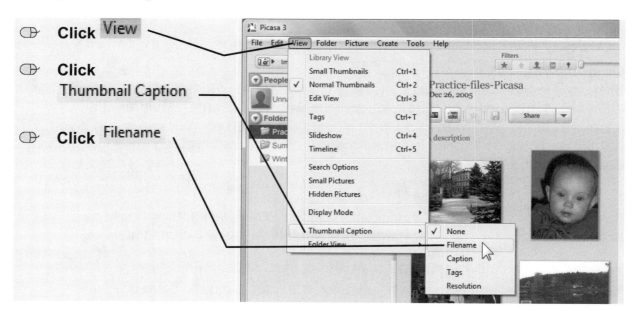

Now the file names appear below the pictures. You can manually change the order of the pictures in the folders. Here is how to do that:

☞ **Click**

☞ **Drag the picture to the left side of**

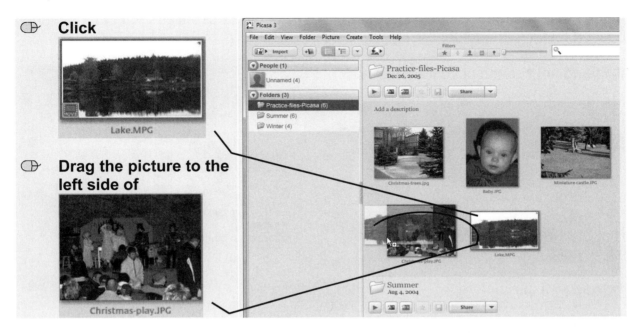

Now the order has been changed:

2.6 Viewing Photos and Videos

In the thumbnail view you can view both photo files and video files. You can open the desired folder in the folder list.

If you do not see the pictures in the 📁 Practice-files-Picasa folder:

☞ **Click the**
   📁 Practice-files-Picasa
   folder

Now you will see the thumbnails in this folder:

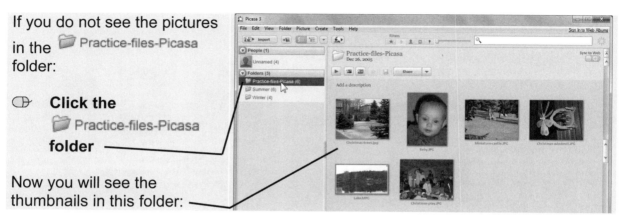

To view a single picture:

☞ **Double-click**

Now you will see this picture in the *edit window*:

Underneath the picture the properties are displayed:
`Practice-files-Picasa > Miniature-castle.JPG`

When you want to view the picture in its actual size:

☞ **Click** `1·1`

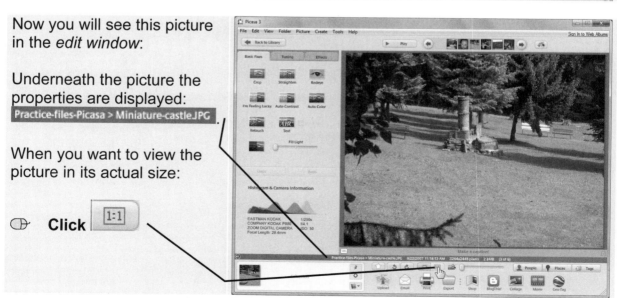

The picture has been enlarged. But only a small portion of the picture appears in the viewing window. You can set the degree of enlargment yourself:

☞ **Drag the slider** next to 🔍 **to the left**

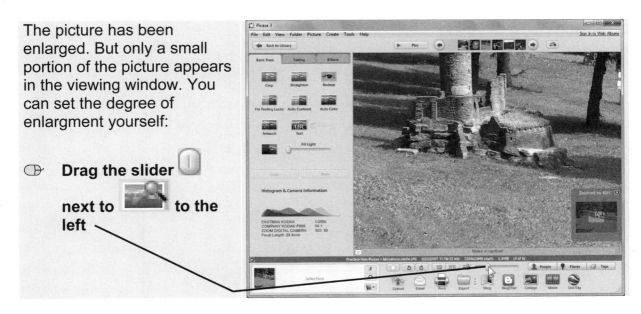

Now you will see a larger portion of the picture. By dragging the selection frame you can determine which part of the picture you want to view:

At the bottom right-hand side of the window:

☞ **Point at the selection frame**

☞ **Drag the selection frame to a different position**

When you want to see the full picture again:

At the bottom of the window:

☞ **Click** 🔳

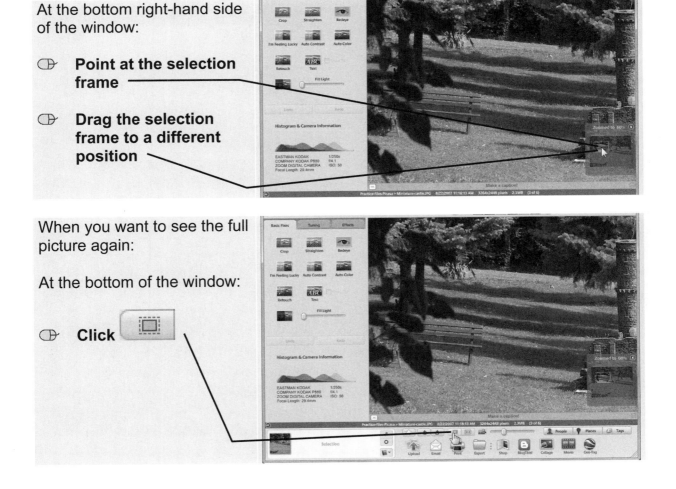

To open the next picture in the folder:

⊕ **Click**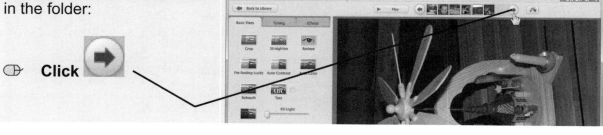

Now you see the next picture in the folder:

⊕ **Click**

The next file in this folder is a video file. This will now be played:

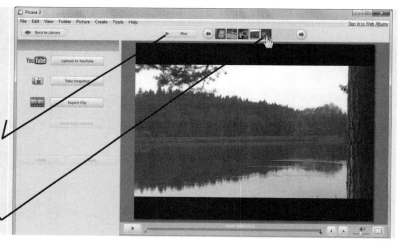

If you want to play the clip

again, click [▶ Play]

You can open a picture in the same way:

⊕ **Click the last picture**

Now you see the picture. It is the last picture in this folder.

You are still looking at the *edit window*.

To return to the *library* window once more:

⊕ **Click**

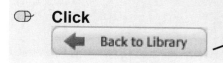

💡 Tip

Browsing with the scroll bars
The scroll bar in the thumbnail view works a bit differently than the way you are accustomed to in *Windows*.

If you want to scroll through the pictures and folders:

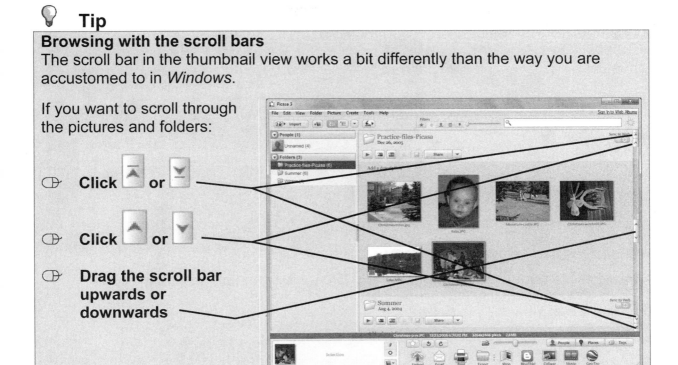

☞ **Click ⏶ or ⏷**

☞ **Click ⏶ or ⏷**

☞ **Drag the scroll bar upwards or downwards**

2.7 Viewing Pictures in a Slide Show

You can also view the pictures and videos contained in a folder as a slide show. You can try that now:

☞ **Click**

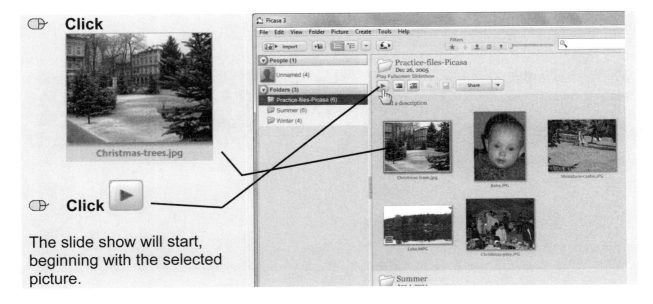

Christmas-trees.jpg

☞ **Click ▶**

The slide show will start, beginning with the selected picture.

You will see the first picture full screen. After a few seconds the next picture appears:

☞ **Position the mouse pointer at the bottom of the window**

Now you will see a toolbar and the slide show will stop playing:

This toolbar contains a number of icons. This is what you can do with them:

- Click to view the next picture.

- Click to view the previous picture.

- Click to continue playing the slide show.

- Rotate the picture by using and .

- Click to display or hide the subtitles.

- You can set the display time of each picture by using .

- Use to zoom in.

- Use to attach a star to a picture (see *section 2.12 Albums*).

When you want to stop the slide show:

☞ **Click**

2.8 Moving Pictures

It is very easy to move your pictures and videos to different folders. Just remember, that when you move a picture in a *Picasa* folder, you are also changing its location on your computer's hard drive.

Click

Drag the picture to the
📁 Summer (6) **folder**

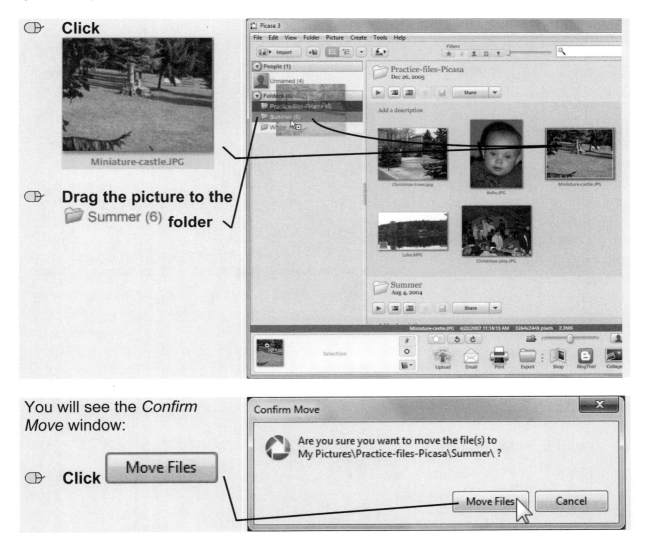

You will see the *Confirm Move* window:

Click [Move Files]

Confirm Move

Are you sure you want to move the file(s) to
My Pictures\Practice-files-Picasa\Summer\ ?

[Move Files] [Cancel]

The 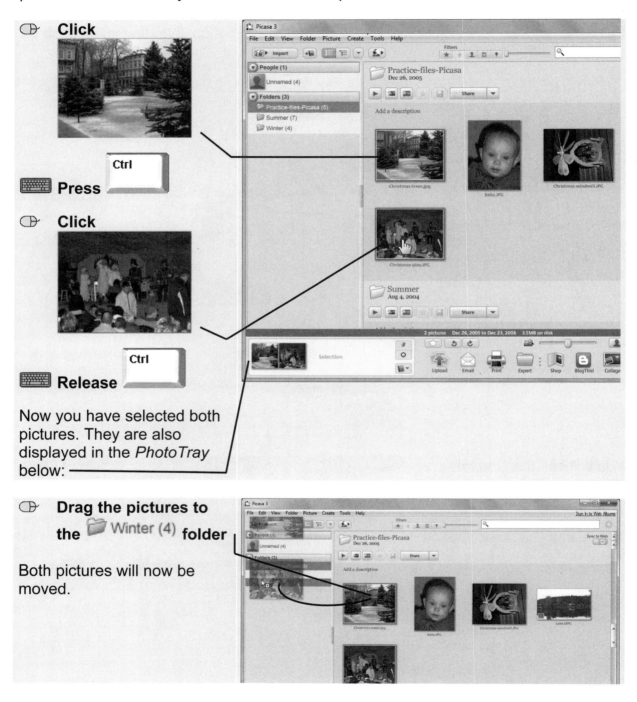 folder now contains seven pictures. You can also move several pictures at once. First you need to select the pictures:

⊕ **Click**

⌨ **Press** `Ctrl`

⊕ **Click**

⌨ **Release** `Ctrl`

Now you have selected both pictures. They are also displayed in the *PhotoTray* below:

⊕ **Drag the pictures to the**  **Winter (4) folder**

Both pictures will now be moved.

First you will see a window that asks your permission to move the files:

⊕ **Click** | Move Files |

2.9 Searching for Pictures

When you have a huge collection of images, it is sometimes difficult to find the one you want. The *Picasa* search engine can help you find your pictures:

☞ **Click the search box**

⌨ **Type:** christ

All of the pictures with 'christ' in their name will be displayed. You will also see the name of the folder where they are stored:

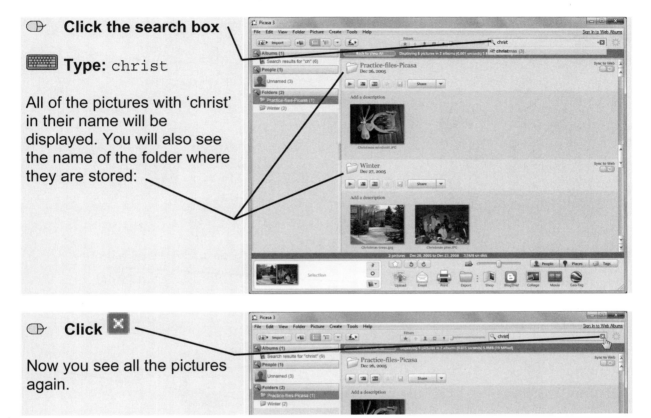

☞ **Click** ☒

Now you see all the pictures again.

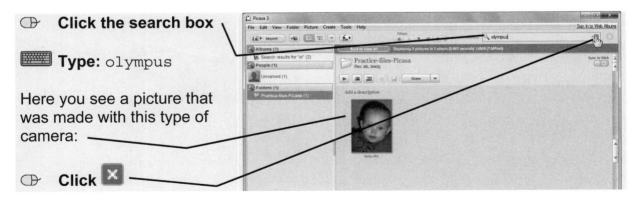

You have searched for the picture by name. You can also search for other characteristics, such as the type of camera. You can try that in the next step:

☞ **Click the search box**

⌨ **Type:** olympus

Here you see a picture that was made with this type of camera:

☞ **Click** ☒

In *section 2.14 Viewing Image Properties* you will learn how to find the camera type, and other attributes of a photograph.

2.10 Searching with Tags

You will be able to find your pictures more easily if you add keywords to them. In *Picasa* this is called adding *labels* (or *tags*) to a picture:

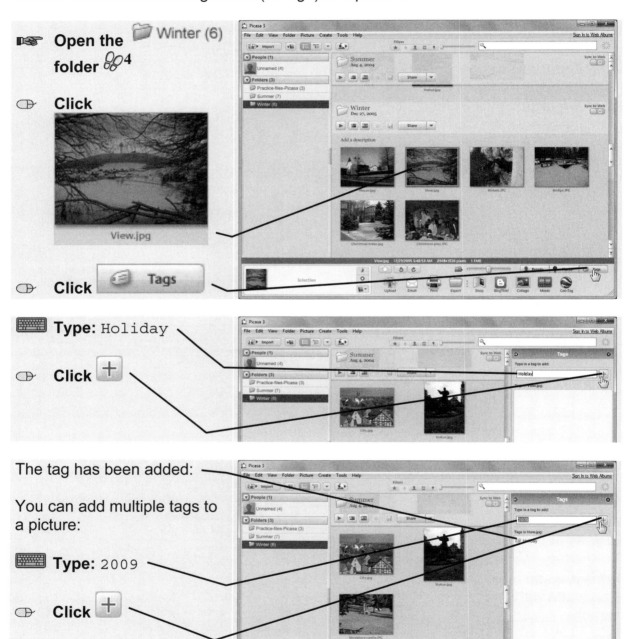

Open the folder Winter (6) ℘4

Click [View.jpg]

Click [Tags]

Type: Holiday

Click +

The tag has been added:

You can add multiple tags to a picture:

Type: 2009

Click +

Now you will see both tags:

⬭ Click ❌

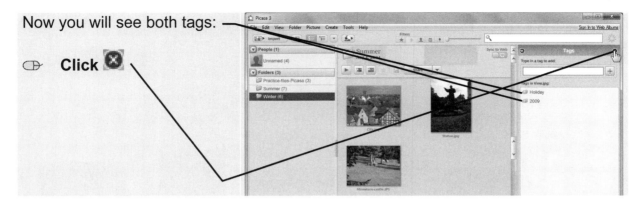

💡 **Tip**

Using first names as tags

The fastest way to find pictures of a particular person is by adding the person's first name as a tag. One of the handiest features in *Picasa*, is its ability to use facial recognition technology when searching folders:

In the *library*:

⬭ **Click the folder you want to search**

⬭ **Click**

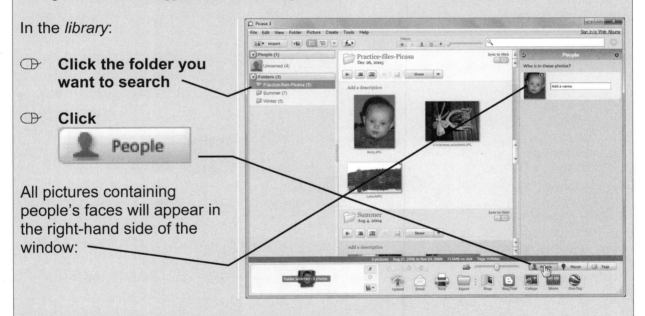

All pictures containing people's faces will appear in the right-hand side of the window:

In *section 5.9 Facial Recognition and Name Tags in a Web Album* you will read more about facial recognition. *Picasa* uses this same technology when searching for faces in a web album.

Click the
🖉 Practice-files-Picasa (3)
folder

☞ Add a *Holiday* tag to

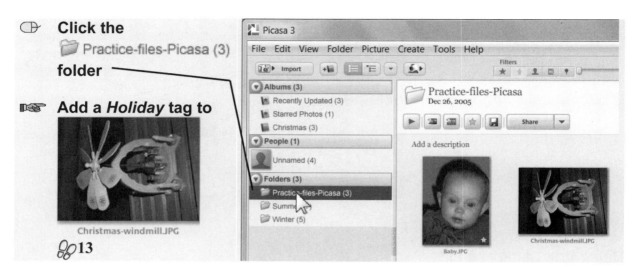

Christmas-windmill.JPG

13

💡 **Tip**

Displaying picture tags
Instead of using file names, you can also try displaying the pictures in the *library* by tags.

Click View

Click
Thumbnail Caption

Click Tags

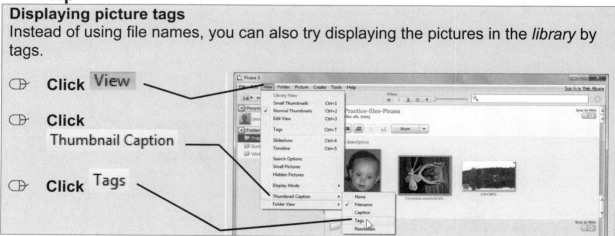

Click the search box

⌨ **Type:** holiday

Now you will see both
pictures:

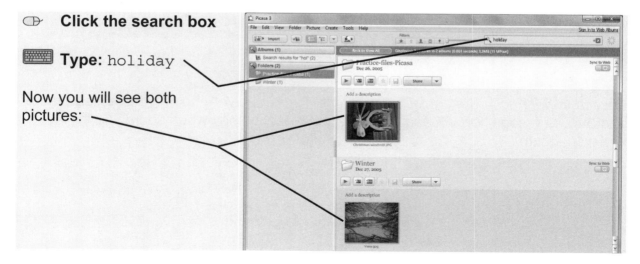

2.11 Deleting Pictures

This is how to delete a picture:

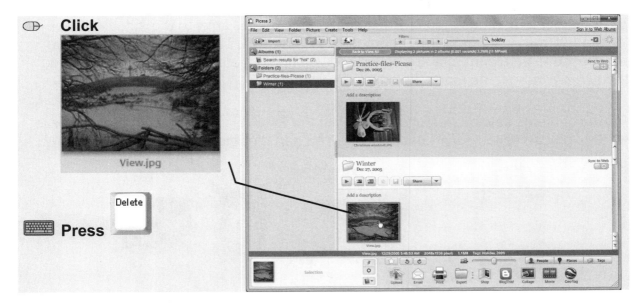

- 👆 **Click**

- ⌨ **Press**

Picasa will prompt you first to make sure you want to delete the file:

- 👆 **Click**  Delete Image

Now the picture has been deleted:

- 👆 **Click** ☒

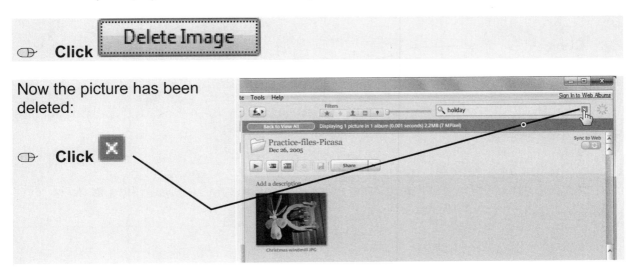

⮱ **Please note:**

If you delete a picture from a *Picasa* folder, it is also deleted from your computer's hard drive. If you have accidentally deleted the wrong picture, you can always restore the deleted file from the *Windows Recycle Bin*.

2.12 Albums

Besides listing your pictures in their regular *Windows* folders, *Picasa* lets you organize and display them in albums as well. You can display a specific selection of pictures together in one album. Such an album contains links to the actual storage location of your pictures on your computer's hard drive. The actual picture files are not moved to an album, but are only *displayed* in the album. You can therefore add the same picture to as many albums as you want.

Picasa contains several default albums, like the 🌟 Starred Photos album for example, where you can collect your best pictures. You add a photo to this album like this:

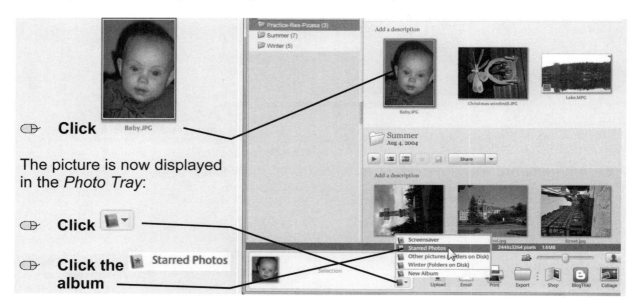

Click Baby.JPG

The picture is now displayed in the *Photo Tray*:

Click 📁▾

Click the 🌟 Starred Photos
album

💡 **Tip**

Using photos as a screensaver
You can use any of your favorite pictures as a screensaver. All you need to do is copy them to the 🌟 Screensaver album.

Now you will see the new
[★] Starred Photos (1) album in
the folder list:

You can also mark a picture
with a star:

☞ **Click**

Christmas-windmill.JPG

☞ **Click** [☆]

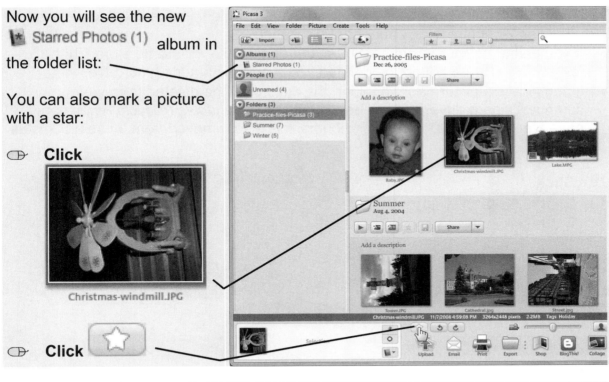

☞ **Click the**
[★] Starred Photos (2)
album

Here you see all of the
pictures that you have
marked with a star. These
pictures can be stored in
different folders.

Pictures from the
[★] Starred Photos album are

easily recognized by the [★]
icon shown in the bottom right
corner:

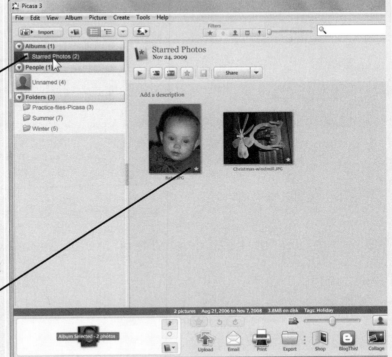

Deleting pictures from an album is pretty much the same thing as deleting pictures from a folder. But there is one important difference:

- If you delete a picture from an album, the original file will still be stored in the folder. This picture will not be deleted from your computer's hard drive.
- If you delete a picture from a folder, the picture will be deleted from your computer's hard drive, and will be moved to the *Windows Recycle Bin*. If you have placed this picture in other albums, it is also removed from these albums as well.

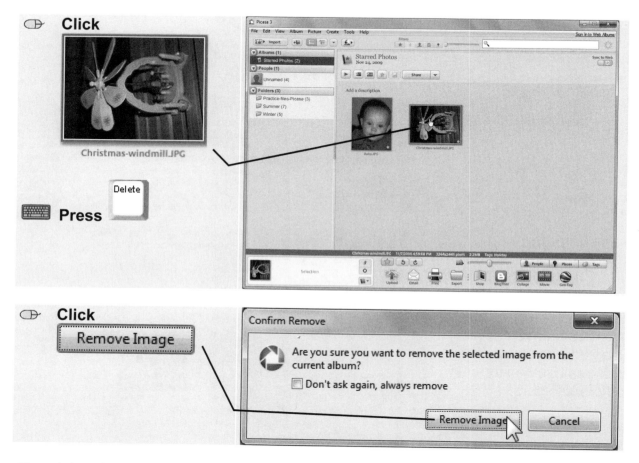

The picture has now been deleted from the album, but is still stored in the folder.

2.13 Creating a New Album

You can also use albums to make your own selection of pictures from the ones you have stored in various folders. You can collect all the pictures of your grandchildren, for example, or all of your Christmas pictures, or pictures of a specific country. Here is how to create a new album:

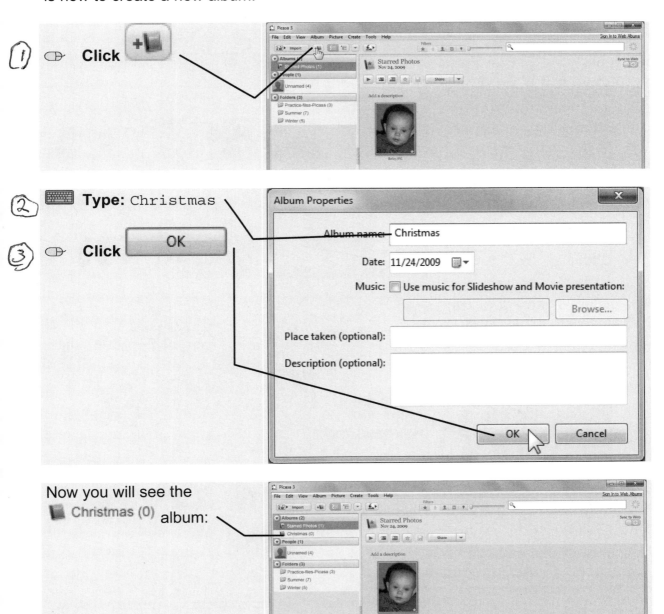

Click

Type: Christmas

Click OK

Album Properties

Album name— Christmas

Date: 11/24/2009

Music: ☐ Use music for Slideshow and Movie presentation:

Browse...

Place taken (optional):

Description (optional):

OK   Cancel

Now you will see the Christmas (0) album:

First, you need to collect the pictures from the various folders, and then you can place them in the new album all at once. You do that like this:

☞ **Open the** 📁 Winter (5) **album** 👓⁴

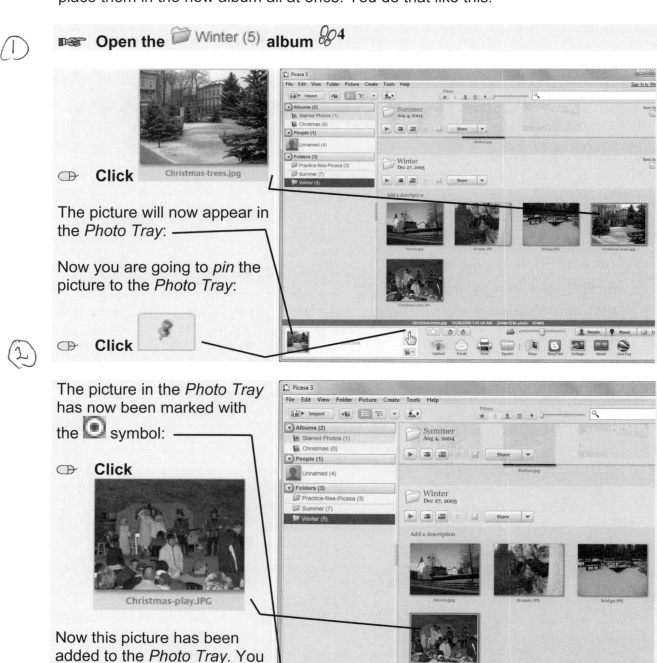

Click

The picture will now appear in the *Photo Tray*: ——

Now you are going to *pin* the picture to the *Photo Tray*:

Click

The picture in the *Photo Tray* has now been marked with the ◉ symbol: ——

Click

Christmas-play.JPG

Now this picture has been added to the *Photo Tray*. You can pin this picture too:

Click

Now you are going to add a
picture from a different folder:

⊕ **Click the**
 📁 Practice-files-Picasa (3)
 folder

⊕ **Click** Christmas-windmill.JPG

This picture is also added to
the *Photo Tray*.

⊕ **Click**

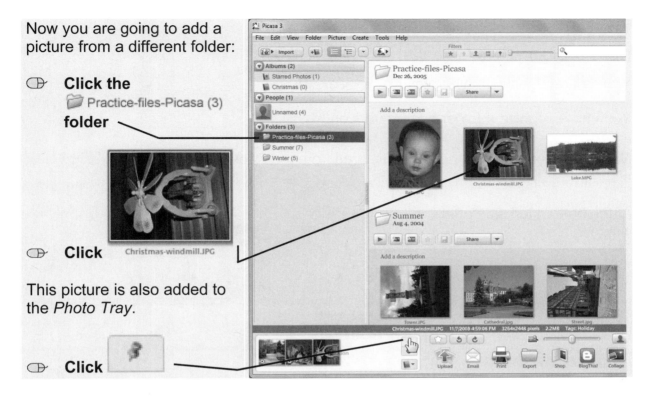

You are going to put all three of these pictures in the new *Christmas* album:

At the bottom left side of your
window:

⊕ **Click**

⊕ **Click the** Christmas
 album

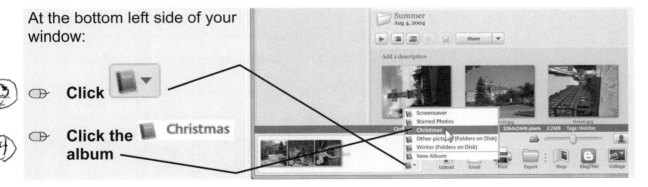

Now all three pictures have been placed in the Christmas album.

⊕ **Click the**
 📖 Christmas (3) **album**

Now you can see the pictures
in this album:

Tip

Icons of albums and folders
You can recognize an album by the 📖 icon.
You can recognize a folder by the 📁 icon.

Now you are going to remove the pictures from the *Photo Tray* of the 📖 Christmas album:

At the bottom left side of the window:

☞ **Click** [O]

☞ **Click** [Clear Tray]

Now the tray is empty:

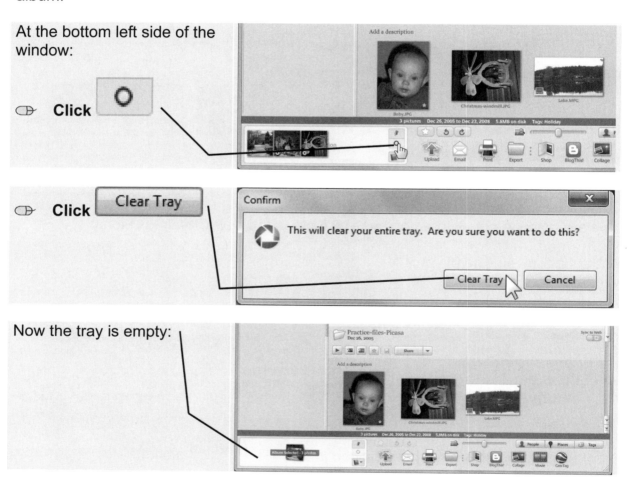

You can delete an album in the same way as you delete a picture. The album will be deleted, but the pictures will still remain stored in the various folders on your computer's hard drive.

 Please note:

The 📷 Starred Photos and 📷 Screensaver albums cannot be deleted, because these are default *Picasa* albums.

2.14 Viewing Image Properties

In *section 2.9 Searching for Pictures* you read about the possibility of searching for images by their properties. Here is how to view the image properties in *Picasa*:

 Double-click

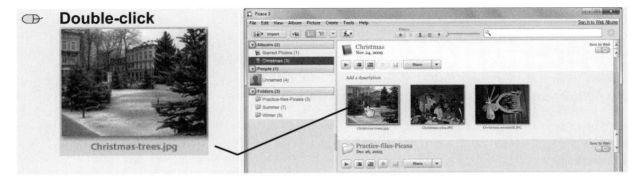

💡 **Tip**

Pictures can be from a folder or an album

Christmas-trees.jpg

It does not make any difference whether you double-click the picture in the *Christmas* album or the one in the *Winter* folder. In both cases the original file from the *Winter* folder will be opened.

Now you will see the picture in the *edit window*:

On the left-hand side of the window you will see the EXIF properties of this image:

EXIF properties

EXIF data contains information about a photograph, such as the date, time and the camera settings (for example, the shutter speed). Your camera stores this data in the image file.

When you double-click a picture, you will see the advanced EXIF data. On the left-hand side of the window you will see a real-time histogram, with the advanced EXIF properties, the RGB color codes and the intensity.
In *Picasa* you can view the following EXIF data:

- date and time of the photo;
- make and model of the camera;
- resolution;
- orientation;
- focus length;
- diaphragm;
- ISO speed;
- GPS location information (longitude and latitude).

Picasa will read the EXIF data for the selected RAW files. However, *Picasa* does not support all RAW file types.

Source: Picasa Help

☞ **Open the *library*** ✇11

Now you will be looking for flash pictures:

☞ **Click the search box**

⌨ **Type:** flash

All of the pictures taken with flash appear very quickly:

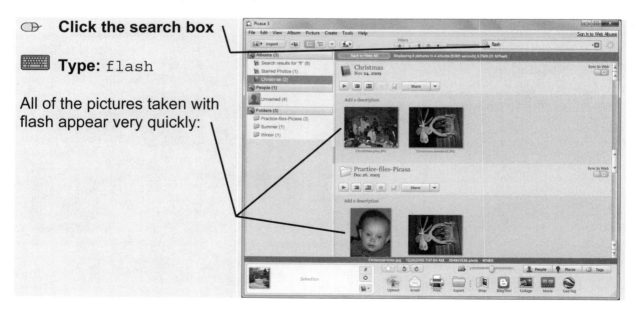

HELP! I see the same picture more than once.

Pictures that have been placed in an album will be displayed both in the album and in their original folder. This means you will see multiple images of these pictures in the *library's* thumbnails.

 Please note:

You need to type the full keyword in the search box. If you are looking for pictures with a setting of ISO:100, you need to type 'ISO'. If you just type '100', the pictures will not be found. The same is true for file names or tags. If you are looking for pictures with the *Holiday* tag, you will not find them if you search for 'day'.

☞ **Click**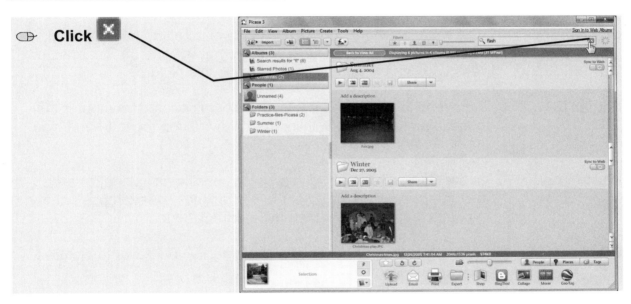

Now you see all the pictures again.

You can now close *Picasa*:

☞ **Click**

In this chapter you have learned how to use folders and albums in *Picasa*.

2.15 Background Information

Dictionary	
Album	Albums are virtual collections of pictures, which only exist in the *Picasa* program. You can combine several pictures in one album, or display the same picture in several albums, without using extra space on your computer's hard drive. When you delete the pictures in an album, or the album itself, the original photo files will still remain stored on your computer's hard drive.
Edit window	The window where you can view the picture you have opened. On the left-hand side of this window you will find the buttons and tabs you can use to edit and enhance this picture.
Folder list	An overview of all the folders and albums on your computer that contain pictures. You will find the folder list on the left-hand side of the *library* window.
Photo Tray	In the *Photo Tray* you can carry out specific actions for one picture, or a whole group of them at a time. For example, printing pictures, sending them by e-mail, or moving them.
Star	By applying the *Star* icon you can classify your favorite pictures in your collection.
Thumbnail view	The view on the right-hand side of the *library* window. The thumbnails of your pictures are displayed here.
Source: Picasa Help	

2.16 Tips

  Tip

Folder order in Windows
You may have already noticed that *Picasa* has its own system for organizing folders. All the folders are lined up one below the other. *Windows* uses a different method of displaying the folders on your computer's hard drive. You may find this annoying, because you cannot see where a specific (sub)folder is located. If you do not like the way *Picasa* organizes its folders, you can select the *Windows* tree view structure:

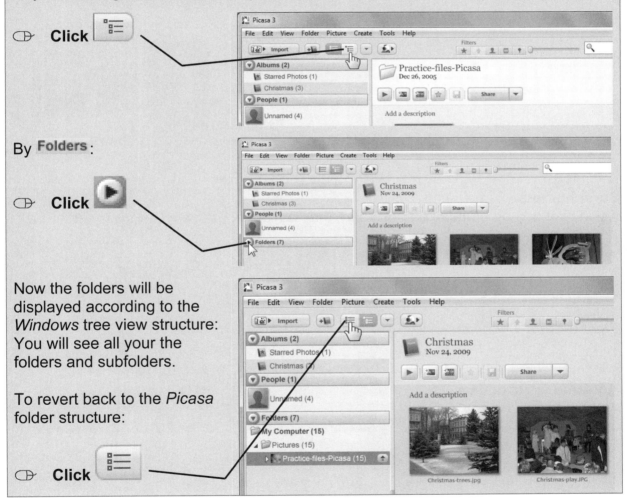

☞ **Click**

By **Folders**:

☞ **Click**

Now the folders will be displayed according to the *Windows* tree view structure: You will see all your the folders and subfolders.

To revert back to the *Picasa* folder structure:

☞ **Click**

Tip

Small thumbnails
If you have many folders and pictures, you can display them as smaller thumbnails.
This allows more pictures (but smaller versions) to be displayed in your window.

☞   **Click** View

☞   **Click** Small Thumbnails

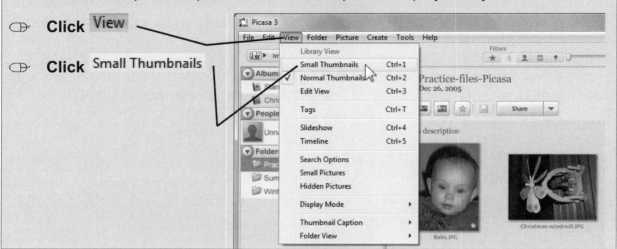

 Tip

Screen shots
If you take screen shots of a full screen, they will appear directly in *Picasa* under the
Projects header:

▦ **Press** Print Screen Sys rq **briefly**

Please note: if you cannot

find the Print Screen Sys rq key on your
keyboard, try to find the key
with the letters *PrtScn* and
use this key together with

⇧ Shift .

Now you will see the
captured screen under
Projects (1) , in the
❘* Screen Captures (1) album:

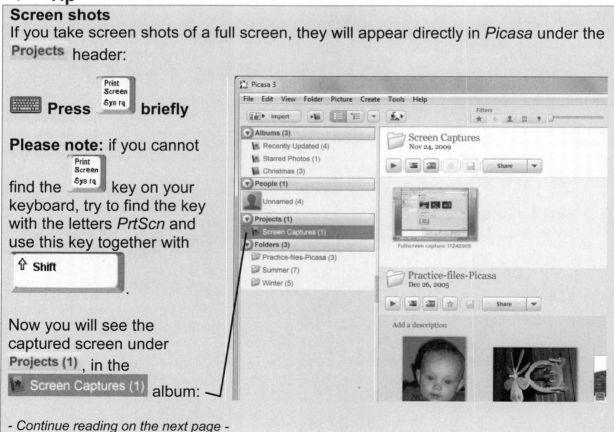

- Continue reading on the next page -

By double-clicking the image, you can open it in *Picasa*.

If you press the + keys together, you can print the active window.

Tip

Disabling the Picasa Photo Viewer
In a standard installation of *Picasa*, the *Picasa Photo Viewer* is also installed. Any photo that is opened in (*My*) *Pictures*, *Windows Explorer*, on your desktop, or in any other program, will automatically trigger the *Picasa Photo Viewer*.

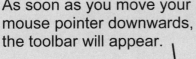 **Double-click a photo**

As soon as you move your mouse pointer downwards, the toolbar will appear.

- Continue reading on the next page -

If you do not want to use the *Picasa Photo Viewer*, you can disable the program in the following way:

☞ **Click** Tools

☞ **Click**
Configure Photo Viewer...

☞ **Click**
Don't use Picasa Photo Viewer

☞ **Click**
OK

Now all of your pictures will be opened in the default program again.

In *Windows 7* and *Windows XP*, the *Windows Photo Viewer* is the default program. In *Windows Vista*, it is *Windows Photo Gallery*.

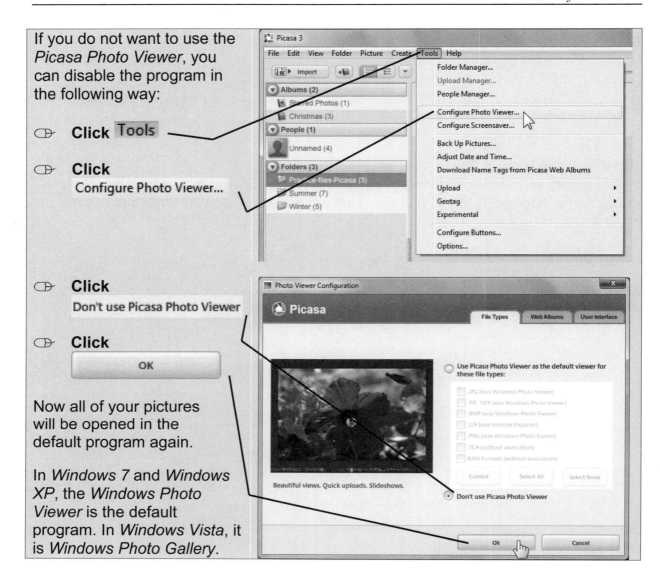

Tip

Importing photos from your camera
You can directly import the photos from your digital camera into *Picasa*. Most digital cameras come equipped with a special cable that can be used to connect to your computer. Here is how you do that:

☞ **Connect the cable to your camera**

Usually, the connection is hidden behind a small flap.

☞ **Connect your camera to your computer's USB port**

☞ **Switch on the camera**

When you see the *AutoPlay* window:

☞ **Close the window** 𝒫𝒫³

☞ **Click**

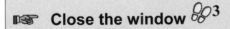

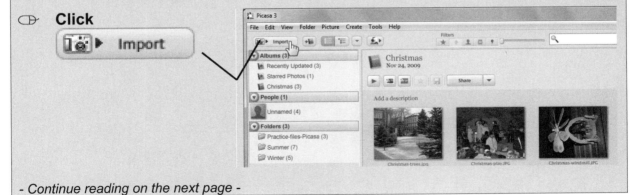

- Continue reading on the next page -

If the camera is recognized by your computer, you will see the name of the camera, and all the pictures:

The pictures will be copied to the (*My*) *Pictures* folder. If you want to store the photos somewhere else, then click ▼, next to Pictures :

⌨ **Type, a folder name, if you wish**

To import all of the pictures:

☞ **Click**

    Import All ✔

If you do not want to import all of the pictures, first select the pictures you want to import.

Afterwards:

☞ **Click**

    Import Selected (1)

Now the pictures will appear in *Picasa*, in the folder you have created.

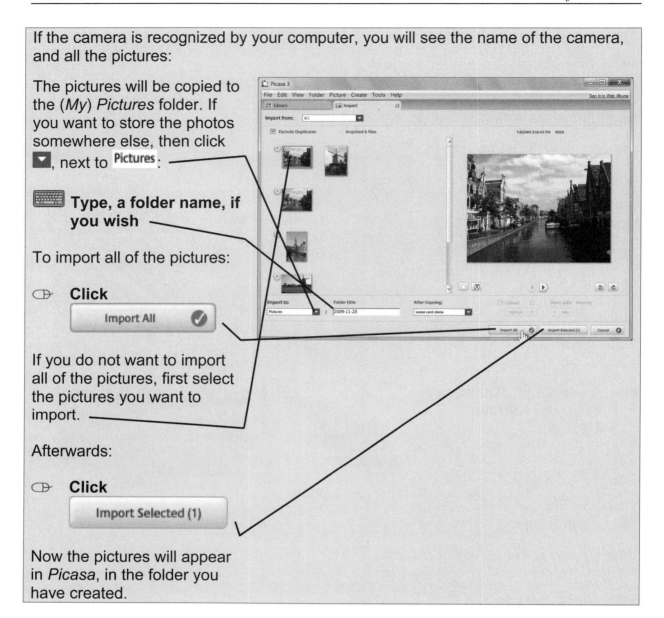

3. Basic Operations

In the old days you often threw away a picture if it was blurred or incorrectly exposed. Nowadays you can use a photo editing program, such as *Picasa*, to correct the flaws and blemishes in your pictures. In most cases, the results are sufficient enough that you can print your pictures in the normal way, or use them in a slide show.

Once in awhile however, no amount of editing will help. If a picture has been taken with a low resolution, you are going to be disappointed when you try to enlarge it. If you have used the wrong exposure, you may be able to make a correction, but the result would have been much better if you had used the correct exposure from the start. This is why it is still a worthy endeavor to try to steadily improve your picture taking skills.

But even the best photographers need to do a small amount of editing at times. Things such as red eye removal, rotating, cropping, retouching …you name it…*Picasa* can do all of this for you.

In this chapter you will learn how to:

- automatically correct your pictures;
- correct the exposure;
- edit pictures by group;
- manually correct pictures;
- rotate a picture;
- straighten a picture;
- add text;
- crop pictures;
- correct red eyes;
- retouch a picture.

 Please note:

If you want to use the exercises in this chapter, you need to download the *Practice-files-Picasa* folder and save it to the (*My*) *Pictures* folder on your computer. You can read how to do that in *Chapter 1 Installing Picasa*.

3.1 Automatically Correct your Pictures

Picasa will allow you to correct your pictures manually, but it also can perform a number of corrections automatically. A well-known example is the discoloration that often occurs with pictures taken in the snow, due to the reflection of the sky. This causes the snow to appear blue, red or grey, instead of white.
Here is how you can correct this problem:

☞ **Open *Picasa*** 🦶6

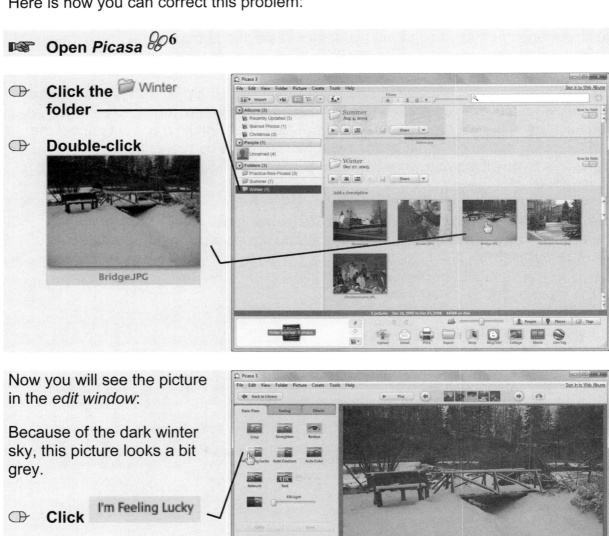

☞ **Click the** 📁 Winter **folder** ————

☞ **Double-click**

Now you will see the picture in the *edit window*:

Because of the dark winter sky, this picture looks a bit grey.

☞ **Click** I'm Feeling Lucky

You will notice that the snow has become whiter, and the picture is much clearer:

 HELP! I cannot see any improvement.

If the picture has not improved, click the Undo I'm Feeling Lucky button, and then click the I'm Feeling Lucky button again. Make sure you notice the difference in color, after you have clicked a button.

Now the I'm Feeling Lucky button is no longer active. You can use this button only once for each picture.

☞ **Click**

Back to Library

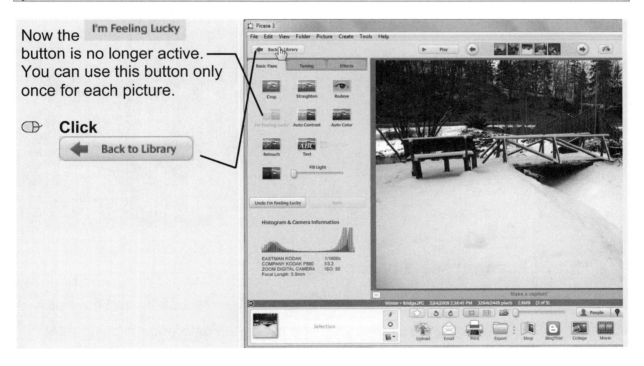

Clicking the I'm Feeling Lucky button can also be helpful when trying to correct pictures that are off color.

☞ **Open the** 📁 Summer
folder 🦶4

☞ **Open**

City.jpg

🦶5

This picture is a bit too red,
due to the late afternoon sun.

👉 **Click** [I'm Feeling Lucky]

Now the picture is much
clearer:

☞ **Open the** *library* 🦶11

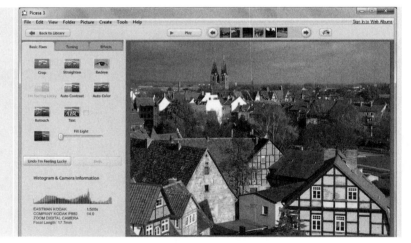

 HELP! I cannot see any improvement.

If the picture has not improved, click the [Undo I'm Feeling Lucky] button, and then click
the [I'm Feeling Lucky] button again. Make sure you notice the difference in color, after
you have clicked a button.

3.2 Correcting the Exposure

The I'm Feeling Lucky button not only improves colors, but it may also help you to correct a bad exposure. This is how you use it:

☞ **Open**

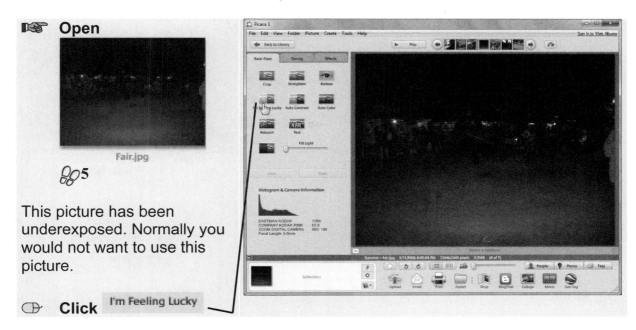

Fair.jpg

This picture has been underexposed. Normally you would not want to use this picture.

👉 **Click**   I'm Feeling Lucky

Now the picture is much brighter, and you can distinguish the horse carriage and the stalls. But you can still see that this picture has been taken at night.

👉 **Click**

        ◀ Back to Library

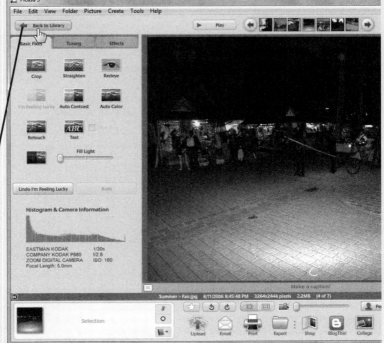

Sometimes, a picture cannot be enhanced.

Open 👣5

Statue.jpg

This picture has been backlit.

👆 **Click** I'm Feeling Lucky

You can hardly see any difference:

👆 **Click**

Undo I'm Feeling Lucky

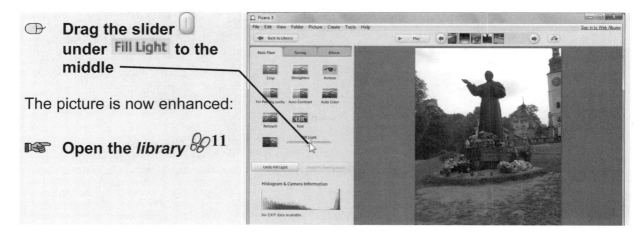

You can still try to correct the exposure manually:

👆 **Drag the slider** under Fill Light **to the middle**

The picture is now enhanced:

Open the *library* 👣11

Tip

First try the I'm Feeling Lucky **option**

If you use I'm Feeling Lucky , *Picasa* will try to correct the picture by using a number of different methods at once. If necessary, the colors, the exposure, and several other corrections will automatically be applied. If you try to do this manually, you will only be able to use one method at a time. This means you will need to try various options in order to achieve the best result.

 Tip

Use the ⬅ **and** ➡ **buttons**
If you want to view or correct more photos, you do not need to return to the *library* each time.

If you want to see the previous photo:

☞ **Click** ⬅

To see the next photo:

☞ **Click** ➡

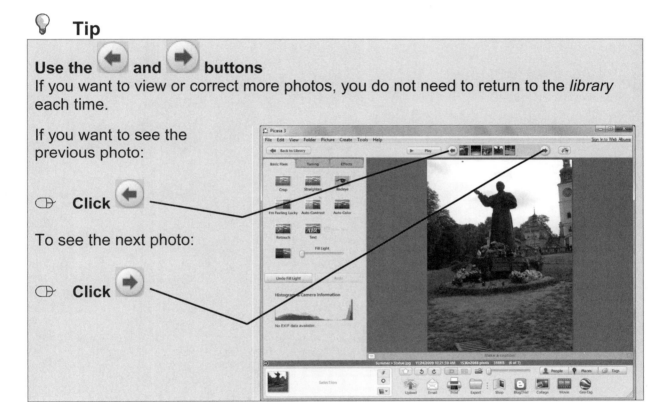

3.3 Group Editing

If you have quite a lot of pictures, correcting each individual picture will be a huge job. This is especially true when you have a whole series of pictures with more or less the same flaw (too dark, too bright, off color). If this is the case, you can first try to apply the same correction to the entire group of pictures. For instance, by using I'm Feeling Lucky . Here is how you do that:

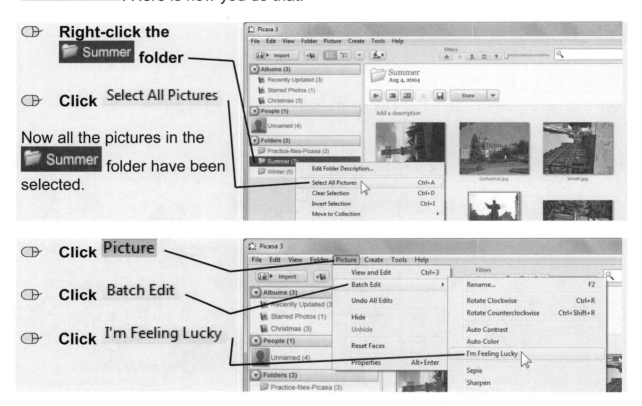

Right-click the Summer folder

Click Select All Pictures

Now all the pictures in the Summer folder have been selected.

Click Picture

Click Batch Edit

Click I'm Feeling Lucky

The editing operation may take a while, depending on the number of pictures.

💡 **Tip**

Only edit selected photos
When you do not want to edit all of the pictures in the folder, first select the photos you want to edit, by clicking them and keeping the Ctrl button pressed down.

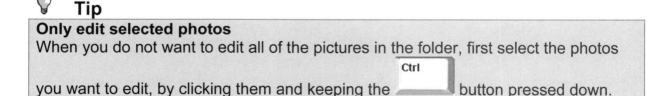

💡 **Tip**

Undoing the editing operation
If you are not satisfied with the result, you can click Picture, and then click Undo All Edits .

♀ Tip

Changing names all at once

Pictures that are transferred from your camera to your computer often have meaningless names, for example *IMG_0039* or *DSCN2058*. You can rename all of these pictures at once:

☞ **Right-click a folder**
☞ **Click** Select All Pictures
☞ **Click** Picture
☞ **Click** Batch Edit
☞ **Click** Rename...

You can type a new file name in the window that appears. For instance: 'Florida Holiday 2009'. Then you click the Rename button. *Picasa* will add this name to all of the selected photos, and will automatically add a sequence number. For instance 'Florida Holiday 2009-1', 'Florida Holiday 2009-2' and so on.

3.4 Manual Corrections

All of the pictures have now been edited in the same way. But the results will vary per photo. Now you are going to check if any of the pictures need to be corrected manually:

☞ **Open**

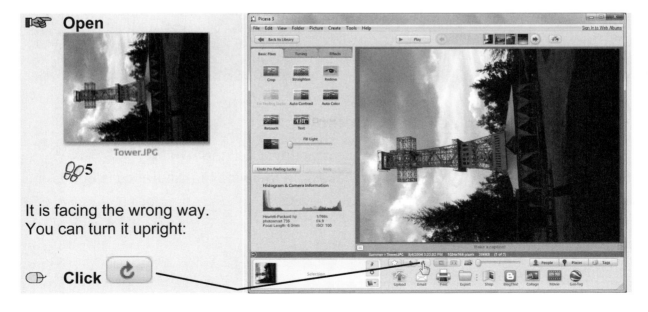

Tower.JPG

👣 5

It is facing the wrong way.
You can turn it upright:

☞ **Click** ↻

Please note:

The Undo I'm Feeling Lucky button is still active. This is due to the batch editing operation from the previous section.

Now the tower has been rotated clockwise and is upright again.

Despite using I'm Feeling Lucky , the exposure is still not very good. You can solve this problem by using Fill Light :

 Drag the slider under Fill Light to the right a little

Now the exposure has been improved:

 Click Auto Color

If you watch carefully, you will see a small difference in color. The white streak of sky will change color.

HELP! I do not see any difference.

Sometimes you cannot see the difference properly. Click the Undo Auto Color button and then click Auto Color again. Make sure to notice the difference in color, after you have clicked a button.

3.5 Straightening

In the next step, you are going to try to straighten the tower in this picture. *Picasa* has a special feature for objects that appear tilted in your pictures, called 'straighten':

 Click Straighten

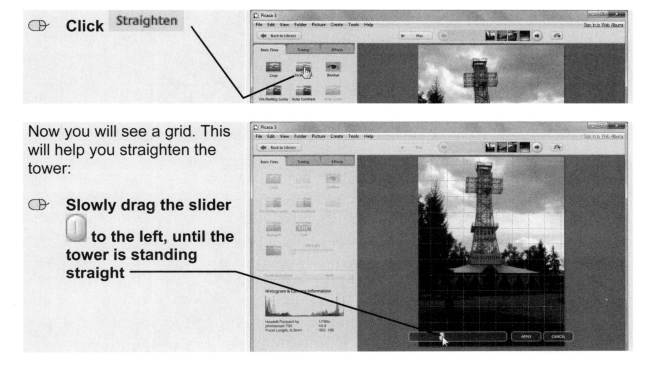

Now you will see a grid. This will help you straighten the tower:

 Slowly drag the slider to the left, until the tower is standing straight

💡 Tip

Watch the horizontal lines
If the object itself is leaning backwards, or is not completely straight, it may be difficult to find the right position. In that case you need to watch the horizontal lines or planes in the photo. Compare these to the horizontal lines in the grid. Or compare the trees and people in the picture to the vertical lines in the grid.

🔖 Please note:

When you straighten a picture, it is rotated somewhat. The height and width no longer fit the picture size that was selected. *Picasa* will crop the picture and adjust the size automatically. You may lose a small piece of the photo border.

If the tower is standing straight:

☞ **Click**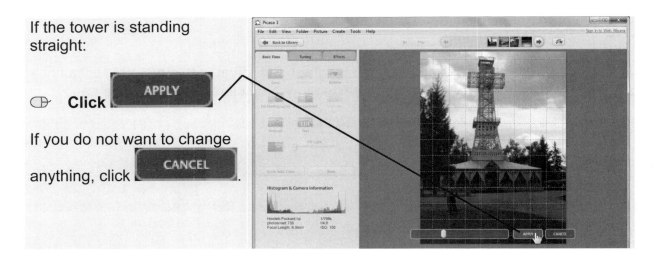

If you do not want to change anything, click .

Now you have done a good job at straightening the tower, but unfortunately you cannot do anything about the fact that the tower inclines slightly backwards.

Also, due to the straightening action, the photo is not quite as sharp as it used to be.

3.6 Adding Text

If you want to use this picture as a header or as a postcard, you can add some text to it. You can position your text anywhere you want, you can rotate the text as well, and choose from several font types, sizes and colors. Here is how you add text to this picture:

☞ **Click** Text

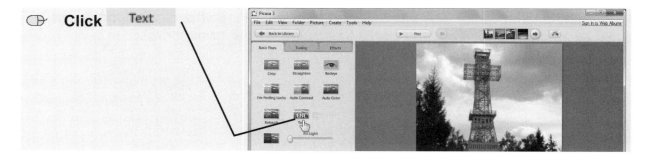

In the middle of the picture you will see a message: ⎯⎯

☞ **Click on the grass in the bottom left corner**

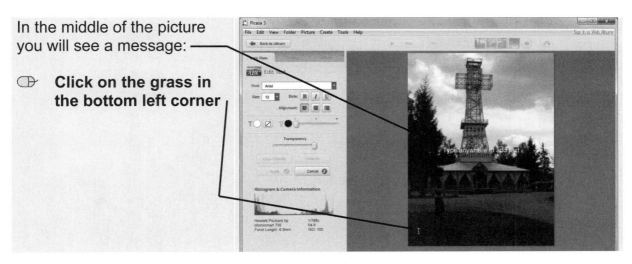

⌨ **Type:** Stolberg, Harz, Germany

Next to Size: :

☞ **Click** ▼

☞ **Click** 16

The text will be adjusted right away:

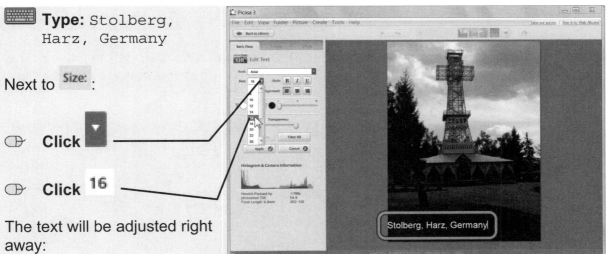

You can change the color of the letters yourself, as well as the outline of the letters. Here is how you do that:

Next to T :

☞ **Click** ○

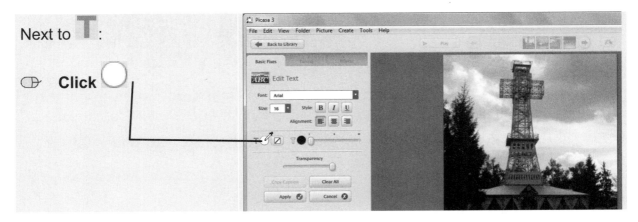

Now you will see a color palette:

☞ **Move the mouse pointer over the colors**

☞ **Click a color**

Now the text color will change:

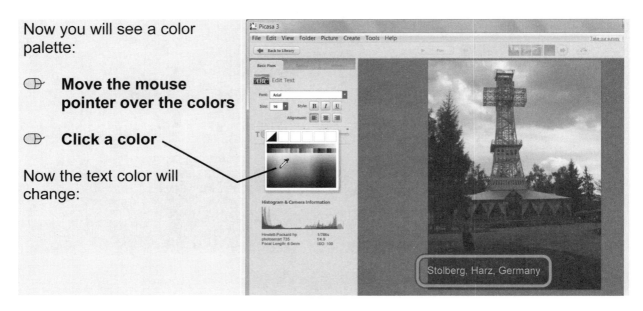

You will only see the color of the letter itself. But you can also change the color of the letter's contours. This is what you are going to do next. First you need to display the outline of the letters. To do this:

☞ **Drag the slider ◖ next to ⊤⬤ to the middle**

This will adjust the outline of the letters and the letters themselves:

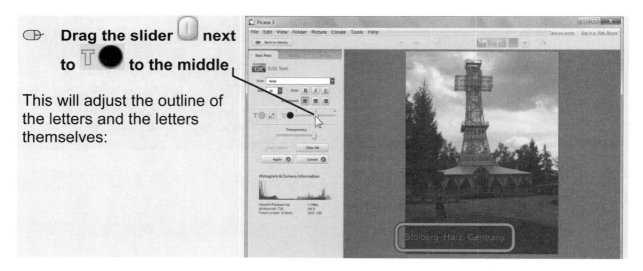

⮞ **Please note:**

If the slider ◖ is positioned on the left-hand side, you will see the color of the letter.
If the slider ◖ is on the right-hand side, you will see the color of the letter's outline.

Tip

Larger letters create more effect
If the letters are quite small, the contours will be so wide that you can barely see the color of the letters. If you select a larger font size, you will be able to see the difference in color between the outline and the letter much easier.

To change the color of the outline:

Next to ⊤ :

☞ **Click**

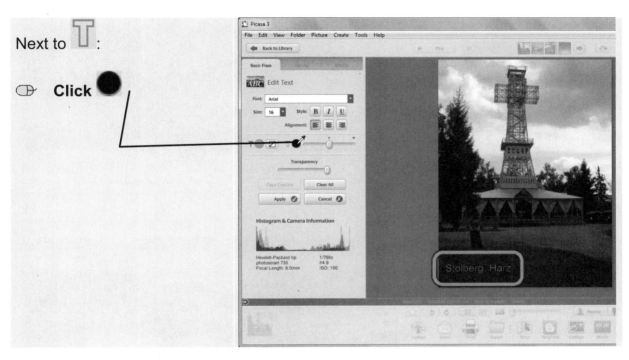

Now you will see a color palette:

☞ **Move the mouse pointer over the colors**

☞ **Click a color**

The color of the letter's outline will change:

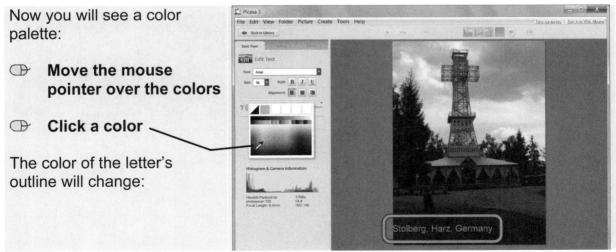

Now you are going to make the text more transparent:

⊕ **Drag the slider** 🖱 **under** Transparency **to the middle** ────

Now the letters will become more transparent, and therefore less visible.

⊕ **Drag the slider** 🖱 **under** Transparency **to the right**

Now the letters are once more clearly visible.

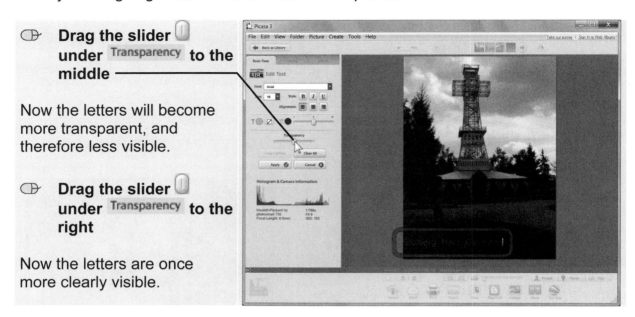

Next you will try moving the text:

⊕ **Position the mouse pointer at the border of the text frame** ╲

The mouse pointer will turn

into ✥:

⊕ **Drag the text frame upwards** ────

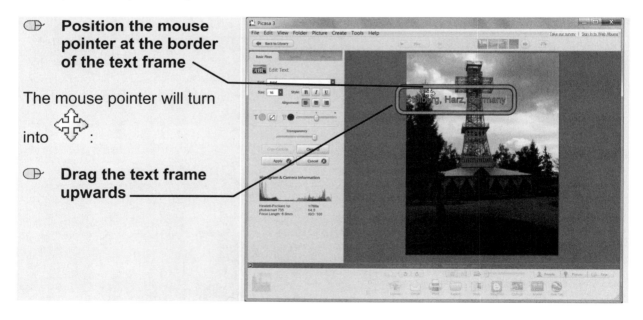

Now you are going to rotate the text:

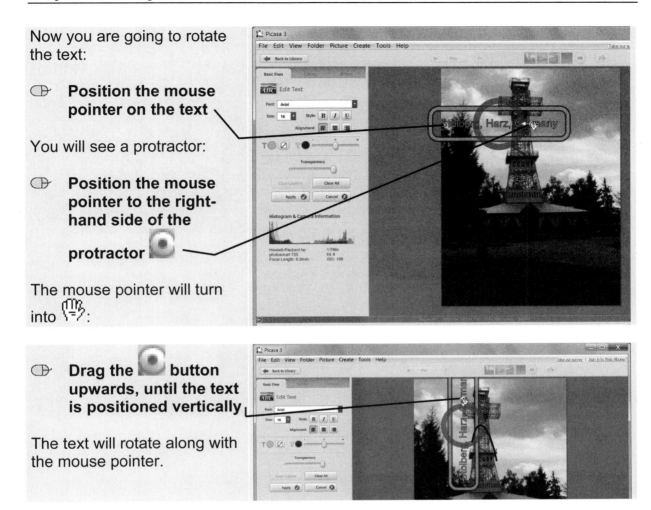

☞ **Position the mouse pointer on the text**

You will see a protractor:

☞ **Position the mouse pointer to the right-hand side of the protractor**

The mouse pointer will turn into 🖑:

☞ **Drag the button upwards, until the text is positioned vertically**

The text will rotate along with the mouse pointer.

💡 **Tip**

Larger or smaller text

If you drag the button inwards or outwards, the text becomes larger or smaller.

The other buttons work the same way as the regular buttons in other *Windows* programs. You can use:

- **Font:** to select a different font type;

- **B**, *I*, or **U** to apply **bold**, *italics*, or underlining;

- ≣, ≣, or ≣ to align the text to the left, to the middle or to the right of the text box.

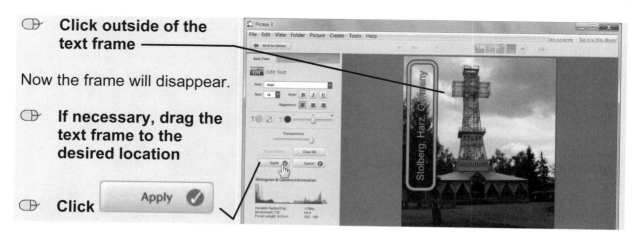

- ☞ **Click outside of the text frame** ———

Now the frame will disappear.

- ☞ **If necessary, drag the text frame to the desired location**

- ☞ **Click** Apply ✓

In just a few steps you have transformed this picture. The picture is no longer too dark and the main subject of the composition (the tower) is nice and straight:

☞ **Open the *library*** ¹¹

3.7 Cropping Pictures

By cropping a picture you can highlight the most important part of your composition and trim away the less attractive parts, such as a lamp post or a billboard. When you do this, you need to maintain the correct height/width ratio, depending on the way you want to use the picture later on. You can crop your pictures like this:

➥ Please note:

If you want to rotate a picture, do so before cropping it. When you rotate a picture, *Picasa* will automatically remove the excess edges of the photo at the same time.

The cathedral is the main subject of this picture. The foreground and the group of people to the right are less important. In fact they actually draw the attention away from the cathedral. By cropping the photo you make the cathedral the dominant feature.

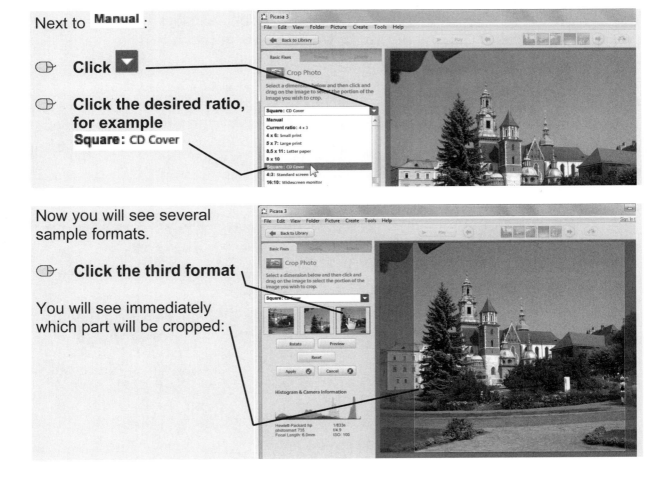

Usually, you will still need to adjust the picture manually. This is how you do that:

 Place the mouse pointer in the left-hand corner

The pointer will turn into 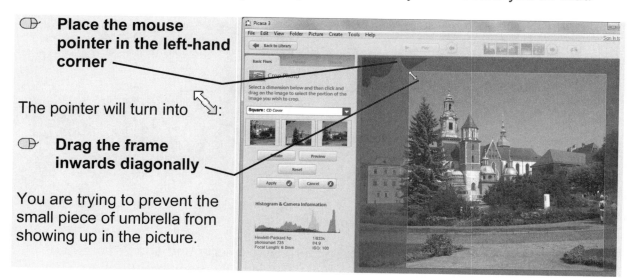:

 Drag the frame inwards diagonally

You are trying to prevent the small piece of umbrella from showing up in the picture.

➡ **Please note:**

When you select a standard preset size, you cannot completely adjust the frame the way you want it. The frame needs to have the height/width ratio that goes with the preset. If you select **Manual** you are free to set your own height/width ratio.

💡 **Tip**

Rotating the cropped frame

If you do not select a square frame, the default frame is always horizontally oriented.

If you click the **Rotate** button, you can create a vertical frame. At first, the size was 5 x 7. Now it will be 7 x 5:

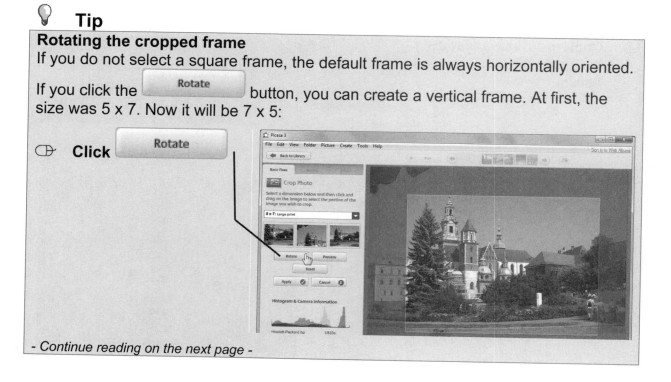 **Click Rotate**

- Continue reading on the next page -

The cropped frame has now been rotated a quarter turn:

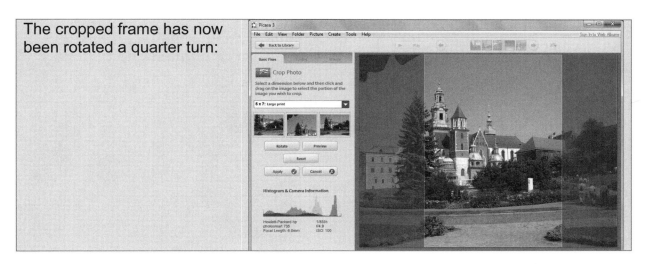

Place the mouse pointer on the right-hand corner ────

The pointer will turn into 🖰:

Drag the frame inwards diagonally

Now the street is no longer visible in the picture.

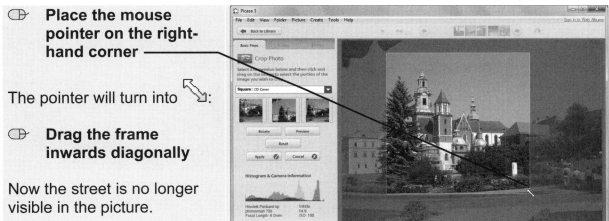

After cropping a picture, it may be necessary to move the cropped frame a little bit, in order to better position the main subject.

Place the mouse pointer on the cropped frame ────

The pointer will turn into 🖐:

Drag the frame slightly to the left

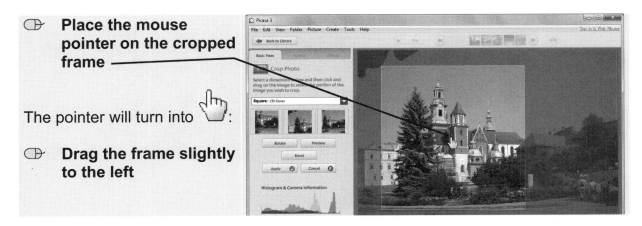

You can watch a preview before you apply the cropping:

 Click [Preview]

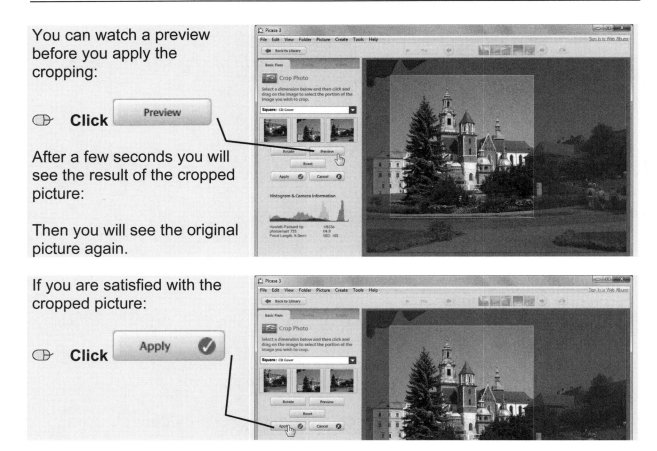

After a few seconds you will see the result of the cropped picture:

Then you will see the original picture again.

If you are satisfied with the cropped picture:

 Click [Apply ✓]

HELP! I do not like the cropped picture.

If you are not satisfied with the result, you can click the [Reset] button. You can repeat the previous steps to crop the picture again.

Here you will see the final cropped picture:

Now you can return to the *library*.

 Click [← Back to Library]

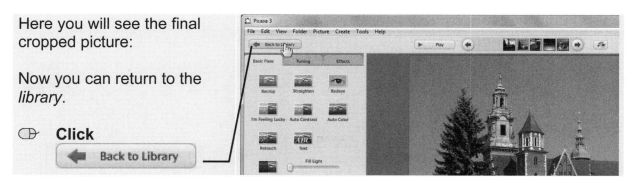

💡 Tip

To the library

You can also return to the *library* by pressing the [Esc] key.

3.8 Correcting Red Eyes

Picasa has a special button for correcting red eyes. First you need to find a picture in the *library*:

⊕ **Click the search box**

⌨ **Type:** baby

The picture appears immediately in the window:

You can see that this picture is stored in the

 Practice-files-Picasa
Dec 26, 2005

folder:

⊕ **Click** ✖

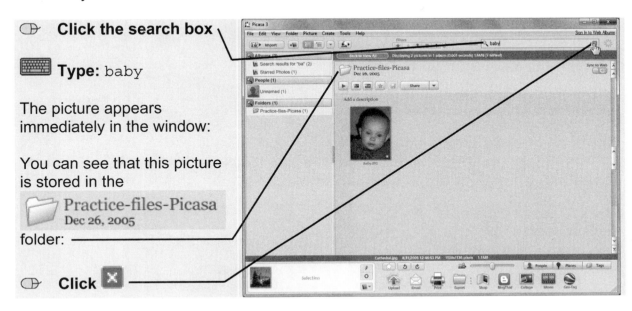

💡 **Tip**

Red eye correction by the camera
Nowadays, many digital cameras have a built-in option to prevent red eyes while using flash. Check the manual of your camera to see if this option is available.

☞ **Open** Baby.JPG ∂∂5

Now you are going to zoom in.

At the bottom of the window:

⊕ **Drag the slider** 🔍 **next to** 🔍 **slightly to the right**

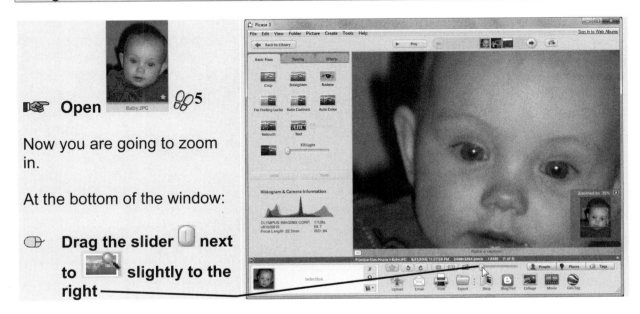

💡 Tip

Moving
If zooming in does not display the baby's eyes:

☞ **Drag the frame in the thumbnail window until you see the eyes**

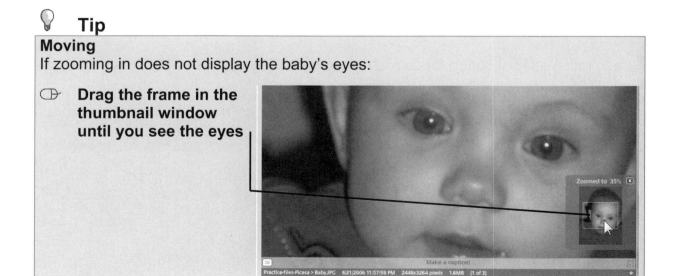

Now you can see the eyes much better:

☞ **Click** Redeye

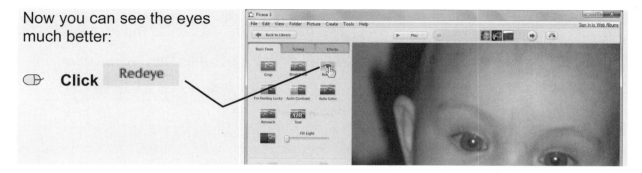

Picasa will analyze the photo and look for red eyes. This may take a few seconds. Subsequently, both red eyes will be corrected:

Here you can see that the red eyes have been corrected:

Sometimes, *Picasa* cannot locate the eyes. Then you need to adjust them manually:

☞ **Click** Reset

The red eyes are back again.

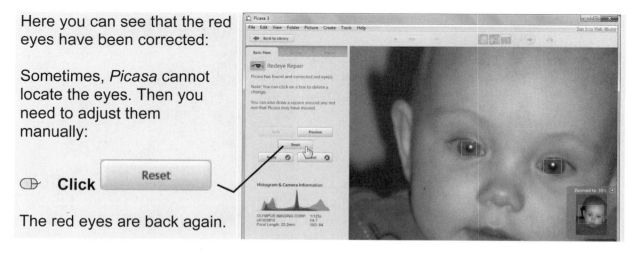

- ☝ **Place the mouse pointer near the top left of the iris of the red eye**

- ☝ **Drag the pointer diagonally over the eye, until the iris is inside the frame**

- ☝ **Release the mouse button**

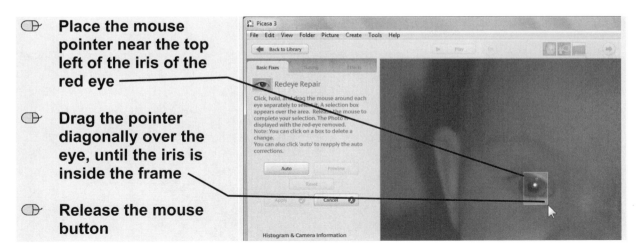

Now you will see the eye, without the red iris:

☞ **Correct the other eye in the same way**

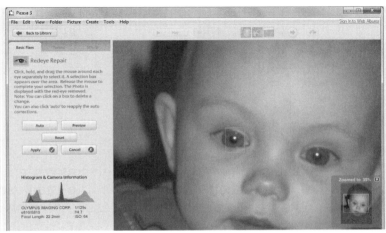

The red eyes have disappeared:

☝ **Click** Apply ✔

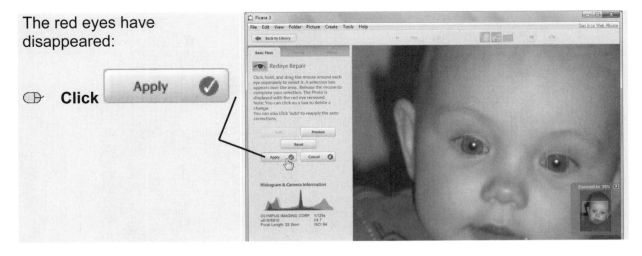

Now you can zoom out again. Here is how you do that:

At the bottom of the window:

👆 **Click**

Now you see the full picture without the red eyes:

☞ **Open the** *library* 📏¹¹

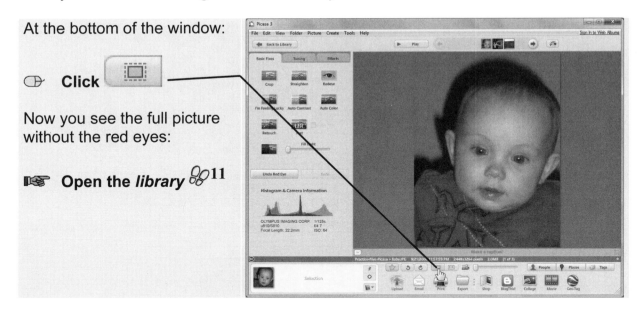

3.9 Retouching Photos

A speck of dust, a hair on your lens, or a scratch mark on a scanned photo or slide can really ruin your picture. In most cases, you can use the *Retouch* option to correct these blemishes. You will get the best results if the blemish occurs in an area that is evenly colored. You can see that in the next picture:

☞ **Find** 📏¹⁴

☞ **Open the picture** 📏⁵

The picture needs to be turned:

👆 **Click** ↻

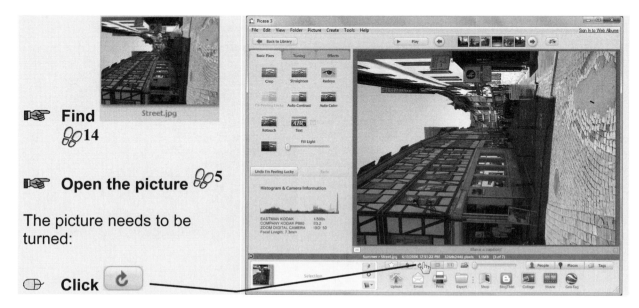

In the bottom right corner of the picture you can see a black dash that does not belong there:

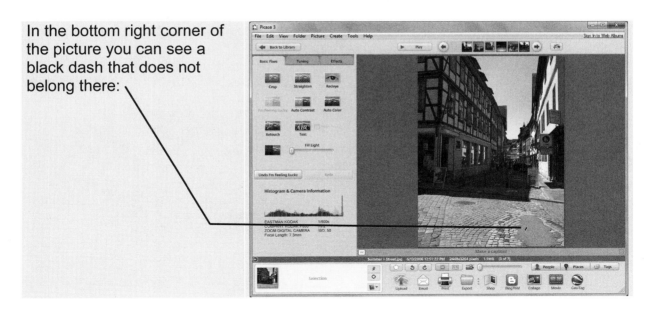

You are going to retouch this dash.

⊂⊅ **Click** Retouch

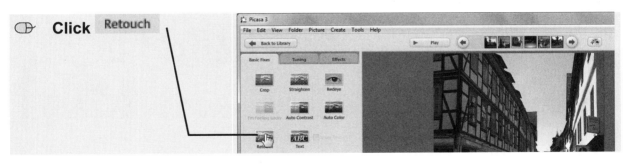

The program will zoom in on the central part of the picture:

At the bottom right side of the window:

⊂⊅ **Drag the zoom frame downwards**

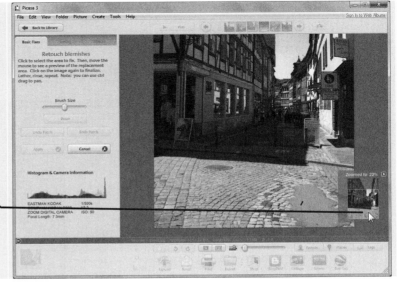

Retouching a picture takes two steps. First, you need to indicate which part of the picture you want to retouch. Here is how you do that:

Position the mouse pointer on top of the black dash ——

A circular selection now surrounds the dash :

The dash is too big for the circle. You will need to enlarge the selection circle.

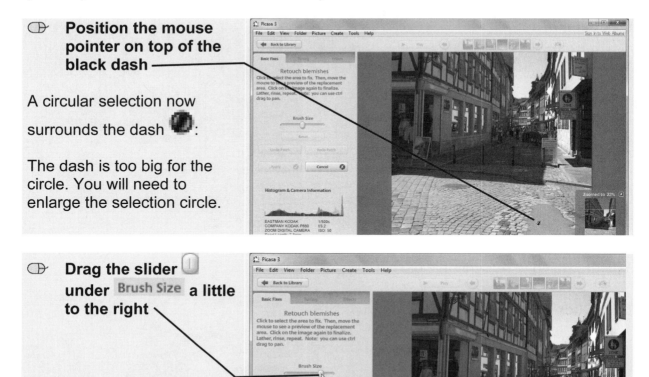

Drag the slider under Brush Size **a little to the right** ＼

➥ Please note:

Try to resize the circular selection just slightly, until the dash fits exactly into the circle. This will give you the best result. If the circle is too big, the retouched area will be more clearly evident.

Position the mouse pointer on top of the black dash ——

Now the dash fits into the circle.

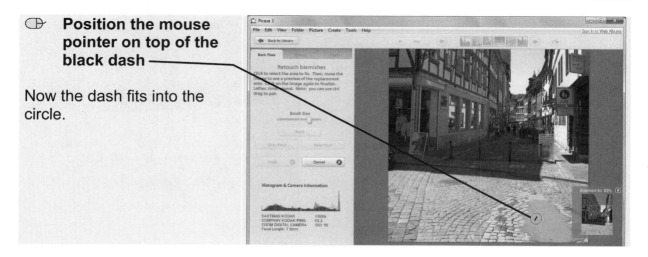

Now you can carry out the first step of the retouching process. You have already indicated which part of the photo you want to retouch. Now you just have to click it:

☞ **Click the dash** ———————

The area in the selection circle is now selected and can be replaced by another part of the photo.

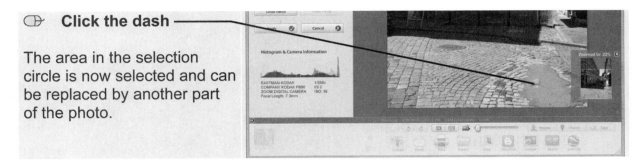

The second step is to choose a part of the photo that will be used to replace the selected retouch area. In this example you will use part of the street next to the selected area.

☞ **Click the desired place in the street** ———————

The part of the photo that you have clicked, will be copied to the retouch area:

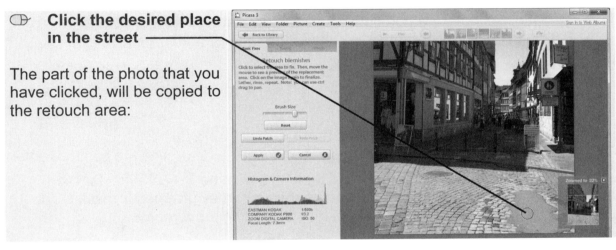

The area where the dash used to be, has now changed color:

If you are satisfied with the result:

☞ **Click** Apply ✔

If you do not like the result:

☞ **Click** Undo Patch

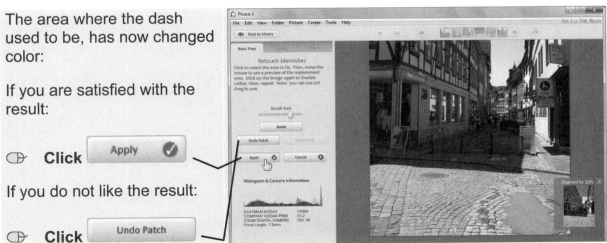

You can view the result better in the full picture:

☞ **Open the** *library* 𝒬𝒬11

☞ **Close** *Picasa* 𝒬𝒬3

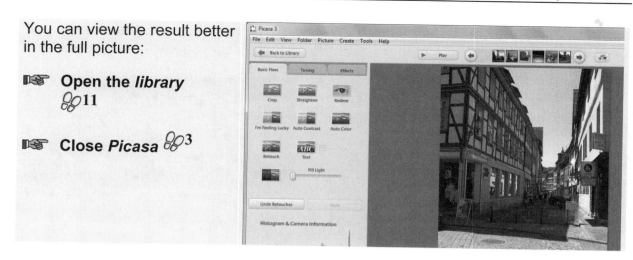

The *Retouch* option lets you replace the selected area by another part of the photo. In photo editing programs, this is often called 'cloning'.

In this chapter you have learned how to use *Picasa's* basic editing features. In general, you will not need to use the Auto Contrast and Auto Color functions, because these will automatically be applied when you use the I'm Feeling Lucky option. But if I'm Feeling Lucky does not give you the results you want, you can try it yourself, by using Auto Contrast or Auto Color .

The function next to Fill Light is used by *Picasa*, to determine the best possible exposure. Even if you have already tried to do this with the I'm Feeling Lucky function, using the slider and correcting the exposure manually may give better results. You can read more about this topic in *section 3.2 Correcting the Exposure*.

3.10 Background Information

Dictionary

Brightness	The amount of light you see in a photo. When you decrease the brightness, the colors will become indistinct. Increasing the brightness will make the colors clearer.
Contrast	The difference in color between adjacent parts of a photo.
Cropping	Cutting out parts of a photo you do not want to see.
Pixel	The smallest element of a digital image. Also called dot or picture point.
Red eyes	The red glow in the eye's iris. This may show on flash photos.
Resolution	The sharpness or definition of a photo. The resolution is determined by the amount of pixels contained in the photo.
Retouching	Getting rid of ugly smudges, scrapes, or blemishes in order to enhance the quality of a photo.
Zooming	Blowing up part of a photo (zooming in) or diminishing a photo (zooming out).

Source: Picasa Help

Searching with Picasa

You can use the *Picasa* search engine to look for photo files, album names, folder names, headers, keywords which you have entered in the *Picasa* search box.

For instance, if you are looking for a folder on your computer called *Mary's pictures*, but you know that you have at least two other photos in other folders, called *Mary at a party* and *John and Mary are fishing*, you can enter 'Mary' in the search box. You will not only find the two separate photos, but all of the pictures contained in *Mary's pictures* folder as well.

Source: Picasa Help

3.11 Tips

 Tip

Hiding and showing photos
You can hide certain pictures in the *Picasa* folders. These pictures will not be visible in the *Picasa library*, but will still be displayed in *Windows Explorer*. This is how you hide a picture:

In the *library*:

☞ **Click the desired picture**

☞ **Click** `Picture`

☞ **Click** `Hide`

Now the picture is no longer visible.

If you want to show the picture again:

☞ **Click** `View`

☞ **Click** `Hidden Pictures`

Now you will see a transparent image of this picture:

☞ **Click the picture you want to show**

☞ **Click** `Picture`

☞ **Click** `Unhide`

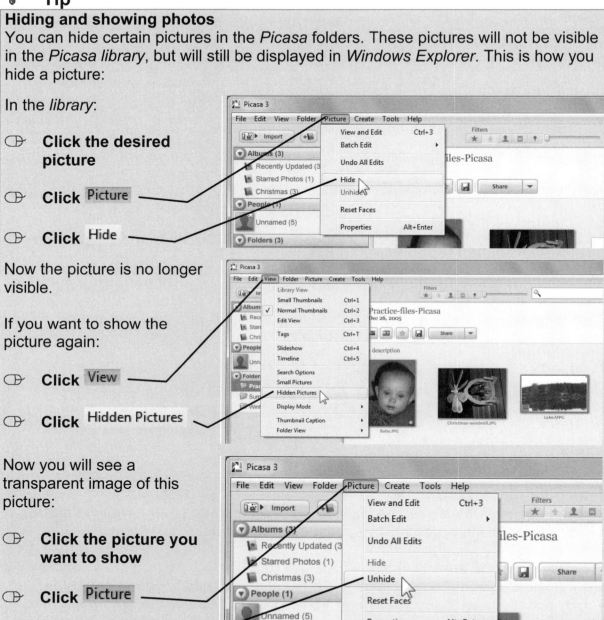

- Continue reading on the next page -

Now the picture is visible in the *library* again.
If you want to make other hidden pictures invisible again:

☞ **Click** `View`

You will see a checkmark next to `Hidden Pictures`:

☞ **Click** `Hidden Pictures`

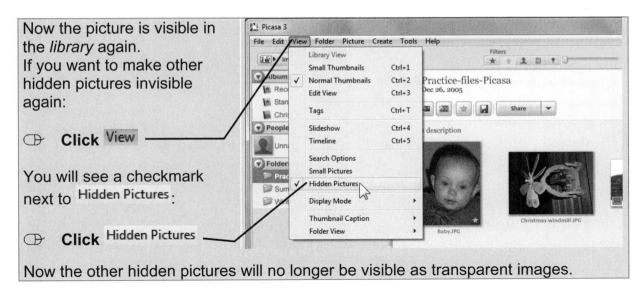

Now the other hidden pictures will no longer be visible as transparent images.

💡 **Tip**

Creating and editing captions
In the *edit window* you can add a caption to a picture. You can use this caption in your search for pictures. Also, you can display these captions in your slide shows or web albums. To add a caption to a picture:

👉 **Open**
👣5

Under the picture:

☞ **Click** `Make a caption!`

⌨ **Type a caption**

⌨ **Press** [**Enter** ←]

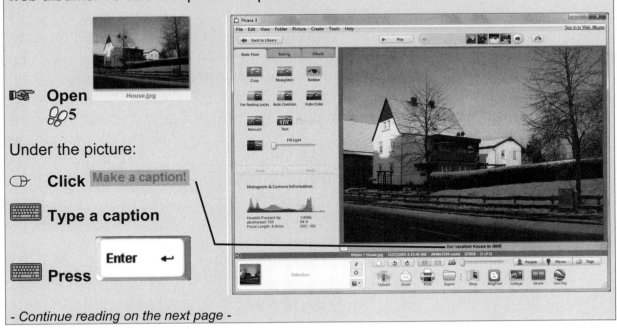

- Continue reading on the next page -

To edit the text:

⬤▷ **Click in the caption text** ——

⌨ **Press** ← Backspace **or** ←

⌨ **Edit the caption**

⌨ **Press** Enter ↵

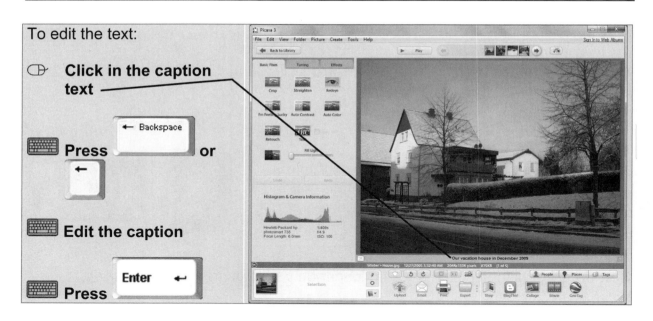

4. Tuning, Saving and Making Backups

In the previous chapter you learned how to apply corrections. Some automatically and others manually. In most cases the application of one or more of these corrections will be all that is necessary to enhance your pictures. But sometimes this is not enough. In this chapter, you will learn more about making manual adjustments and how to add special effects to your pictures.

You will also learn about the different ways you can save the pictures you have enhanced. Using the correct storage method is important, especially if you want to save your original unmodified pictures for later use in other programs.

Finally, you will learn how to use *Picasa* for making backups of your pictures, and for restoring them. Making backups of your pictures for safekeeping is becoming increasingly important, because nowadays with the increasing popularity of digital cameras, the digital file format is often the only storage method being used. For your important pictures it is a good idea to have a copy of them somewhere separate from your computer.

In this chapter you will learn how to:

- fine tune pictures;
- adjust the colors;
- make a picture look warmer or cooler;
- apply special effects;
- sharpen a picture;
- save pictures in *Picasa*;
- restore a picture to its original version;
- export pictures;
- make a backup of your pictures;
- restore the backup.

Please note:

If you want to use the exercises in this chapter, you need to download the *Practice-files-Picasa* folder and save it to the (*My*) *Pictures* folder on your computer. You can read how to do that in *Chapter 1 Installing Picasa*.

4.1 Fine Tuning

At times your pictures may display unnatural colors. This often happens when the wrong exposure has been used, particularly when pictures are made in a tricky lighting situation, such as at the beach or in the snow. If you have tried applying automatic corrections and you are not satisfied with the result, or if after applying them, other unwanted effects appear, you can try using *Picasa's Tuning* option instead and correct your pictures manually. Here is how to do that:

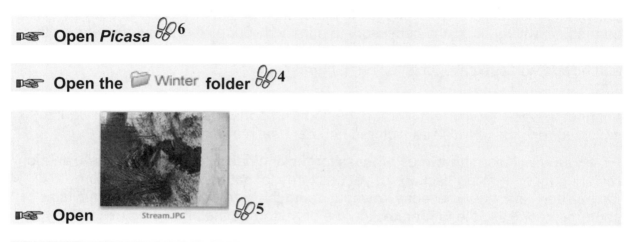

☞ **Open *Picasa*** 🐾⁶

☞ **Open the** 📁 Winter **folder** 🐾⁴

☞ **Open**   Stream.JPG   🐾⁵

☞ **Rotate the photo clockwise** 🐾⁹

Due to the snow, there are fewer details in the picture and it is very pale. You can correct these things yourself:

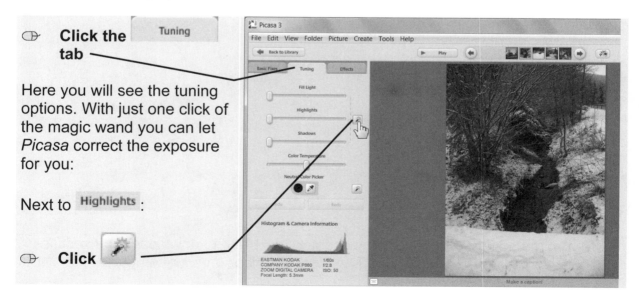

🖱 **Click the** Tuning **tab**

Here you will see the tuning options. With just one click of the magic wand you can let *Picasa* correct the exposure for you:

Next to Highlights :

🖱 **Click** 🪄

The sliders  under **Highlights** and **Shadows** have changed position: ——

Now the details in the picture become more visible:

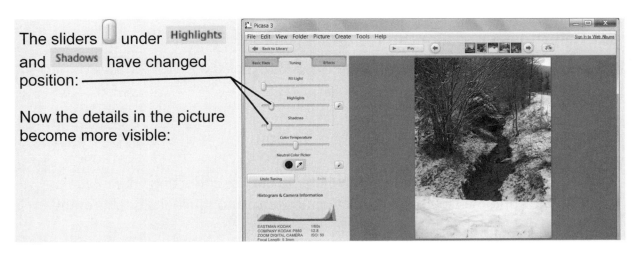

Please note:

If you have previously altered a photo by using **I'm Feeling Lucky** or **Auto Contrast**, the option will already have been applied automatically and you will not see any changes.

Now you can try to enhance the photo further:

☞ **Drag the slider under Fill Light to the right a bit** ——

The picture will become clearer:

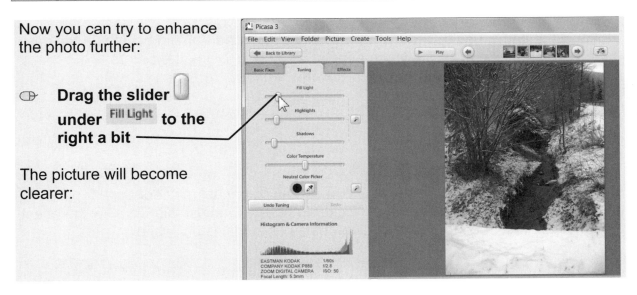

If you want to use a photo for an album or an enlargement, it may be useful to use the *Tuning* tool's sliders a bit more and try to fine tune the photo as best you can. For use in a simple slide show, the automatic tuning option will usually produce a satisfying result.

HELP! I do not like the result.

If you do not like the correction and want to undo it, click the | Undo Tuning | button.

Which slider should you use?
Use the following list to determine which slider to use for correcting your pictures:

- Fill Light : to lighten a backlit photo, or a dark photo, and retain the details in the brighter areas of the photo.
- Highlights : to lighten the entire photo, whereby the lighter areas will become even lighter. For the best results, use Highlights together with Shadows .
- Shadows : to darken the entire photo, whereby the darker areas will become clearer. For the best results, use this option together with Highlights .

Often, you will need to combine several functions, in order to achieve the best result. The magic wand will help you with the initial corrections. This button works in the same way as the Auto Contrast function on the Basic Fixes tab, but in this case you will still be able to edit the effects yourself, by using the sliders.

Source: Picasa Help

4.2 Adjusting Colors

Snow or clouds depicted in pictures with a certain color cast may not appear pure white. You can use the *Neutral Color Picker* to help you adjust this. To view the effect properly, you first need to click a portion of the photo that is not white:

☞ **Click**

The mouse pointer will turn into :

☞ **Click the bush**

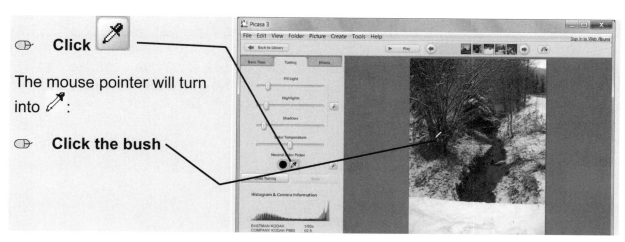

The degree of discoloration will depend on the spot you have clicked. *Picasa* will consider this spot to be white or light grey (which was not the case in this photo), and will adjust the other colors accordingly. If you want to correct the photo once more, you can click the portion of the photo that was supposed to be white. You can also try using the magic wand.

The colors in the photo have changed:

Next to Neutral Color Picker :

⊕   **Click**

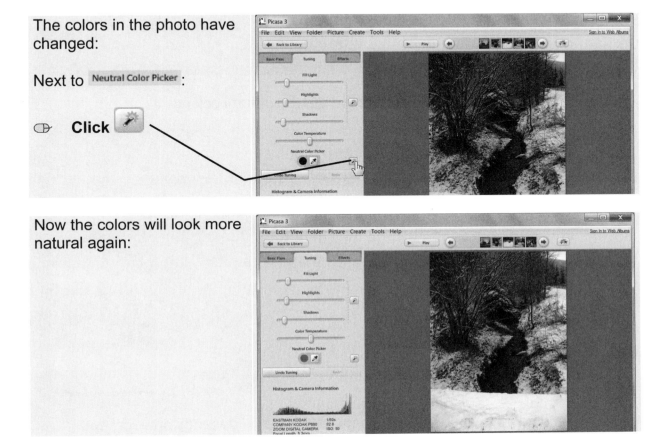

Now the colors will look more natural again:

With the color temperature slider you can make a photo appear warmer or cooler.

⊕   **Drag the slider under Color Temperature to the left**

The colors will become bluer and make the photo appear 'cooler'.

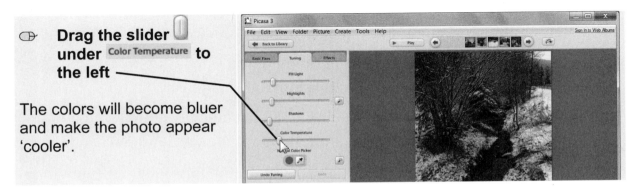

👆 **Drag the slider under** Color Temperature **to the right**

The colors will become 'warmer':

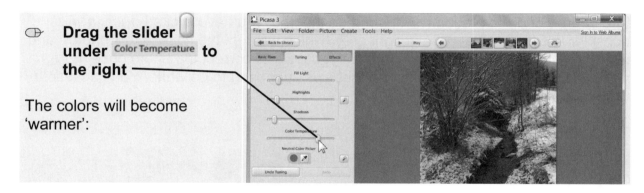

Again, you can use the magic wand to revert to the natural colors:

Next to Neutral Color Picker :

👆 **Click** 🪄

The colors will appear more natural and the slider under Color Temperature will once again be positioned in the middle.

☞ **Open the** *library* 𝒪ℓ11

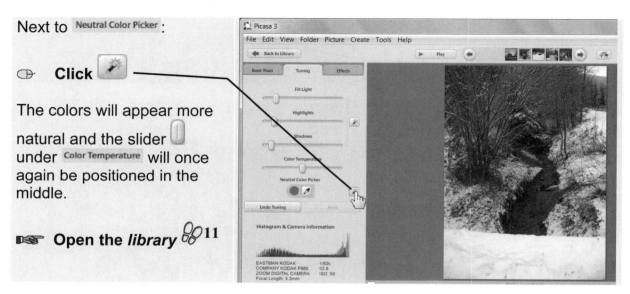

Getting the colors right is not always easy and obviously depends on your own preferences. Do you want to create a warmer picture, a crisper picture, or a picture with a lot of contrast? *Picasa* can help you improve the general appearance of nearly all of your pictures. But sometimes, you just cannot get the result you want. This is illustrated in the following example:

☞ **Open** House.jpg 𝒪ℓ5

The photo has a bluish cast.

You want to try to correct this:

☞ **Click the Tuning tab**

☞ **Click**

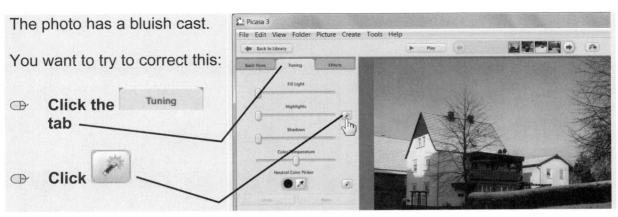

This photo is still too blue.

Now try looking for a neutral color:

Next to Neutral Color Picker :

☞ **Click**

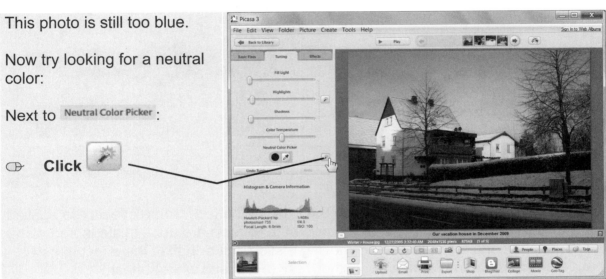

Now the photo has become redder, but the snow is still not pure white.

☞ **Click** Undo Tuning

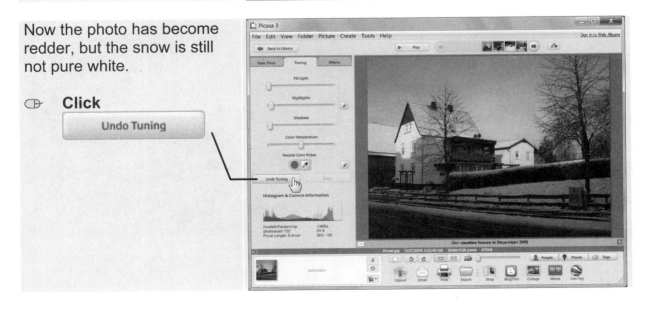

4.3 Effects

Although you may not be wholly satisfied with the color adjustments for a given photo, you may be quite happy with the end result when you apply special effects. *Picasa* offers a number of standard effects for you to try out.

☞ **Click the Effects tab**

Here you will see twelve various effects:

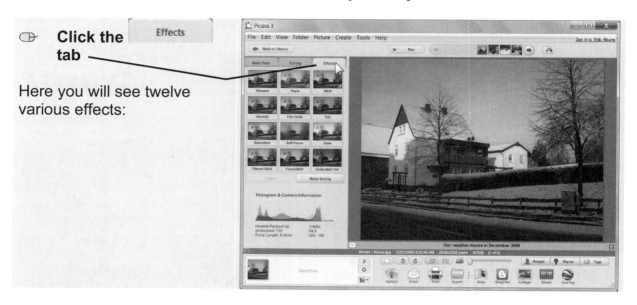

The way each effect works depends on the particular effect. Some effects are applied to the whole image with just one click, while other effects are done in steps and you can make additional adjustments by moving a slider left or right. One effect that will change a picture quite dramatically is the *B&W* (black and white) effect:

☞ **Click B&W**

Now the photo becomes black and white:

☞ **Click Undo B&W**

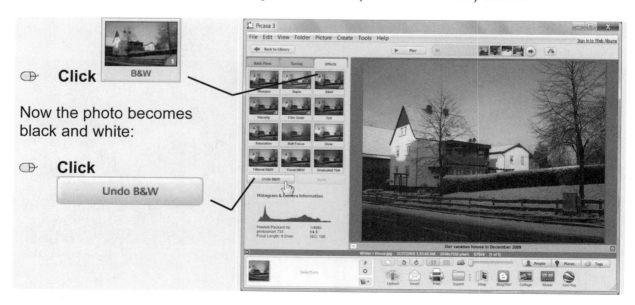

Tip

One-click effects

You will recognize these effects by the icon in the bottom right-hand corner of the effect. These effects will change the entire photo at once.

The adds a sepia tone and gives the appearance of an aged photo:

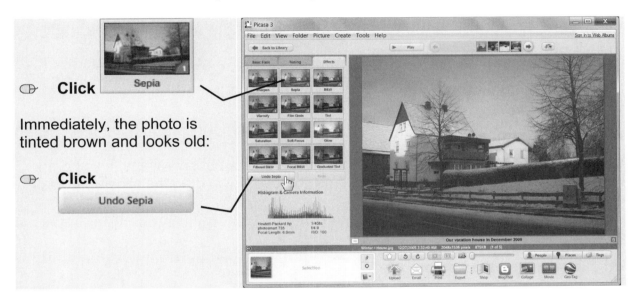

☞ **Click** Sepia

Immediately, the photo is tinted brown and looks old:

☞ **Click**

Undo Sepia

If you apply the sharpen effect to the photo, you can see how out of focus some of the objects in the original photo were:

☞ **Click** Sharpen

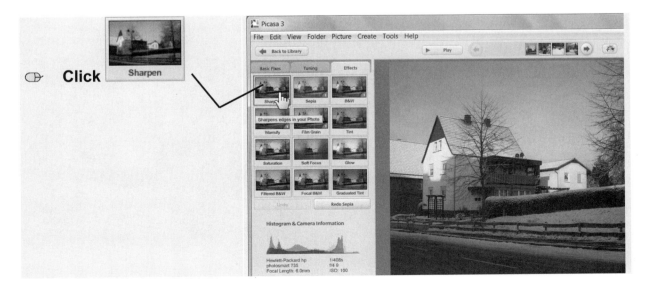

If you watch closely, you will
see that the house and the
trees have become sharper:

 Click Apply ✓

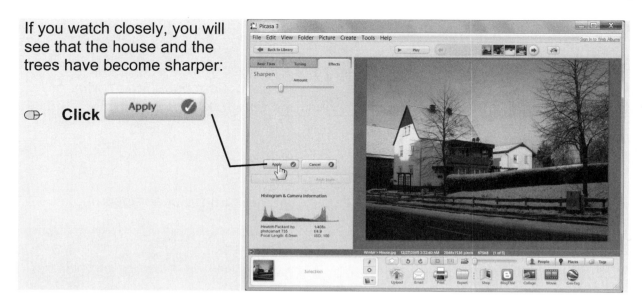

💡 Tip

Amount of sharpness

You can use the slider 🔲 under Amount to set the amount of sharpness. If you drag
the slider to the right, the photo will become sharper. If you drag the slider to the left,
the photo will become less sharp.

💡 Tip

No difference on the screen

If you cannot see any difference on your screen:

 Click Cancel ✗

Now you can try again.

Here you will see the sharper
picture:

Please note:

You can combine several effects one after the other, but if you want to be able to see the results properly, you need to undo any previous effects first. Try experimenting and applying more than one effect. You may be pleasantly surprised at the results.

Instead of black and white, or sepia, you can also give the photo a different color. You can choose any color you want:

⊕ **Click** Tint

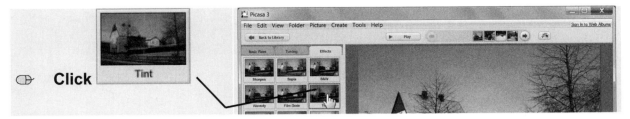

At first the photo becomes black and white:

⊕ **Click**

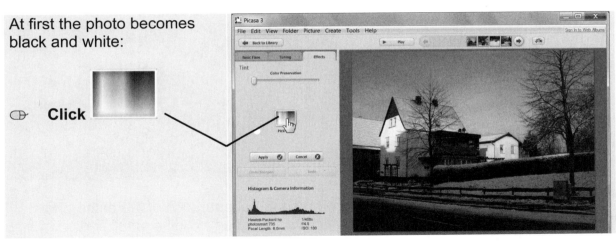

⊕ **Hover the mouse pointer over the color palette**

You will see the photo change colors.

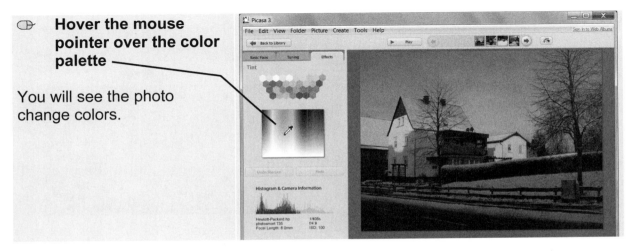

Now you can pick a color:

👉 **Click a tint** ——

You will see the selected tint.

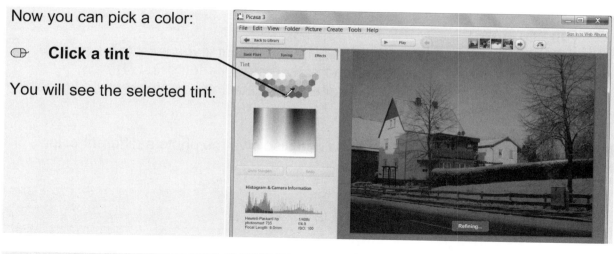

You can apply the tint: ——

👉 **Drag the slider under** Color Preservation **to the right** ——

The original colors will be restored.

👉 **Click** Cancel ✖

The effects you have tried so far have changed the appearance of the entire photo. There are also other effects available which can be used to edit a small portion of a photo. In the following section, you will learn about some of these fun and interesting effects:

👉 **Click** Focal B&W

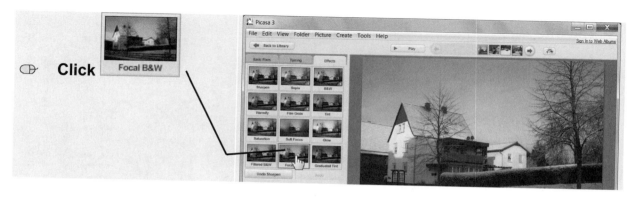

The center of the photo will remain in color, while the rest of the photo becomes black and white.

In the middle of the photo you

will see  :

☞ **Click the tree to the right of the picture**

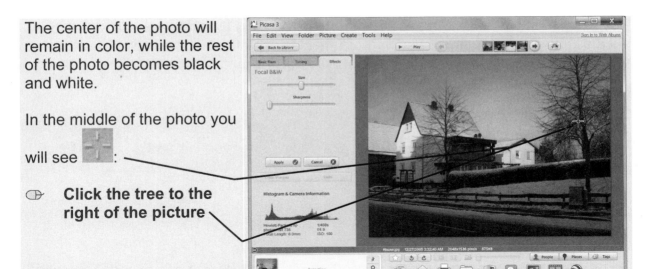

Now the tree will be colored and the center of the picture becomes black and white:

☞ **Click the side of the house**

The side of the house becomes colored again.

☞ **Drag the slider under** `Sharpness` **completely to the right**

Now you can clearly see a colored circle:

☞ **Drag the slider under** `Size` **to the right a bit**

The circle will become larger:

☞ **Click** Apply ✓

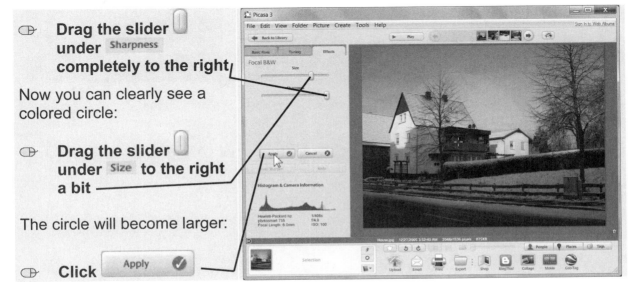

The special effects shown in this section are particularly suited for special occasions, such as Christmas cards, or wedding pictures. These effects may also help you to reclaim an otherwise 'ruined' picture that previously would simply have been deleted.

 Tip

Which effects can you use?
In the *Background Information* at the end of this chapter you will find an overview of all of the effects along with a short explanation.

4.4 Saving Edited Photos

So far all of the changes you have applied in *Picasa* have not been saved. They will only be visible when you view the photo in *Picasa*. When you have save the edited photo, it will also be visible in other programs.
In the next section you will learn how to save an edited photo:

☞ **Click** File

☞ **Click** Save

 HELP! I cannot click Save.

The Save option will not be available if the photo has not changed.

In *Picasa* you can also use the Save As... option. This option lets you save a copy of the photo as a different file, with a different file name:

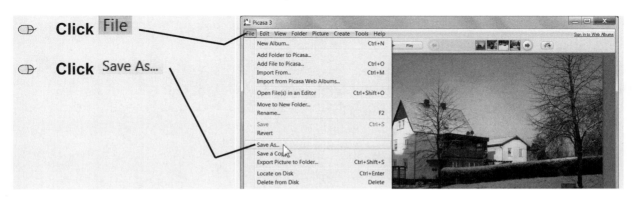

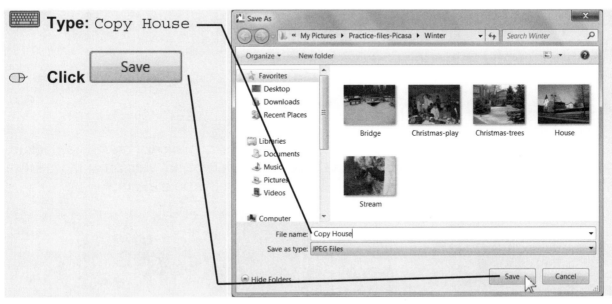

 Please note:

Picasa always stores images in the JPG file format, even when the original file format was different.

☞ **Open the *library*** 👣11

Now you will see the original
photo and the copy of this
photo, with its new file name:

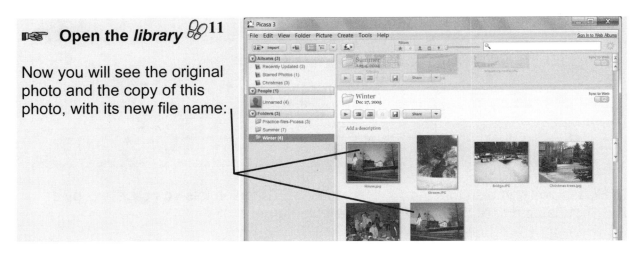

💡 **Tip**

Saving changes for an entire folder
If you have edited several photos within the same folder, you can save these files all
at once. These changes will then apply to the folders on your computer's hard drive,
as well as those shown in *Picasa*.

👉 **Click** 💾

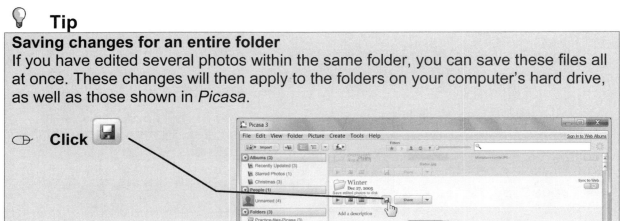

4.5 Restoring the Original Photo

Each time *Picasa* saves an edited photo, the program automatically creates a backup
copy of the original file. This enables you to revert to the original version of the photo,
should this be necessary. You will see how to do this in the next example:

☞ **Open**
👣5

👉 **Click** File

👉 **Click** Revert

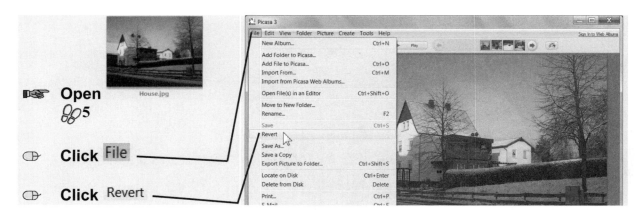

Now you will see the *Revert* window. Click the 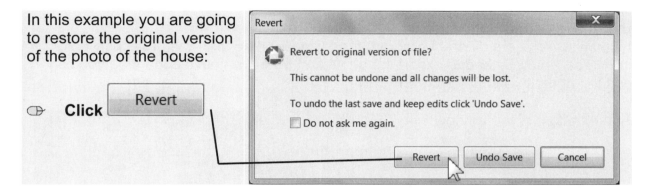 button if you want to restore the original version of the photo. Click the **Undo Save** button if you want to retain the changes you have made to the photo. When you do this you will be able to undo the changes you have made in *Picasa* one by one, or use this photo to try out some of *Picasa's* other editing options.

In this example you are going to restore the original version of the photo of the house:

 Click Revert

Revert

Revert to original version of file?

This cannot be undone and all changes will be lost.

To undo the last save and keep edits click 'Undo Save'.

☐ Do not ask me again.

[Revert] [Undo Save] [Cancel]

Please note:

These options will only work in *Picasa*. If, in the meantime, you have edited the photo in a different program, you will no longer be able to revert to the original photo.

Now you will see the original photo of the house once more:

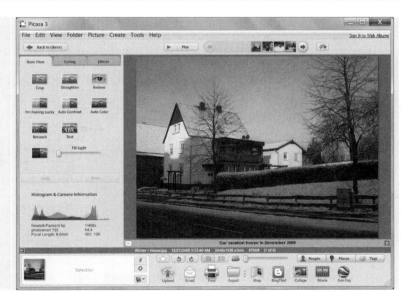

4.6 Exporting Images

You can use the *Picasa Export* function to save copies of the photos you have edited. You can select a different location for the export file, and select the file format and picture quality for this file.

💡 Tip

Exporting to another program
If you want to use a different program for editing a photo that was previously edited in *Picasa,* you will need to export the photo first. After you have done that, you can edit the photo in another program.

At the bottom of the window:

☞ **Click** 📁 Export

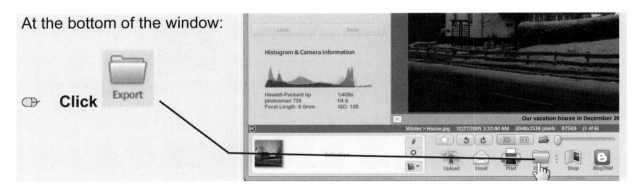

💡 Tip

Exporting multiple photos
When you need to export more than one photo, it is not necessary to do it one at a time. Just select all the photos in the *library* that you want to export and then export them all at once:

☞ **Select the photos**
    𝒪𝒪15

The three selected photos are now shown in the *Photo Tray:*

☞ **Click** 📁 Export

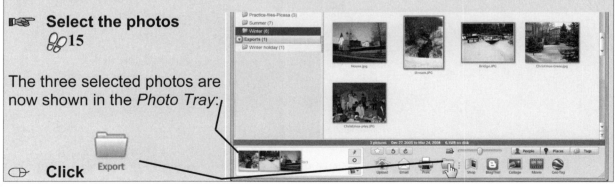

Now you can give a name to the folder where the files will be exported:

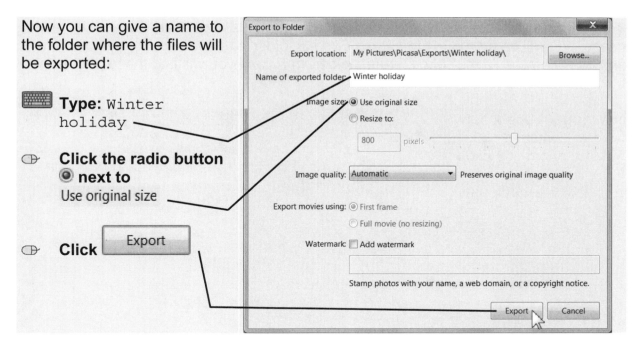

 Type: Winter holiday

 Click the radio button ⊙ next to Use original size

☞ **Click** Export

📖

Options for the image size

By Image size: you can select the original size of the photo, or select a different pixel size by moving the slider. The number of pixels you select with the slider determines the length or height of your photo (whichever is longer). The other dimension is determined automatically to maintain the aspect ratio of the photo.
The quality and resolution of the original photo determines whether a high-quality enlargement can be produced.

Source: Picasa Help

📖

Image quality

Select the desired image quality for your photo using the Image quality: drop-down menu:

- Automatic : preserves the original image quality.
- Normal : balances quality and size.
- Maximum : preserves fine detail for large file sizes.
- Minimum : yields some quality loss for small file sizes.
- Custom (85) : enables you to select your own value.

Rule of thumb: The higher the quality, the larger the file will be.

Source: Picasa Help

Your exported images will be stored on your computer's hard drive. Copies of these image files will be stored in the *Picasa Exports* folder. In *Windows Explorer*, you will find this subfolder in the *(My) Pictures* folder. In *Picasa* you will find these photos in the *Exported Pictures* collection.

Now you will see a new window containing a folder with the photo you exported:

☞ **Double-click the**

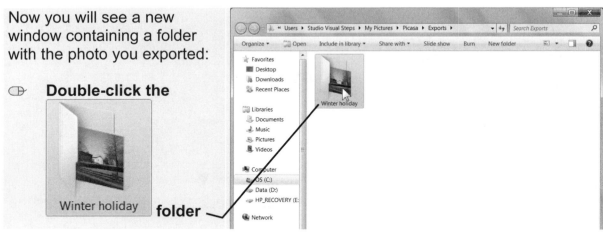

Winter holiday folder

☞ **Double-click**

House

By default, the photo will be opened in *Windows Photo Viewer*:

Your computer may have a different setting for the default photo viewer, or you may see the photo in full screen mode. That is ok.

You can close the window now.

☞ **Click**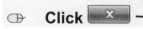

☞ **Close the *Winter holiday* window** 𝄞3

Now you will see the *edit window*:

⊕ **Click**

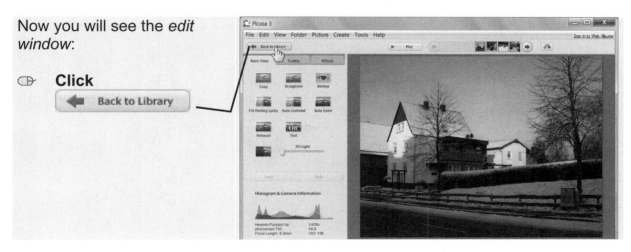

In the folder list you will also see the exported photos:

⊕ **Click the** 📁 Winter holiday (1)
folder

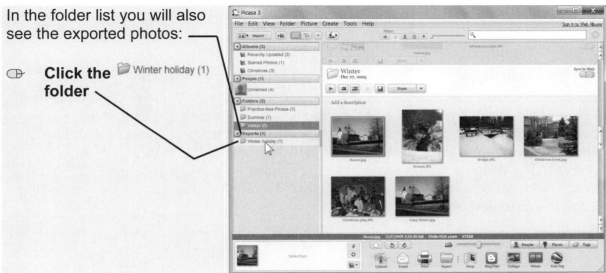

You will see the photo in the
📁 Winter holiday
   Nov 25, 2009
                   folder:

Next to **Exports**:

⊕ **Click** 🔽

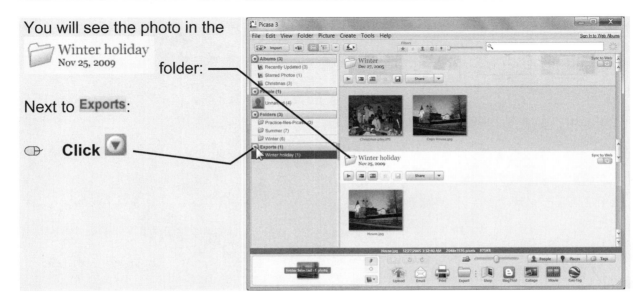

 has now turned into .
The list with the exported
photos has been closed: ——

You can open the list by

clicking ▶ again.

4.7 Making Backups

If your computer is the main place where you store your pictures, it is a good idea to
get in the habit of making regular backups. A backup is a safety copy of your image
files.

➥ **Please note:**

When you back up your photo files, *Picasa* will back up your original photos, as well
as the photos you have edited and the albums you have made. These items will be
stored separately. If you have restored photos from a backup CD, all of your photo
edits and any altered albums will be available in *Picasa* once more.
But if you use *Windows Explorer* to view the photos on a backup CD or DVD, or on
an external hard disk, your photos will be displayed in the original format without the
alterations or album changes.

Here is how to create a backup:

☞ **Click** Tools

☞ **Click** Back Up Pictures...

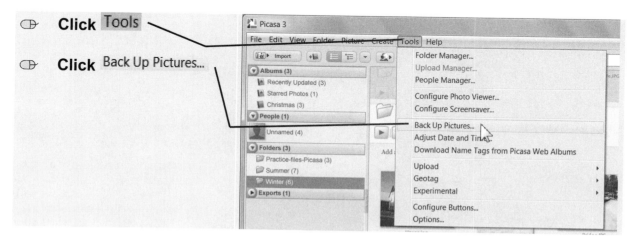

Backups are stored in *sets*. The first time you will create a new set:

At the bottom left-hand corner of the window:

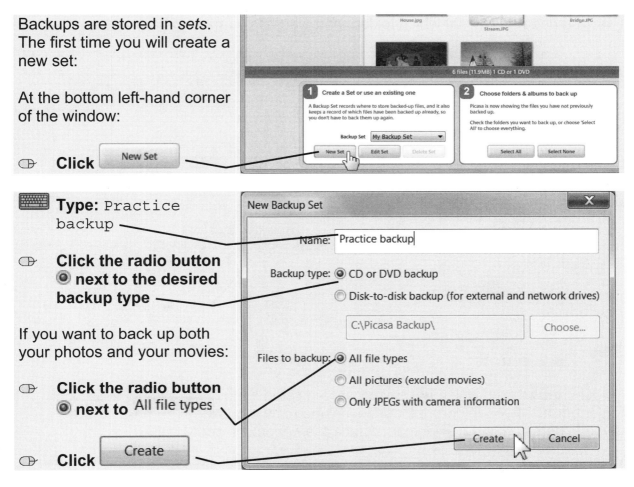

 Click New Set

 Type: Practice backup

⊕ **Click the radio button ⦿ next to the desired backup type**

If you want to back up both your photos and your movies:

⊕ **Click the radio button ⦿ next to** All file types

⊕ **Click** Create

🐾 Please note:

If you only store your backup on your computer's hard drive, you will not be able to use it in case your computer crashes or is stolen. That is why you need to save a backup copy on a CD, DVD, or an external hard disk.

💡 Tip

Just your own pictures
If you just want to back up your own photos, and not all the other icons or images you downloaded from the Internet, select Only JPEGs with camera information . Make sure that the photos you made with your camera are stored in the JPEG file format.

First you need to indicate which folders and albums you want to back up:

☞ **Click** [Select All]

You will see a checked box ☑ next to each folder: ―

If you only want to select specific folders. Check the box ☑ next to these folders.

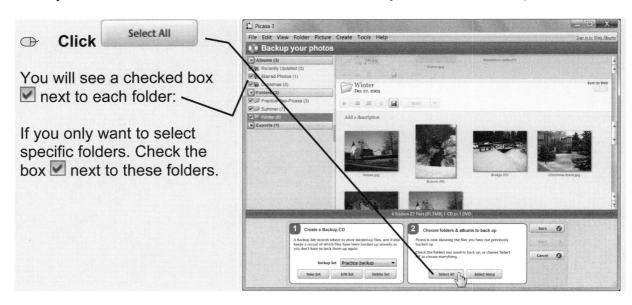

Please note:

Folders and albums which are closed are indicated by the symbol next to the folder name. These folders will not be included in the backup. You need to open these folders first, before you can include their photos in your backup.

At the bottom of the window you will see the overall size of the backup, and the number of CDs or DVDs you need to use: ―

☞ **Click** [Burn ✓]

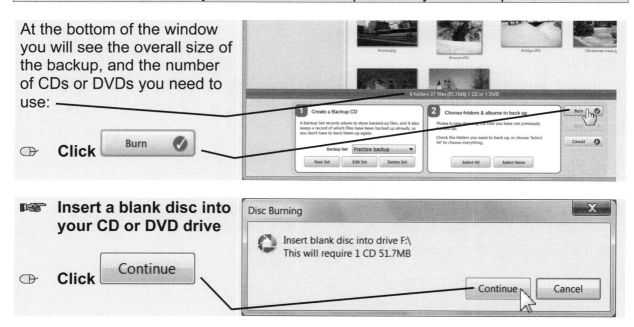

☞ **Insert a blank disc into your CD or DVD drive**

Disc Burning

Insert blank disc into drive F:\
This will require 1 CD 51.7MB

[Continue] [Cancel]

☞ **Click** [Continue]

Instead of a blank disk, you can also overwrite a previous backup, if this has been saved to a rewritable disk. First, you will see a message warning you that the contents of the disk will be deleted.

At the bottom right-hand corner of the window you will see a progress bar:

 Please note:

During the burning or repairing process, you will see several indications for the size of your backup. These may differ. This is due to the storage of various additional files to the disk, such as indexes.

When the burning process has finished, you will see this window:

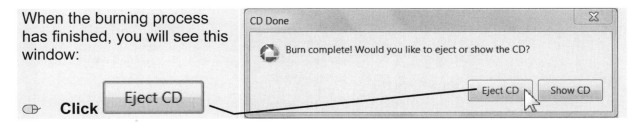

☞ **Click** Eject CD

Your CD or DVD tray will open.

4.8 Restoring a Backup

Whenever you insert a *Picasa* backup disk into your CD or DVD drive, you will be asked if you want to restore the files:

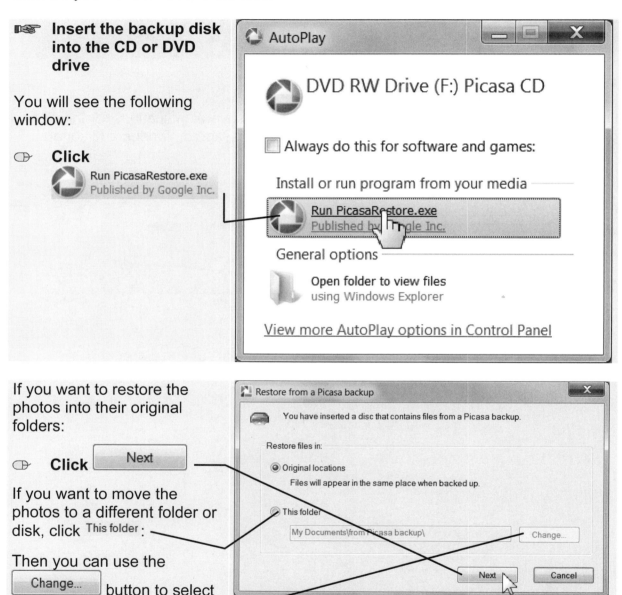

☞ **Insert the backup disk into the CD or DVD drive**

You will see the following window:

☞ **Click**

Run PicasaRestore.exe
Published by Google Inc.

If you want to restore the photos into their original folders:

☞ **Click** Next

If you want to move the photos to a different folder or disk, click This folder :

Then you can use the
Change... button to select
a different location: ─────

Picasa will compare the files on the backup disk to the files on your computer:

☞ **Click** Restore

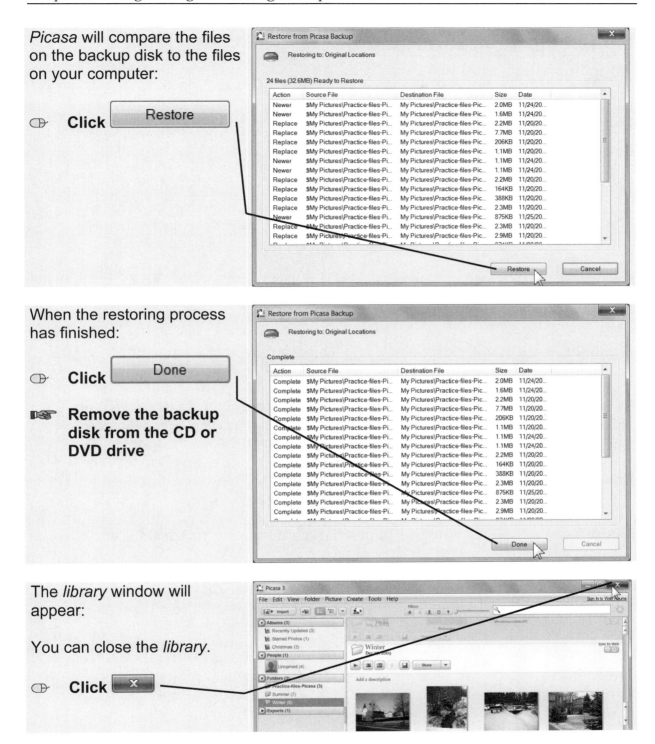

When the restoring process has finished:

☞ **Click** Done

☞ **Remove the backup disk from the CD or DVD drive**

The *library* window will appear:

You can close the *library*.

☞ **Click** ✕

In this chapter you have learned how to improve your pictures with *Picasa's* built-in fine tuning tools and special effects. You have also learned how to save your edited photos, how to export them, and how to create a backup.

4.9 Background Information

Dictionary	
Backup	A safety copy of your photo files.
Effects	Filters that can be applied to alter the sharpness, color, or resolution of the entire image or a portion thereof. *Picasa* contains twelve different effects that you can use separately, or in combination with each other.
Exporting	Storing a photo for use in a different program. The *Export* option allows you to select a different location for your photo, and change the file format or photo quality of the exported copy.
Highlight	Method for amplifying the lighter areas of your photo. The lighter parts of the photo will become more vibrant.
Neutral color picker	The parts of the photo that *Picasa* should regard as grey or white. *Picasa* will then tune the surrounding colors in accordance with the selected color.
One-click fix	A 'magic' button you can use to let *Picasa* automatically correct some settings, such as lighting and colors.
Restoring	Restoring files from a backup disk to the computer's hard drive.
Sepia	Brownish tint that gives a picture the appearance of being old.
Tuning	Adjusting the color, lighting, and contrast in your pictures.
Source: Picasa Help	

Twelve tools you can apply

The `Effects` tab contains twelve effects that can be applied to any still photo. *Picasa* will save the original photo, so you can always undo the changes you have made. The effects are added to your photo in layers, one on top of the other. This makes it possible to 'undo' your edits one step at a time, if needed.

Sharpen
Make the edges of objects in your photos crisper and less fuzzy.

Sepia
Create an 'old-fashioned' effect by changing the photo to a reddish brown tint.

B&W
Turn any color photo into a black and white photo.

Warmify
Warm up a cool photo, improving skin tones. To adjust manually, you can also use the `Color Temperature` slider on the *Tuning* tab.

Film Grain
Add a 'grainy' appearance to your photo, also looks great when you print.

Tint
Strip the color out of your photo and apply a colored tint over the top. Use the `Color Preservation` slider to add the original color back to your photo underneath the tint.

Saturation
Use the slider to adjust color saturation. Slide it all the way to the left to make the picture black and white. Slide it all the way to the right to make it appear 'radio-active'.

Soft Focus
Soften the focus around a center point that you select.

Glow
Brightens the white areas of a photo, giving a dreamy effect.

Filtered B&W
Add the effect of shooting black and white film with a color filter. The filter blocks or enhances certain colors in the photo depending on the color filter you choose.

Focal B&W
Turn a photo to black and white, while keeping one circular area of color intact. You can define the size and sharpness of the colored spot.

Graduated Tint
Similar to a graduated color filter on a camera, this allows you to apply a colored tint to the top half of a photo. This is useful for enhancing a sunset or making gray skies blue.

Source: Picasa Help

Save options for photos that have been edited in Picasa

You can edit your pictures in *Picasa* in numerous ways. For instance, you can crop them or make color adjustments. If you do not save these edits, the changes will only be visible in *Picasa*.

If you are viewing your pictures directly from your computer's hard drive with *Windows Explorer*, or if you open them with a different program, you will see the original photo files without the changes you have made in *Picasa*. This can be annoying if you want to use your edited photos in other programs. In that case you can choose to save your edited photos in a separate location. *Picasa* offers various save options.

Picasa always saves the original photo in a hidden folder called 'Originals' each time you use the save command. A new file containing your edits is created as you work on your pictures. The original file never changes, when you click 'Undo Save', *Picasa* retrieves the original from the hidden folder and puts it back in the file position. Just keep in mind that you will need enough storage space on your hard disk when you want to save edited copies. This is because you are actually storing two photo files instead of one.

Here you will see a brief overview of the save commands available in *Picasa,* based on how they affect the location of your original photos.

Moving the original picture

If you use the 💾 button and File , Save options, *Picasa* will make a copy of the edited photo and move the original photo file to the *Windows Originals* subfolder. By default, this subfolder is a hidden folder and you will not be able to view this folder in *Picasa* (see also the *Tip* on page 140). You can use this automatic backup file to undo all edits or to restore the original photo.

- **Save to disk**

When you have edited a photo or an album, you will see the 💾 button under the album name. This is a useful option if you want to save all edits at once (this could apply to different photos in any given folder or album).

- **File > Save**

You can use the Save option if you only need to save the edits of a single photo, or a group of photos you have selected.

- Continue reading on the next page -

Saving the original photo in the current location

If you use the following options the original files will not be moved. A new version of the photo will be created and saved and will include any changes you have made to it. This means the original photo will not be moved to a different location. The new, edited version will be stored in a different location, depending on the option you select.

- **Export**

If you need to create edited versions of a large number of pictures, the best and easiest thing to do, is to export them to a different location. You can choose any location you like. When you export your pictures, you will be able to resize them and control the JPEG compression level when applying photo edits.

- **File > Save a Copy**

This option will automatically create a copy of the original photo in the same folder, including all the changes you have made. The photo's filename will have '-1' appended to the end of the name to distinguish it from the original.

- **File > Save As**

This option is similar to Save a Copy , in that a copy will be made of the original photo, including all the edits. But before the file is saved, you can choose the file name and the location of the new copy yourself.

Source: Picasa Help

JPEG-quality

When you save a copy, *Picasa* tries to match the JPEG quality level of the original photo. *Picasa's* default JPEG quality level is 85%, and will be applied if it is unable to determine the JPEG quality. If you are saving a non-JPEG photo (for example a TIF or BMP file), it will be converted and saved as a JPEG file.

Source: Picasa Help

Undoing saved edits

There are two ways to retrieve the original version of a photo after you have saved

your edits: Undo Save   and Revert .

Undo Save

With this option, your photo edits will still be visible in *Picasa*, but these edits are no longer saved to disk. To undo a save, follow these instructions:

In the *library*:

☞ **Double-click the image**

At the bottom of the   Basic Fixes   tab:

☞ **Click**   Undo Save

Revert

This option will revert the file to its original state, discarding any edits you have made. To revert a photo, follow these instructions:

☞ **Select the photo(s) you would like to revert**

☞ **Click** File , Revert

If this option is grayed out, the photo has not been previously edited.

Please note: In order to undo or revert to an edited photo, the original photo file must be located in the '.*picasaoriginal*' subfolder.

If you are unable to undo or revert to a saved photo, most likely the original version of the photo has been moved or deleted from your computer's hard drive. When you save an edited photo in *Picasa*, an edited copy of this photo will be made and the original photo will be moved to the *Originals* subfolder. The *Originals* subfolder is not visible in *Picasa*, but you can always view the original photo in *Windows Explorer* (see also the *Tip* on page 140).

Source: Picasa Help

4.10 Tips

 Tip

Save a copy of a photo
To quickly save different versions of the same photo, just save a copy of it:

☞ **Click** File

☞ **Click** Save a Copy

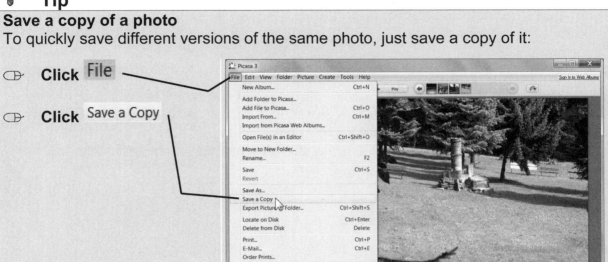

A copy of the photo will be saved, in the same folder as the original photo. The file name of the copy is the same as the original file name, appended with '-1'. For example, the copy of the *Miniature-castle.jpg* photo will be called *Miniature-castle-1.jpg*.

 Tip

Watermarks
Picasa has a watermark feature. You can help protect your images by adding a watermark to your photos. A watermark in *Picasa* is white text that is added to the lower-right corner of photos during the export or uploads process. This is how you add a watermark to a photo:

In the *Export to Folder* window:

☞ **Check the box ☑ next to** Add watermark

⌨ **Type the desired text**

☞ **Click** Export

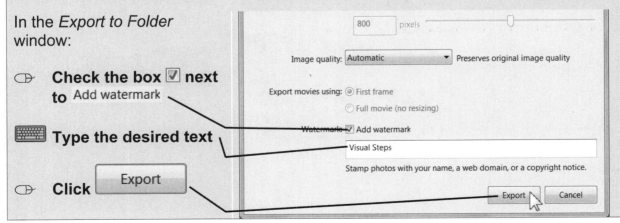

Tip

Using photos in other programs
If you want to use the photos that you have edited in *Picasa* in another program, you will need to export these photos from *Picasa*.

 Tip

Creating backup copies of original files
When saving an original photo, *Picasa* automatically creates a backup copy of the original photo file. This backup copy is stored in a subfolder called *Originals*, in the same folder location as the original file. By default, the subfolder is not visible in *Windows Explorer* or in *Picasa*. But you can make this hidden folder visible:

In *Windows 7* and *Vista*:

☞ **Click**

In *Windows XP*:

☞ **Click** start, 🖼 **My Pictures**

You will see the contents of the (*My*) *Pictures* folder. In *Windows XP*, the window below appears a bit different, but the operations are exactly the same.

☞ **Double-click the** ***Practice-files-Picasa*** **folder**

⌨ **Press** `Alt`

Now you will see a toolbar:

☞ **Click** Tools

☞ **Click** Folder options...

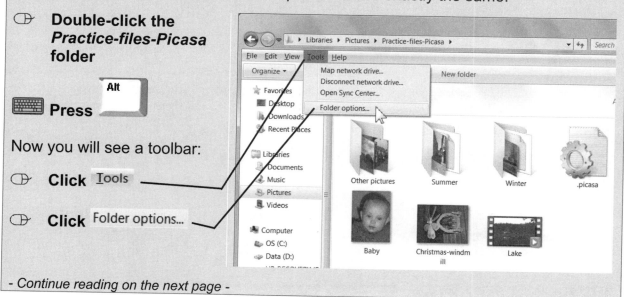

- Continue reading on the next page -

Now you will see the *Folder Options* window:

☞ **Click the** View **tab**

☞ **Drag the slider downwards**

Under ⬛ Hidden files and folders :

☞ **Click the radio button ◉ next to** Show hidden files, folders, and drives

At the bottom of the window:

☞ **Click** OK

You will now see all of the hidden subfolders and photo files in the *Practice-files-Picasa* folder:

In the .picasaoriginals folder you see all of the original photo files:

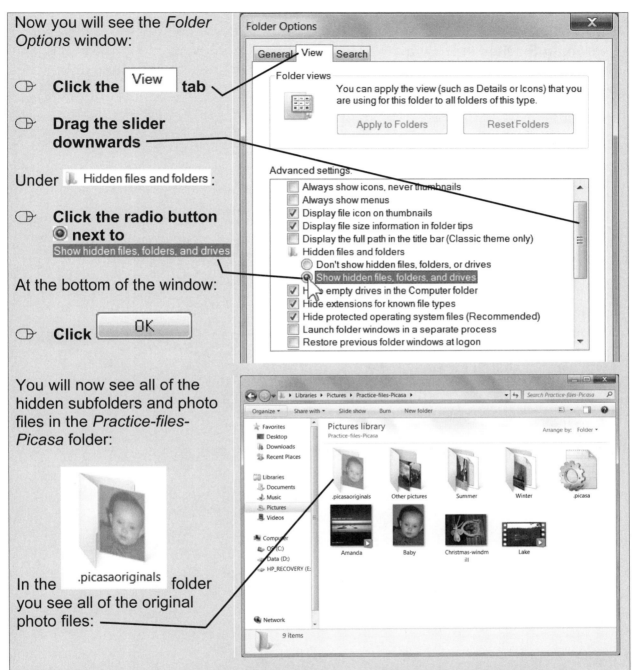

The photo files which you have edited and saved in *Picasa*, will be stored in the *Practice-files-Picasa* folder.

Please note: the *.picasaoriginals* folder will occupy extra space on your hard disk. This means that you are now saving the same photo file twice. If you do not need to view your original photos, you can use the *Folder Options* window to hide the folders and files again.

Tip

Searching for files in Picasa
Picasa also offers a search utility for locating files on your computer's hard drive. Here is how to use the search feature:

In the *library*:

☞ **Right-click the photo**

☞ **Click** Locate

If you want to search for the edited file:

☞ **Click** File on Disk

Now the folder which contains the edited photo will be opened.

If you want to search for the original file:

☞ **Click** Original on Disk

Now the folder which contains the original photo will be opened.

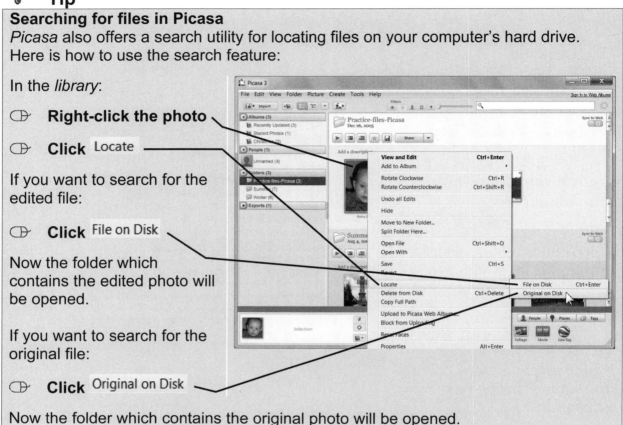

5. Printing and Publishing

Most likely you will want to share your pictures with other people. *Picasa* lets you print your photos or photo collage yourself, or you can send your photos to an online printing service. It is very easy to select the format and printing method for your photos.

Furthermore, there are several ways to distribute digital copies of your photos. You can do this by e-mail, and you can create web albums as well. In this chapter you will learn how to create a web album and how to synchronize this album with an album on your computer. This way, your web album will always be up-to-date.

In this chapter you will learn how to:

- print photos;
- adjust print formats;
- make photo collages;
- send photos by e-mail;
- create a web album;
- upload photos to a web album;
- synchronize the web album;
- share your web album with others;
- upload photos using the *Drop Box*;
- recognize faces in a web album;
- append name tags;
- print photos at a print service.

Please note:

If you want to use the exercises in this chapter, you need to download the *Practice-files-Picasa* folder and save it to the (*My*) *Pictures* folder on your computer. You can read how to do that in *Chapter 1 Installing Picasa*.

5.1 Printing

You can print one photo or multiple photos in various sizes and formats. This is what you are going to do now. First you need to select the photos you want to print and put them in the *Photo Tray*:

☞ **Open** *Picasa* 𝒪𝒪⁶

☞ **Open the** 📁 Summer **folder** 𝒪𝒪⁴

☞ **Put** Cathedral.jpg **in the** *Photo Tray* 𝒪𝒪⁸

☞ **Put** Miniature-castle.JPG **in the** *Photo Tray* 𝒪𝒪⁸

Now you will see two photos in the *Photo Tray*: ——

At the bottom of the window:

☞ **Click** Print

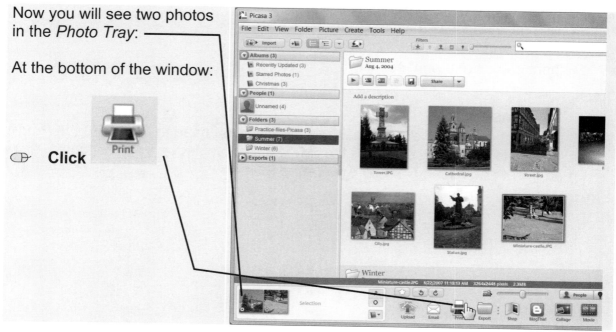

Here you will see the print options:

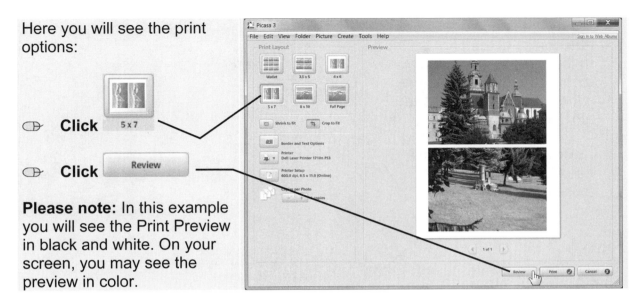

 Click

 Click Review

Please note: In this example you will see the Print Preview in black and white. On your screen, you may see the preview in color.

HELP! My Print Preview looks different.

It is possible that your own photo has been cropped differently from the photo in this book. This can result in a different Print Preview. This does not matter. The operations described in this chapter will still be the same.

Please note:

If you have selected more than two pictures, or have chosen a larger print size, you can scroll to the other

pictures by clicking the ▶ button:

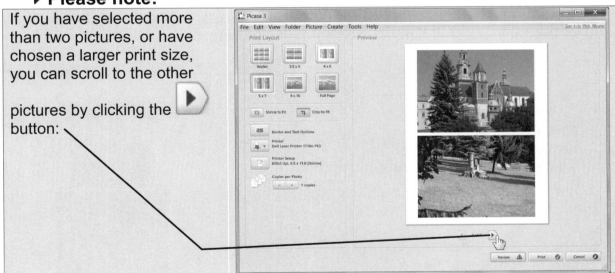

Picasa recommends checking the quality of the photos first. If the quality is too poor, you could experience problems when you try to enlarge the photos.

Here you will see that the photos are of the best possible quality:

☞ **Click** OK

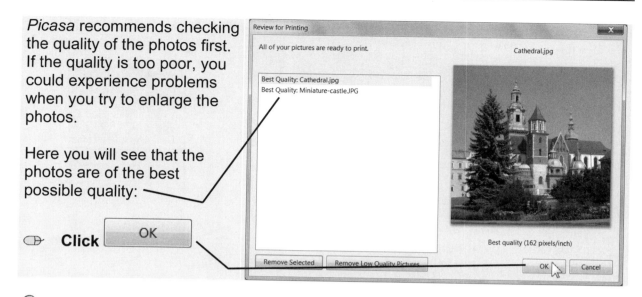

💡 **Tip**

Removing low quality pictures

Use the Remove Low Quality Pictures button to automatically remove photos with a poor quality.

In the example below you will see that part of the cathedral tower is not included in the Print Preview. This is because the photo is square, while the selected print format is 5 x 7. This means the photo will be made to fit by cropping the top and bottom half of the photo. Here is how you can solve this problem:

☞ **Click**

Now the photo of the cathedral will be displayed with the original dimensions, in the 5 x 7 format.

The button lets you crop the photos to the 5 x 7 format.

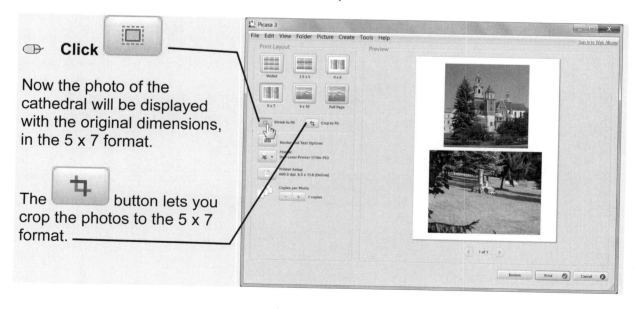

Before printing for the first time, you need to adjust the printer settings:

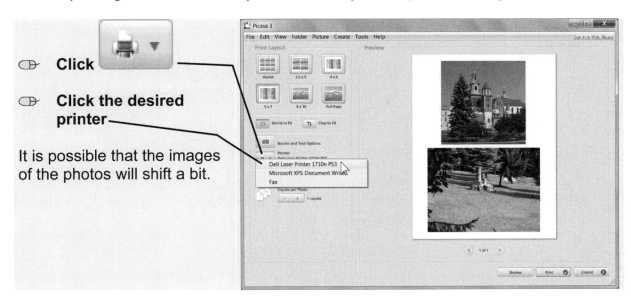

☞ **Click**

☞ **Click the desired printer**

It is possible that the images of the photos will shift a bit.

Above or below the photos you can print the title, or other data:

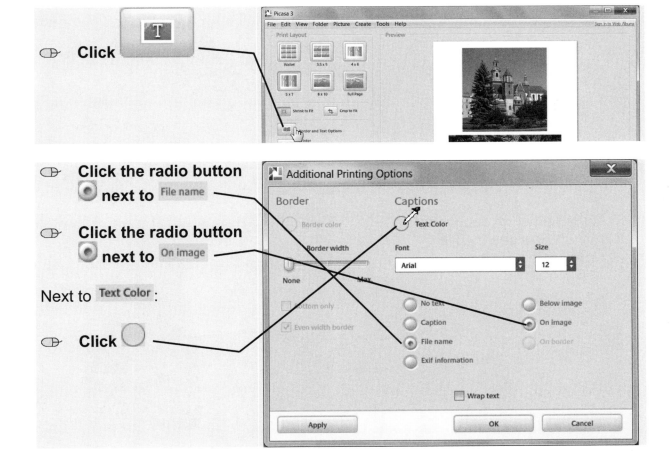

☞ **Click**

☞ **Click the radio button next to** File name

☞ **Click the radio button next to** On image

Next to Text Color :

☞ **Click** ◯

☞ **Click the desired color**

Please note: keep in mind that the text color should match the color of the photos.

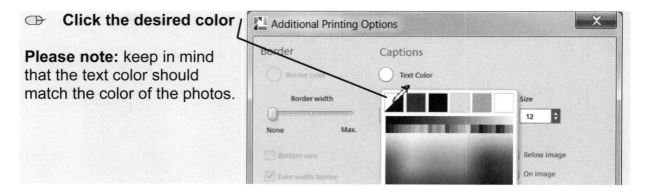

The font size has been set to twelve. The file name will be displayed in very small letters and is not clearly visible. You can use the *Additional Printing Options* window to adjust the font. Here is how you do that:

Next to **12** :

☞ **Click** ▲▼

☞ **Click 20**

☞ **Click OK**

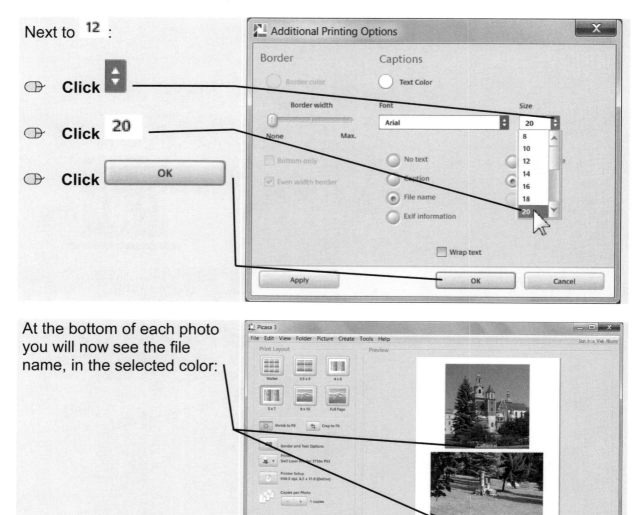

At the bottom of each photo you will now see the file name, in the selected color:

Tip

Changing the printer settings

If you want to print the photos horizontally (in landscape format), you need to change the settings in the following way:

Next to *Printer Setup* :

☞ **Click**

You now see the print setup window of your printer. Here you can select the orientation and the print quality.

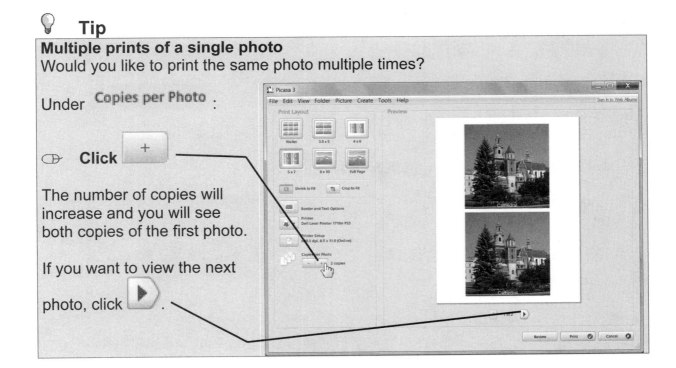

Tip

Multiple prints of a single photo

Would you like to print the same photo multiple times?

Under *Copies per Photo* :

☞ **Click** +

The number of copies will increase and you will see both copies of the first photo.

If you want to view the next photo, click ▶.

Do you want to print the photos?

☞ **Click** Print ✓

If you do not have a printer, or do not want to print the photos, click Cancel ✗ .

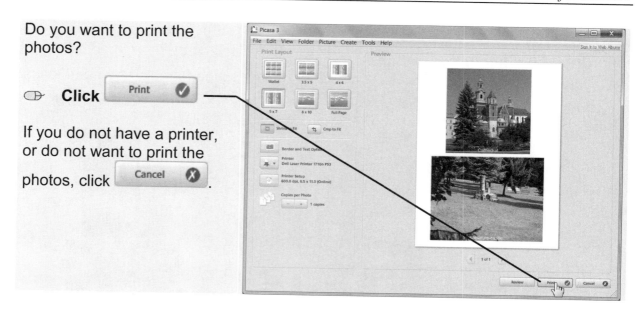

5.2 Collages

You can display and print your photos in a more creative way by making a collage of various photos. Here is how to do that:

☞ **Put** Tower.JPG **in the *Photo Tray*** 🦶8

The *Photo Tray* now contains three photos:

At the bottom of the window:

☞ **Click** Collage

Now you see all the photos together in one image:

⊕ **Click** Scramble Collage

Please note: the photos in your window may be placed a bit differently.

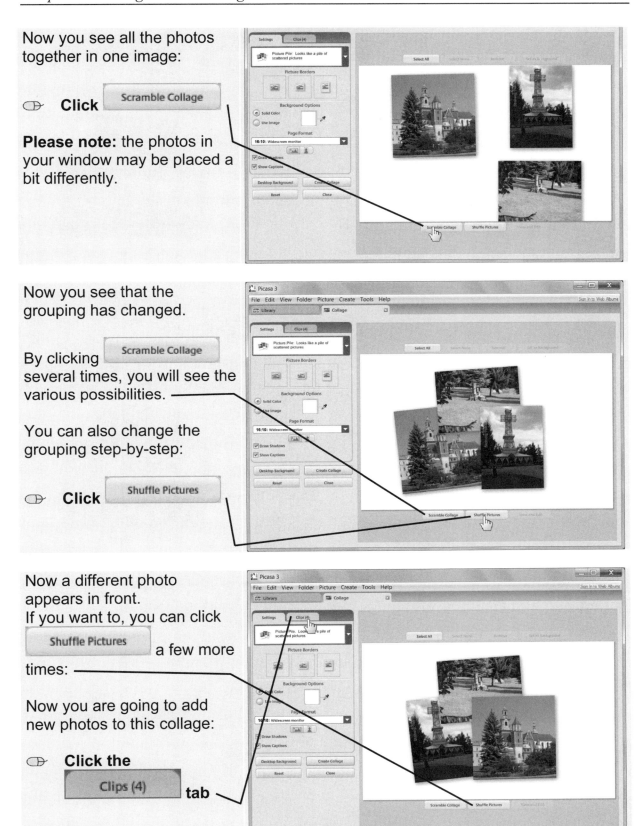

Now you see that the grouping has changed.

By clicking Scramble Collage several times, you will see the various possibilities.

You can also change the grouping step-by-step:

⊕ **Click** Shuffle Pictures

Now a different photo appears in front.
If you want to, you can click Shuffle Pictures a few more times:

Now you are going to add new photos to this collage:

⊕ **Click the** Clips (4) **tab**

You will see the other photos in the folder. By default, all photos have been selected.

☞ **Click the grey area**

Now the photos are no longer selected:

☞ **Click**

☞ **Click** ➕

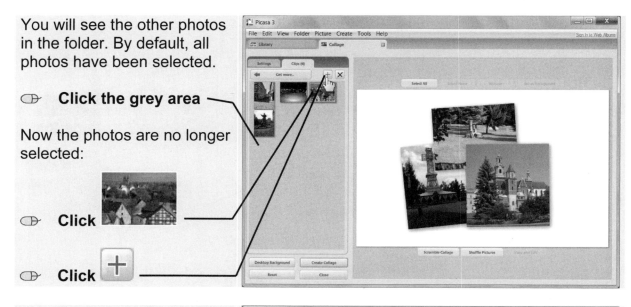

The photo has been added to the collage:

You are now going to move this photo:

☞ **Place the mouse pointer on the photo**

The pointer will turn into ✥ :

☞ **Drag the photo to the desired location**

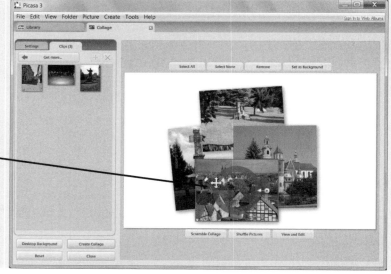

You now see a protractor and you will be able to rotate the photo:

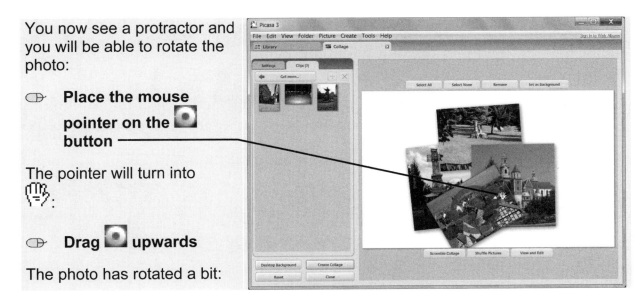

☞ **Place the mouse pointer on the 🔘 button** ⎯⎯⎯⎯⎯⎯⎯⎯⎯⎯⎯⎯⎯

The pointer will turn into 🖐:

☞ **Drag 🔘 upwards**

The photo has rotated a bit:

➤ **Please note:**

If you drag 🔘 inwards or outwards, the photo becomes smaller or larger.

You are now going to add a photo from a different folder:

☞ **Click**

You will see the *library*:

☞ **Empty the *Photo Tray* ✇16**

☞ **Click the 📁 Winter folder** ⎯⎯⎯⎯⎯

☞ **Click** Christmas-trees.jpg

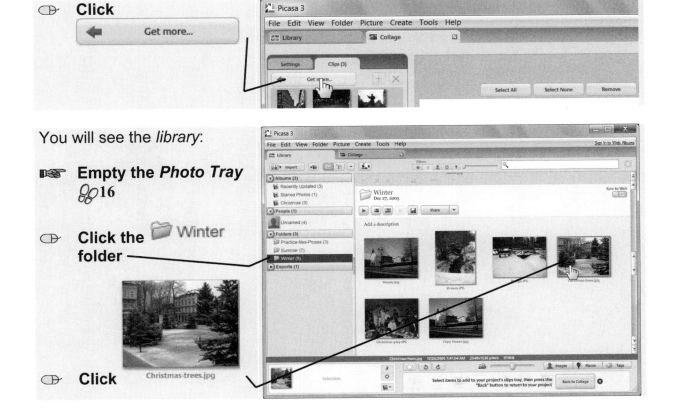

The photo has now been put in the *Photo Tray*:

At the bottom right of the window:

☞ **Click** Back to Collage

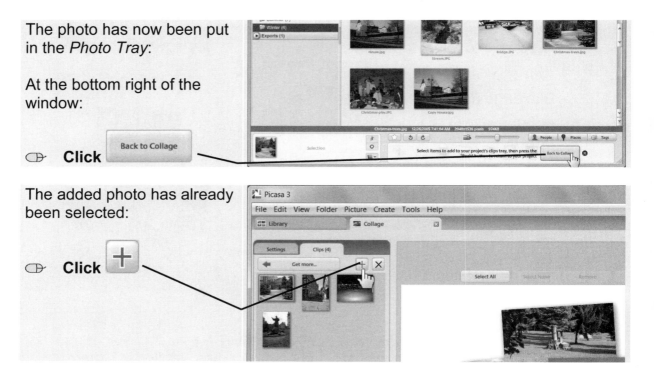

The added photo has already been selected:

☞ **Click** ➕

The photo has now been added to the collage.

You can also remove photos from a collage:

☞ **Click the photo you have just added**

☞ **Click** Remove

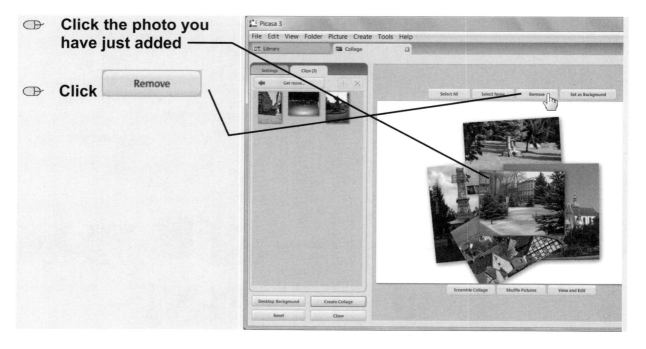

You can replace the collage's white background by a different color, or set one of the photos as a background image:

Click the Settings **tab**

Under Background Options :

Click

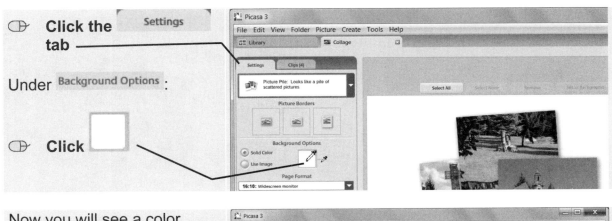

Now you will see a color palette:

Click a color

You will see the selected color appear as a background color for the collage:

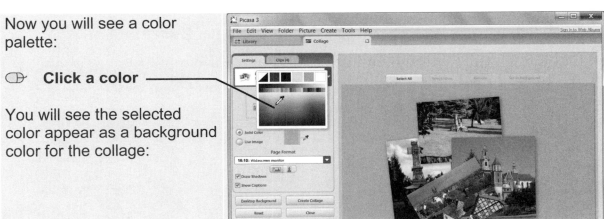

Now you are going to select a background photo:

Click a photo

Click

Set as Background

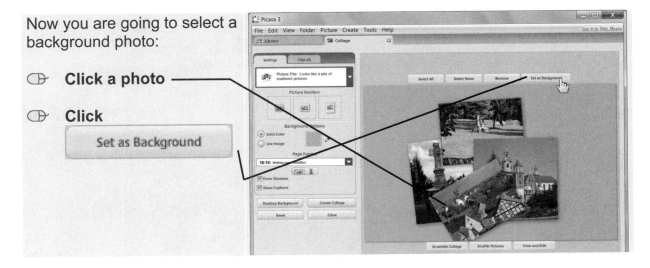

You will see the new background:

Now you are going to remove this background again:

Next to Solid Color :

☞ **Click** ⬤

The background will again have the same color as before.

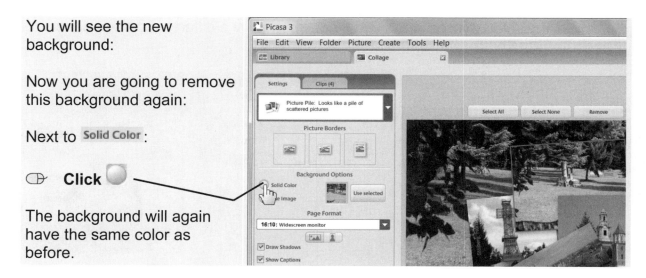

Apart from the collage, *Picasa* contains various other formats:

☞ **Click** ▼

☞ **Click**

Grid: Arrange pictures into reg columns

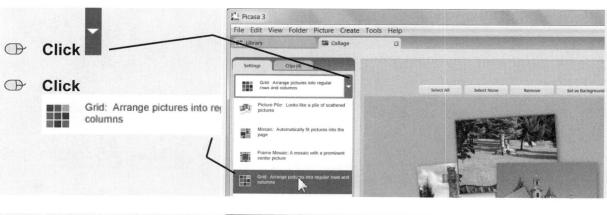

Now the photos are placed in a grid:

Due to the landscape orientation, the tops of the cathedral and the tower have been cut off.

Now you are going to select the portrait orientation:

☞ **Click**

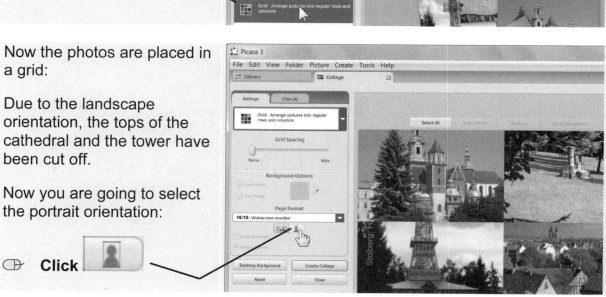

The page will be rotated and you can see the photos better:

Now the collage is finished:

 Click

Create Collage

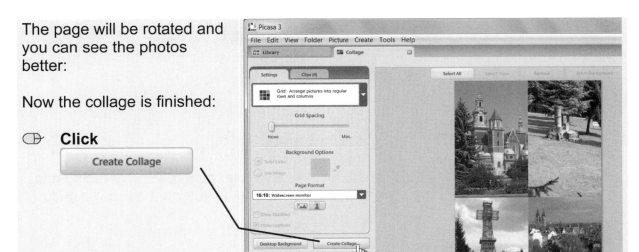

💡 Tip

Collage for widescreen monitors or a CD cover
By default, the collage is created for screens with a 4:3 aspect ratio. If your screen uses a different aspect ratio, or if you want to use the collage for a CD cover, you can change the settings:

Under Page Format :

 Click 🔽

 Click the desired ratio

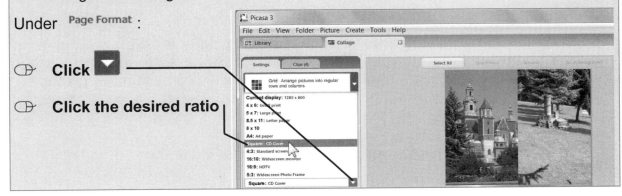

💡 Tip

Collage as desktop background

If you click the Desktop Background button, the collage will immediately be set as a desktop background for your computer.

When the collage is finished, you will see this message at the bottom right of the window:

Collage Finished! (click to view)

☞ **Open the** *library* 🦶11

In the *library*, you will see the collage under Projects (1):

You can edit the collage in *Picasa*, just like a regular picture. You can also add effects. You can print the collage in the same way as you print a regular photo.

5.3 Sending By E-mail

Instead of printing the photos, many people send their photos to each other digitally. By e-mail, for example. You can send photos by e-mail directly from *Picasa*:

☞ **Open the** 📁 Winter **folder** 🐾4

➥**Please note:**

Photo files are often very large, and many e-mail programs have a maximum file size for their messages of 1 MB, for example. *Picasa* will automatically reduce the file size of photos that are sent by e-mail. However, if you send many photos at once, the message may still become too large. In that case, it is better to distribute the photos over several different messages.

First, you place the photos you want to send in the *Photo Tray*:

⊕ **Click a picture** ────

☞ **If you want, you can add more photos to the *Photo Tray* 🐾8**

⊕ **Click** E-mail

Click your e-mail program

If you use a different e-mail program, this default program will be at the top of the list.

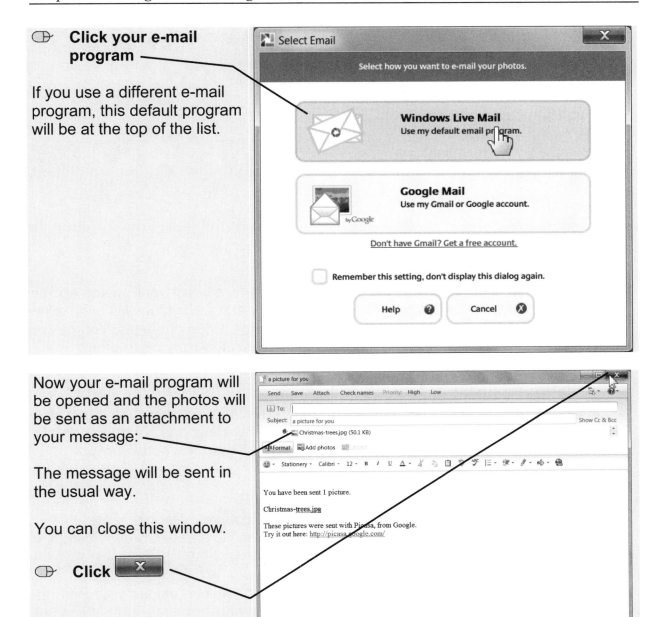

Now your e-mail program will be opened and the photos will be sent as an attachment to your message:

The message will be sent in the usual way.

You can close this window.

Click

🩹 HELP! The e-mail program does not open.

Does your e-mail program not open, or do you receive error messages? Check the *Picasa* help topics and learn how to set your e-mail program for use in *Internet Explorer* and *Picasa*.

The photos you have sent, are now put in the Emailed (1) album: ———

Because you have not sent the e-mail message in this example yourself, you will not see this album.

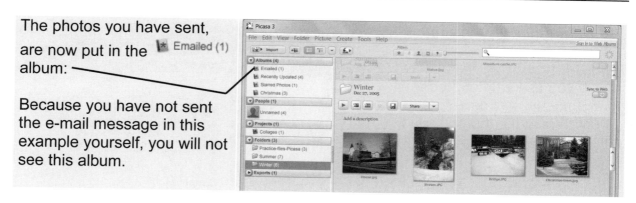

5.4 Creating a Web Album

A web album is a location on the Internet, where you can put your photos and show them to others. To do this, you need to register first. A web album will often allow various options for creating slide shows, with a wide range of effects. You can display the photos you have edited in *Picasa* on every web album on the Internet.

Please note:

In the following sections we will only explain how to upload your photos to a web album. You can find more information about additional options and functions of the web album program you are using by going to the program's help function.

Please note:

If you want to create a web album, you will need to have a *Google* account. If you do not yet have such an account, then read *Appendix A Create a Google Account* first, and learn how to create a *Google* account.

If you already have a *Picasa* web album, you will be able to upload your pictures at once, as is described in the next section. If you do not yet have a web album, you will need to create one first before uploading the photos:

At the top right-hand side of the window:

 Click Sign In to Web Albums

⬚ **Click**
Sign up for Web Albums

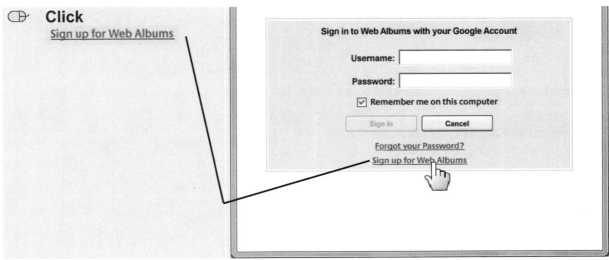

Now you will see the following window:

⬚ **Type the e-mail address**

⬚ **Type the password for your *Google* account**

⬚ **Click** Sign in

⬚ **Type the user name**

Now you are going to check if this name is still available:

⬚ **Click** check availability!

If the name is already in use, you will see a message, and you will need to think of a different name.

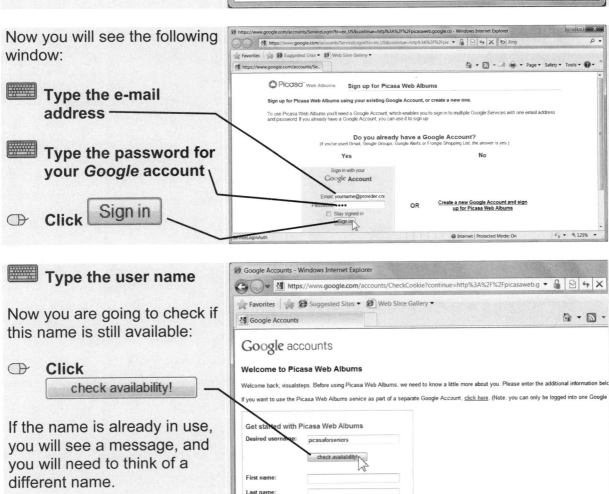

Type your first name

Press ⊢ Tab

If necessary, drag the scroll bar downwards

Type your last name

Click Continue

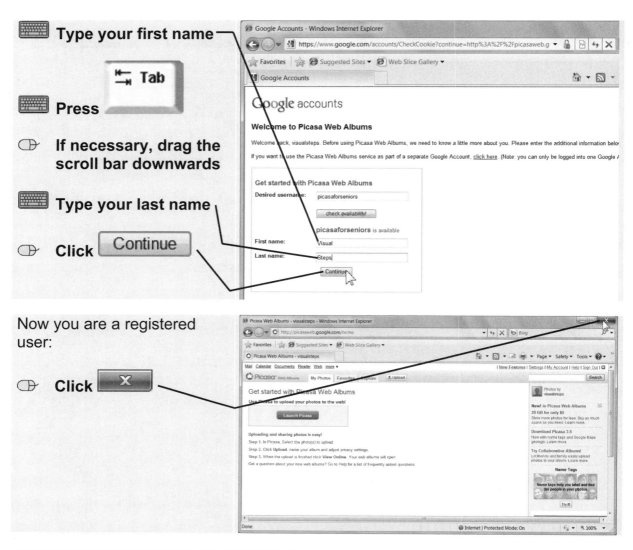

Now you are a registered user:

Click ✕

☞ **Close the next window as well** ⏎³

5.5 Uploading Photos

If you have a web album, you can upload photos to this album.

 Tip

| **Put the photos for your web album in separate albums** |
| It is recommended to place the photos you want to use in your web album in a separate album. In the web album, these photos will be stored in the same album, and in this way it is much easier to manage the photos and maintain all the changes. |

Open the Christmas (3) **album** 4

In the *Photo Tray* you will see

Click Upload

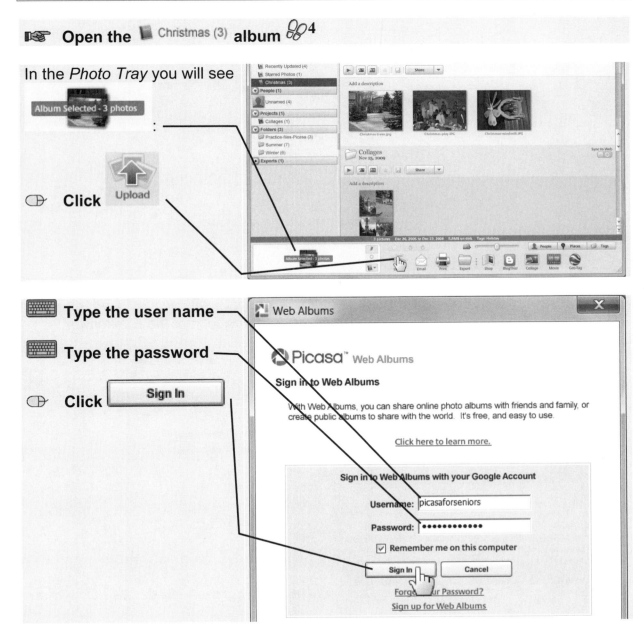

Type the user name

Type the password

Click Sign In

Here you will see the number
of photos you are going to
upload: ──────

⊕➔ **Click**   Upload

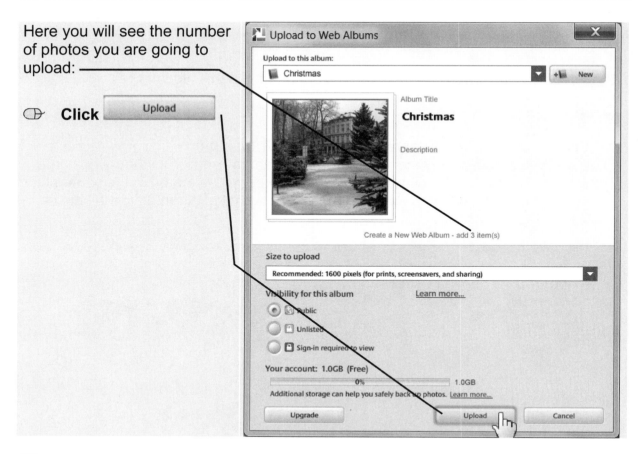

➔Please note:

You can determine which people are allowed to view your photos, by setting the
visibility options. You can choose one of three options: *Public*, *Unlisted*, or *Sign-in
required to view*. You can read more about these options in the *Background
Information* at the end of this chapter.

During the upload process
you will see this window:

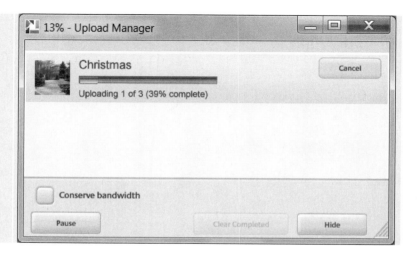

Now you are going to check if
you have uploaded the right
photos:

⊕ **Click** View Online

You will see the photos in
your web album:

⊕ **Click** X

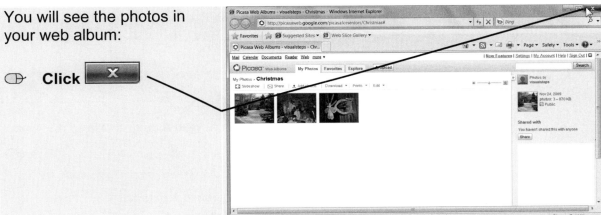

⊕ **Click**

Clear Completed

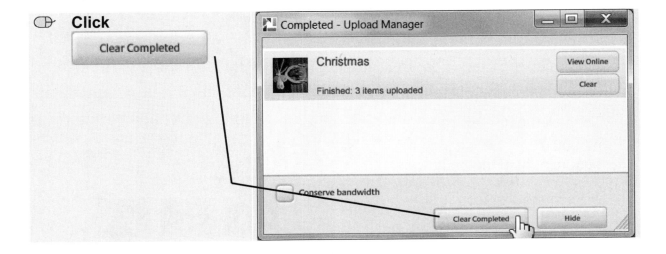

5.6 Synchronizing Your Web Album

If you want to add new photos to your web album, or replace edited photos, you will need to upload them again. By synchronizing your *Picasa* album with your web album, the changes you make to your album will automatically be applied to your web album as well. To enable this, you will need to activate the web synchronization option for the *Picasa* album:

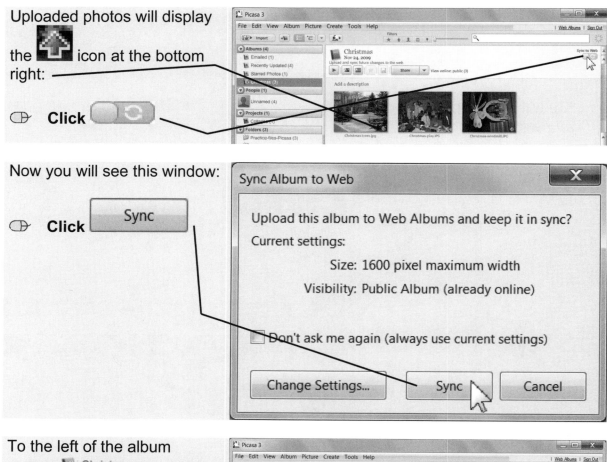

Uploaded photos will display the ⬆ icon at the bottom right:

☞ **Click**

Now you will see this window:

☞ **Click** Sync

To the left of the album named 🖼 Christmas and at the bottom right of the photos you will see the 🔄 icon:

☞ **Open the** 📁 Summer **folder** 🦶4

 Add Fair.jpg **to the** Christmas **album** 🐾17

Please note:

If you have added multiple pictures to the album, the synchronizing process may take a little while.

 Open the Christmas **album** 🐾4

You will see the photo you just added, as well as the icon on the photo.

⊕ **Click** View online: public (4)

Now you will also see the new photo appear in your web album:

⊕ **Click** ⨯

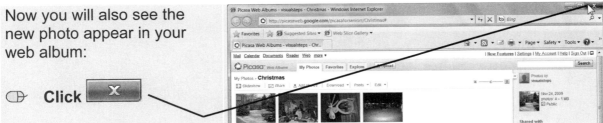

💡 Tip

Disable web synchronization

In order to (temporarily) disable the web synchronization option, for instance if you want to finish the *Picasa* album first, you need to click ⟲ once more. The photos that have already been uploaded will remain stored in the web album, but any changes will no longer be synchronized.

5.7 Sharing a Web Album

By clicking View online: public you can only view your album yourself. If you want to share this album with others, you need to activate the share option:

👉 **Click** | Share |

Now you are going to send an e-mail message and invite people to view your web album:

⌨ **Type the e-mail addresses**

Please note: Type a semi-colon (;) between the various addresses.

⌨ **If you want, you can change the subject and the message**

👉 **Click** | Send |

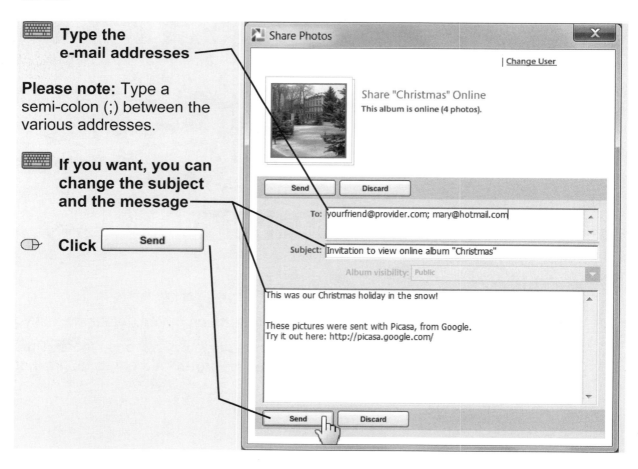

After you have uploaded the message you will see the following window:

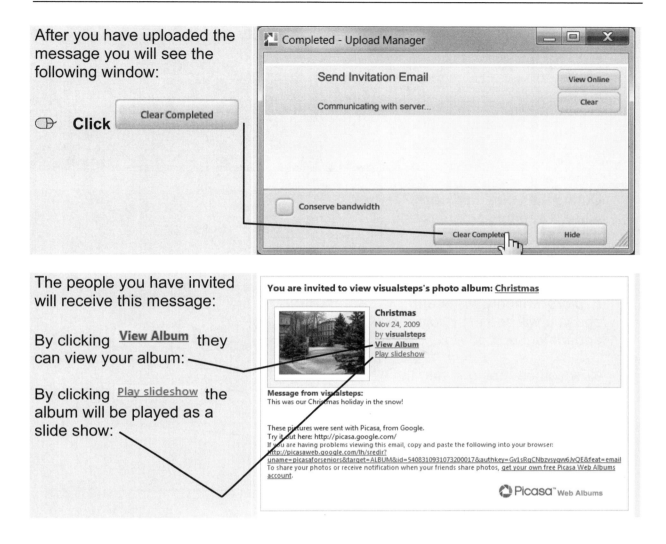

⟜ **Click** [Clear Completed]

The people you have invited will receive this message:

By clicking **View Album** they can view your album:

By clicking Play slideshow the album will be played as a slide show:

You are invited to view visualsteps's photo album: Christmas

Christmas
Nov 24, 2009
by **visualsteps**
View Album
Play slideshow

Message from visualsteps:
This was our Christmas holiday in the snow!

These pictures were sent with Picasa, from Google.
Try it out here: http://picasa.google.com/
If you are having problems viewing this email, copy and paste the following into your browser:
http://picasaweb.google.com/lh/sredir?
uname=picasaforseniors&target=ALBUM&id=5408310931073200017&authkey=Gv1sRgCNbzvsyqvw6JvQE&feat=email
To share your photos or receive notification when your friends share photos, get your own free Picasa Web Albums account.

⟁ Picasa™ Web Albums

5.8 Uploading Photos With the Drop Box

The *Drop Box* is a quick and easy way of uploading your photos. This is a temporary web album to which you can upload photos from different folders, after which you can add them to the appropriate web album.

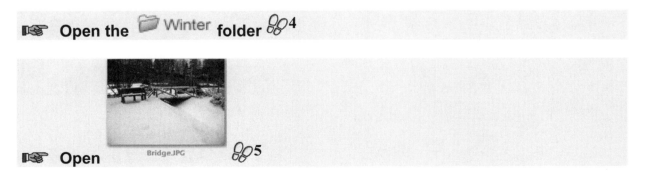

☞ **Open the** 📁 Winter **folder** 👣⁴

☞ **Open** Bridge.JPG 👣⁵

⊕ **Click**

During the upload process
you will see this progress bar:

Uploading Bridge.JPG

Afterwards, the *Internet
Explorer* window will open
and you will see the photo
appear in the *Drop Box*.

Now you are going to add the
photo to a different album:

⊕ **Click** Edit ▼

⊕ **Click** Organize & Reorder

⊕ **Click the picture**

⊕ **Click** Move

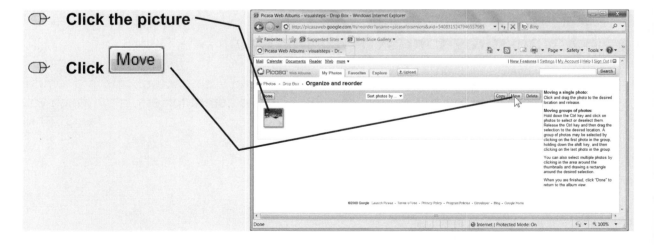

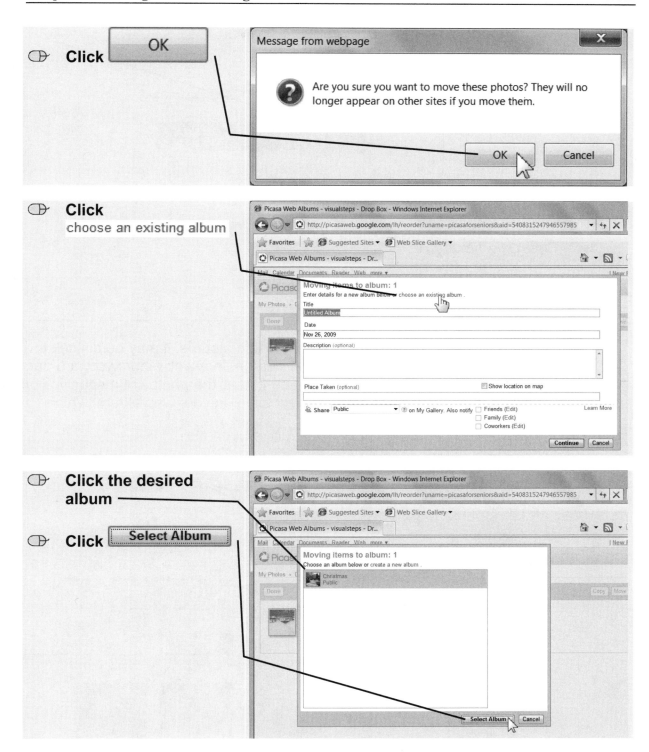

Now you will see the photo
appear in this album:

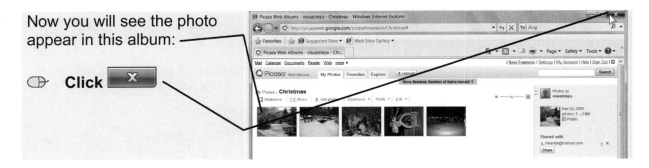

Click ⊞ [X]

Now you will return to the *Picasa* window.

☞ Open the *library* 𝄜 11

5.9 Name Tags in a Web Album

Even if you have neatly organized your photos into albums, it may be difficult to
quickly find all the pictures of one particular person. In a web album you add name
tags to these people. These tags will help you find all the photos of a specific person
more quickly. First, you need to create a new folder in your web album, which
contains the photos of various people.

Click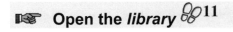

Click Folder Manager...

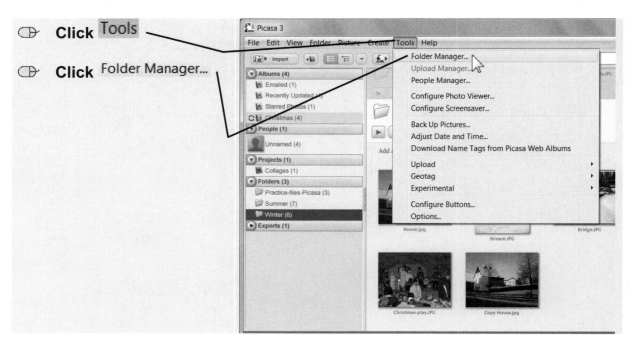

⊕ **If necessary, click** ▷ **next to**

📁 Practice-files-Picasa

⊕ **Click** 📁 Other pictures

⊕ **Click** Scan Once

⊕ **Click** OK

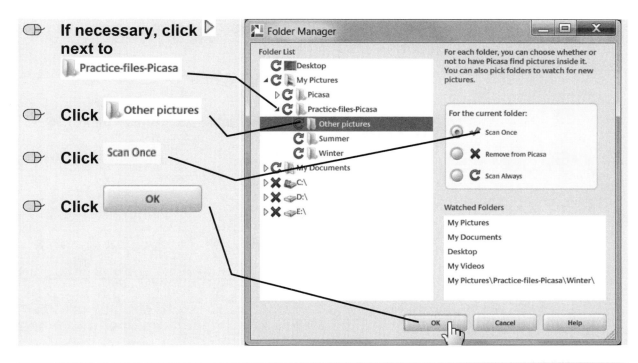

At the bottom right of the window you will see a bar:

☞ **Open the** 📁 Other pictures **folder** 👣4

Now you will see various pictures of people, but also some photos which do not contain people:

⊕ **Click**

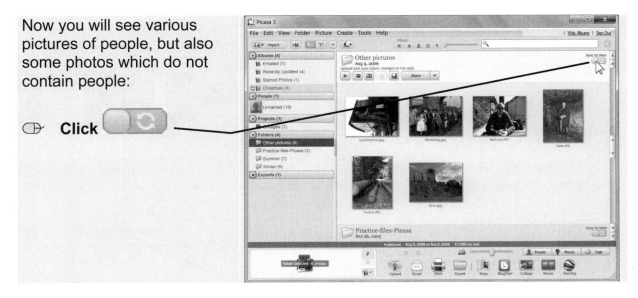

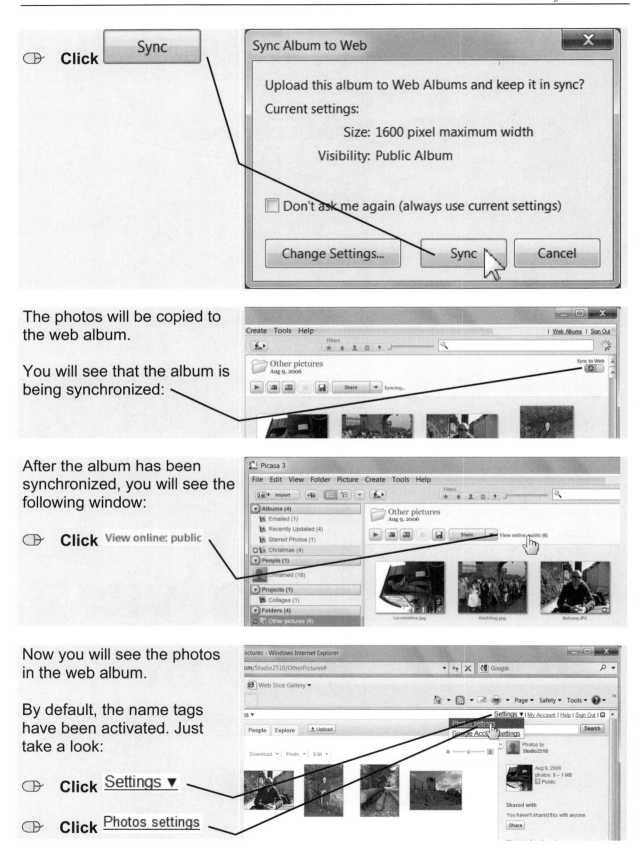

Click Sync

Sync Album to Web

Upload this album to Web Albums and keep it in sync?

Current settings:

   Size: 1600 pixel maximum width

   Visibility: Public Album

☐ Don't ask me again (always use current settings)

Change Settings...   Sync   Cancel

The photos will be copied to the web album.

You will see that the album is being synchronized:

After the album has been synchronized, you will see the following window:

Click View online: public

Now you will see the photos in the web album.

By default, the name tags have been activated. Just take a look:

Click Settings ▼

Click Photos settings

👆 **Click**
Privacy and Permissions

You will see that the box is checked ☑ at
Hide name tags in my *public alt*

You can close this window:

👆 **Click** Cancel

👆 **Click the** My Photos
tab

👆 **Click** Other pictures

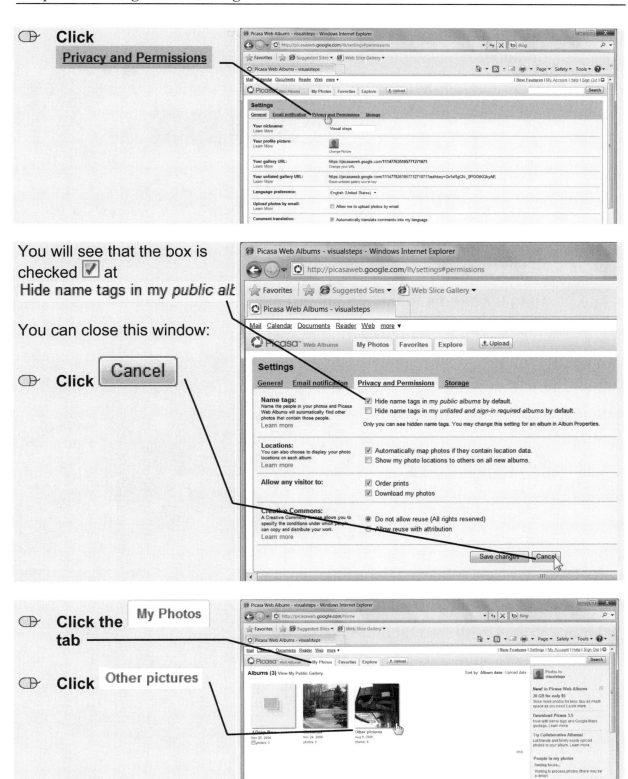

Click a photo with a person in it

Click **+**

Drag the handle to the desired location

Type the name

Click Apply

If you want, you can type a name and an e-mail address

Click Save

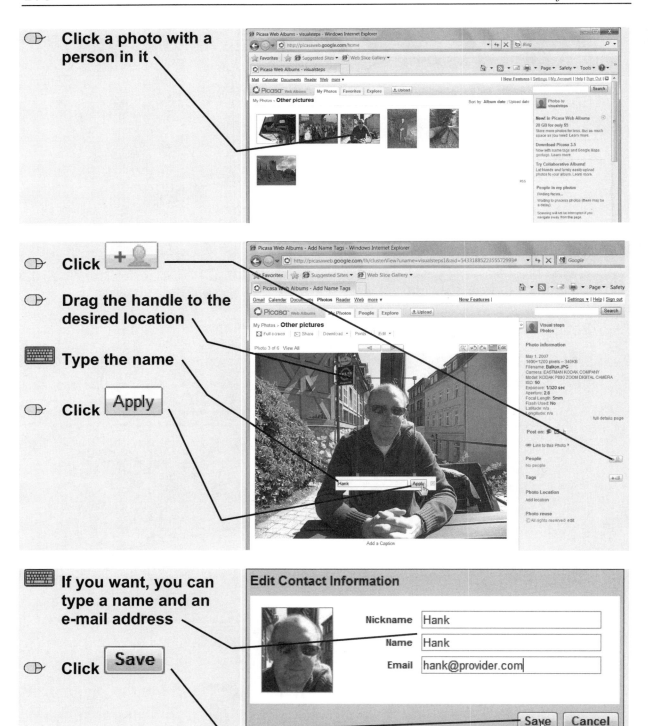

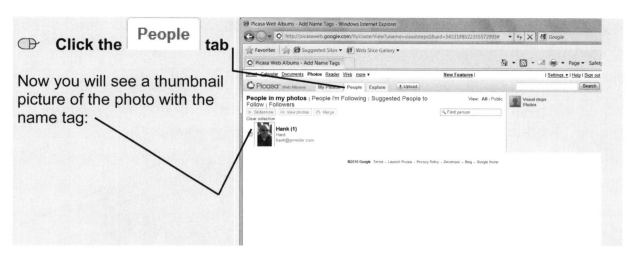

☞ **Click the** People **tab**

Now you will see a thumbnail picture of the photo with the name tag:

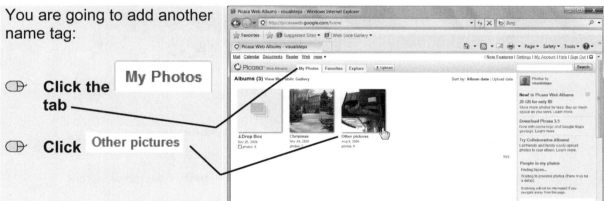

You are going to add another name tag:

☞ **Click the** My Photos **tab**

☞ **Click** Other pictures

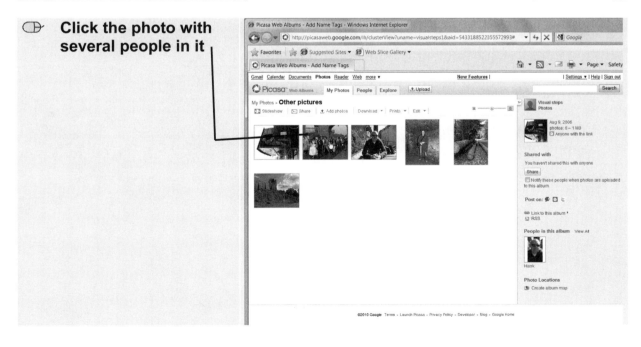

☞ **Click the photo with several people in it**

Give the bride a name:

Click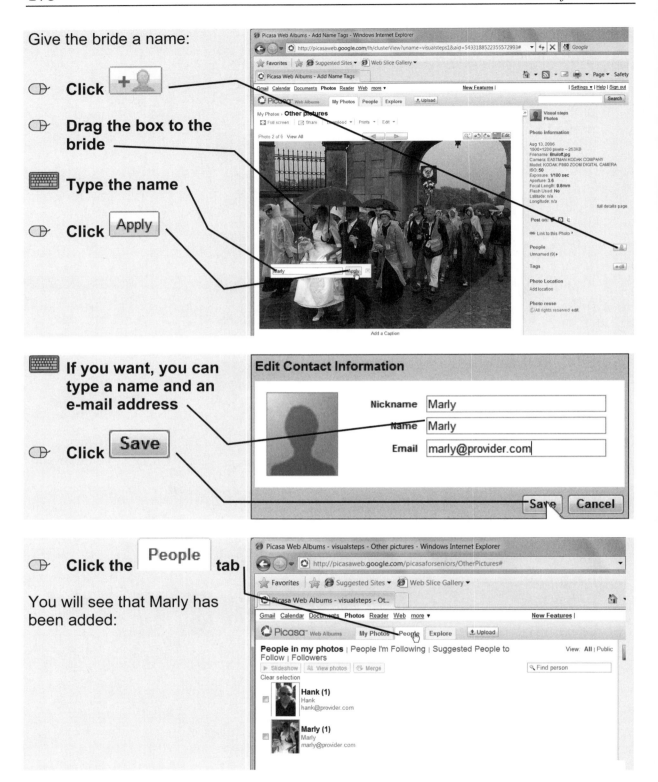

Drag the box to the bride

Type the name

Click Apply

If you want, you can type a name and an e-mail address

Click Save

Click the People tab

You will see that Marly has been added:

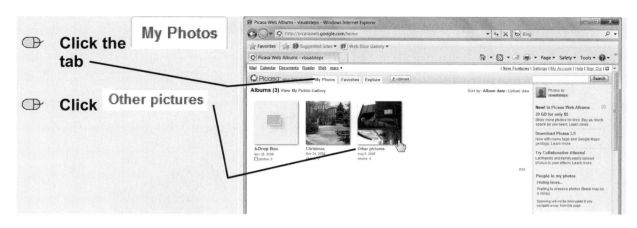

⊕ Click the My Photos **tab**

⊕ Click Other pictures

Now you see all the photos in the album:

In a web album you can also straighten a photo:

⊕ Click the first photo

⊕ Click

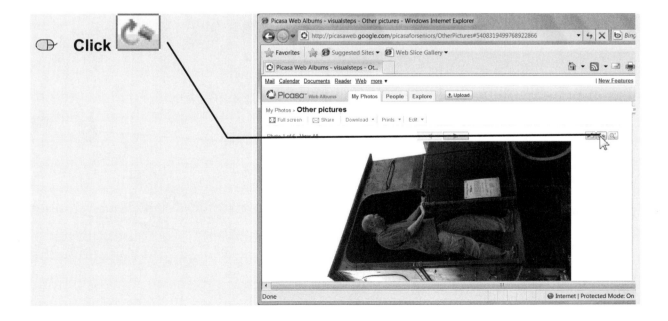

After the photo has been
rotated:

☞ **Click** View All

Now you can search for all
the photos with Hank in it:

☞ **Click the photo with**
Hank

Now the photos will be found.

☞ **Click** ☒

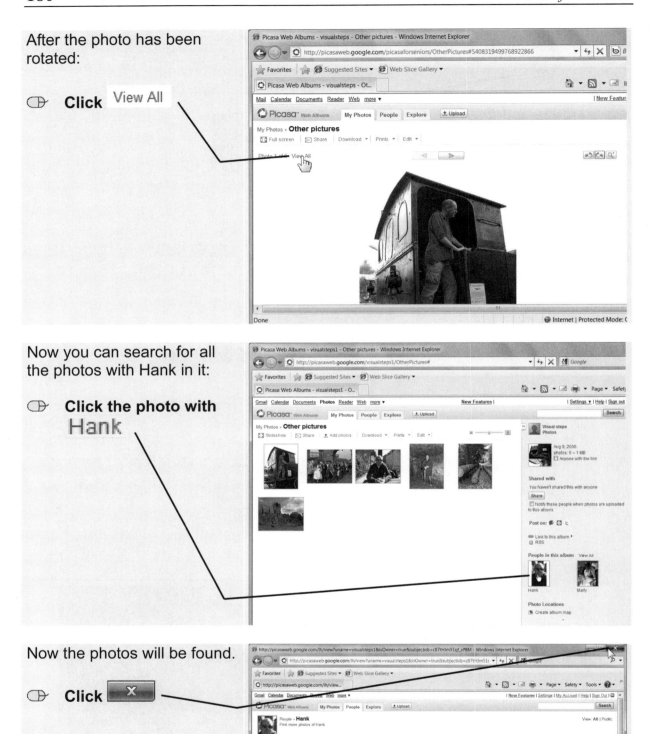

Tip

Rotate the photo in Picasa first
If you rotate the photo in *Picasa* first, before adding the name tags in your web album, the program will be able to find the rotated photo.

You do no longer need the ☼ 📷 Other pictures (6) folder, so you can delete this folder:

☞ **Right-click**
   ☼ 📷 Other pictures (6)

☞ **Click**
   Remove from Picasa...

☞ **Click**
   Remove Folder

☞ **Click** Sign Out

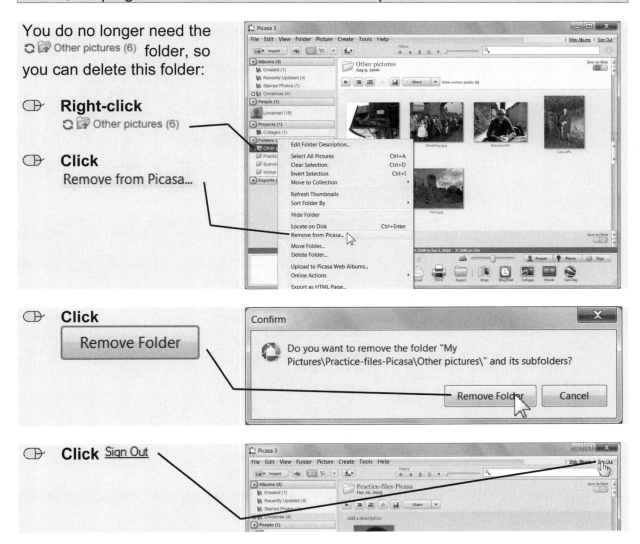

Currently, the facial recognition function has not been fully perfected yet, but in the next editions of *Picasa* this function will undoubtedly be improved.

5.10 Online Order of a Photo Print

Instead of printing your photos yourself, you can also send them to an online printing service. Of course this is a little more expensive, but you will get high quality prints printed on special photo paper. Usually, the result is a lot better than the prints you make with your own printer.

☞ **Put the photos you want to print in the** *Photo Tray* 🦶🦶8

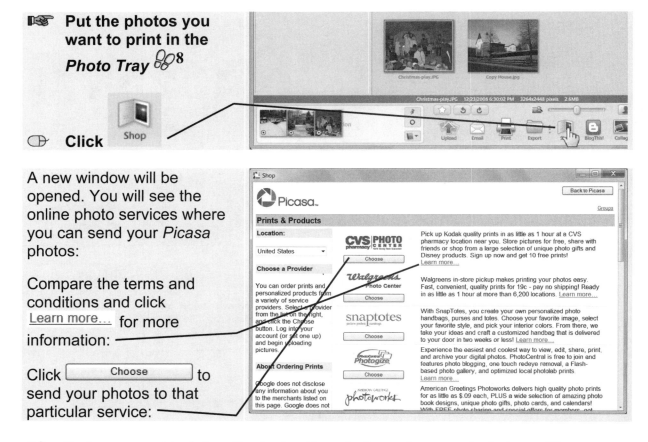

☞ **Click** Shop

A new window will be opened. You will see the online photo services where you can send your *Picasa* photos:

Compare the terms and conditions and click Learn more... for more information:

Click to send your photos to that particular service:

After that, you need to follow the instructions in the subsequent windows. These instructions may differ per service.

Please note:

When you check the costs, make sure to pay attention to the additional charges, such as ordering costs or shipping and handling fees.

☞ **Close all windows** 🦶🦶3

5.11 Background Information

Dictionary	
Collage	Collection of photos which you creatively shuffle and print together on the same page.
Drop Box	The *Drop Box* is an online album you can use to collect various types of photos, and to quickly upload photos. You can easily move these *Drop Box* photos to other online albums. The *Drop Box* will only be visible in your *Picasa* web albums after you have actually added a photo to the box.
Visibility	The visibility options allow you to determine the degree of privacy for your albums. You can set these visibility options during the uploading process, and change them in *Picasa* and in the *Picasa* web albums whenever you want.
Web album	Location on the Internet, where you can show your photos to other people. Before you can create a web album, you need to register with the administrator of this album first. Often these web albums are free of charge, but sometimes you need to pay for additional services.

Source: Picasa Help

Photo Sizes and Image Sizes
Conventional photos have an aspect ratio of 2:3 or 3:2.
Other well-known standard formats are:
4" x 6"
5" x 7"
8" x 10"

Digital cameras, however, often have a different aspect ratio, such as 4:3.
The following sizes are standard digital photo sizes:

640 x 480
1024 x 768
1152 x 864
1280 x 960
1600 x 1200
2048 x 1536

This means that not every digital photo can be printed on conventionally sized photo paper. In certain situations part of the photo will be omitted, or conversely, the photo may acquire a white border. You can compare this to viewing a widescreen picture on a regular television set. Unless the display is corrected, you will see a black bar. If you crop the photo in *Picasa* first, and take into account the size you want to use for your print, you will be able to see how the photo will turn out before printing it. You can also use the *Shrink to Fit* and *Crop to Fit* options while printing your photos (see *section 5.1 Printing*).

Album privacy: visibility options for your album

With the *Picasa* web albums you can easily share your photos with the rest of the world. But you can also choose to keep them for yourself, and a few friends. Use the visibility options to determine the degree of privacy for your options. You can set these options while uploading the photos, and you can change them in *Picasa* and the *Picasa* web albums whenever you want.

 Public

Use this option if you want your photos to be visible to anyone who knows the web address (URL) of your public photo gallery. The web address is based on the user name of your *Google* account: http://picasaweb.google.com/username/albumname. By default, your public albums will also appear when people are searching public albums.

 Unlisted

Set your album to *Unlisted* to limit who can see your album. All unlisted albums have an authorization key in the web address. The key is a combination of letters and numbers which makes the web address very difficult to guess. Anyone that has the exact web address will be able to see your unlisted album.

 Sign-in required to view

Select the *Sign-in required to view* option to set the highest level of privacy for your album. You specify who has permission to view it, and those viewers must sign in to their *Google* account to verify their identity. Users without a *Google* account will be prompted to create one. Anyone not included on the album's *Shared with* access list will be unable to view the album. In *Picasa Help* you will find more information on adding and removing visitors from your *Shared with* access list.

Source: Picasa Help

5.12 Tips

 Tip

Save as HTML document
If you want to view your photos in *Internet Explorer*, or display them on your own website, you can export them to the HTML file format:

☞ **Click the desired photo, folder, or album**

☞ **Click** Folder

☞ **Click**
Export as HTML Page...

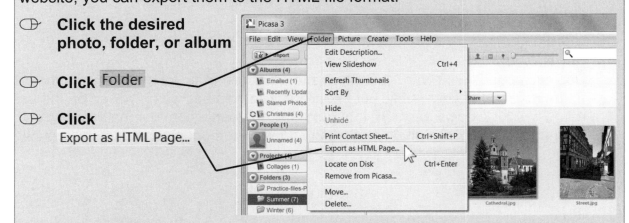

In the following windows you can select the desired name, resolution and formatting.

 Tip

Use your photo as a desktop background
Just as a collage, you can also use a single photo as a desktop background:

In the *library*:

☞ **Click a picture**

☞ **Click** Create

☞ **Click** Set as Desktop...

☞ **Click** Set Desktop

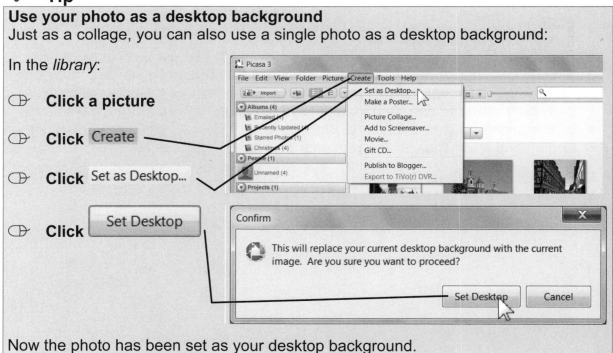

Now the photo has been set as your desktop background.

Tip

Album as a screensaver
Picasa has a special album for the photos you can use as a screensaver:

In the *library*:

⊕ **Click a folder, album, or photo**

⊕ **Click** Create

⊕ **Click** Add to Screensaver...

⊕ **Click** Settings...

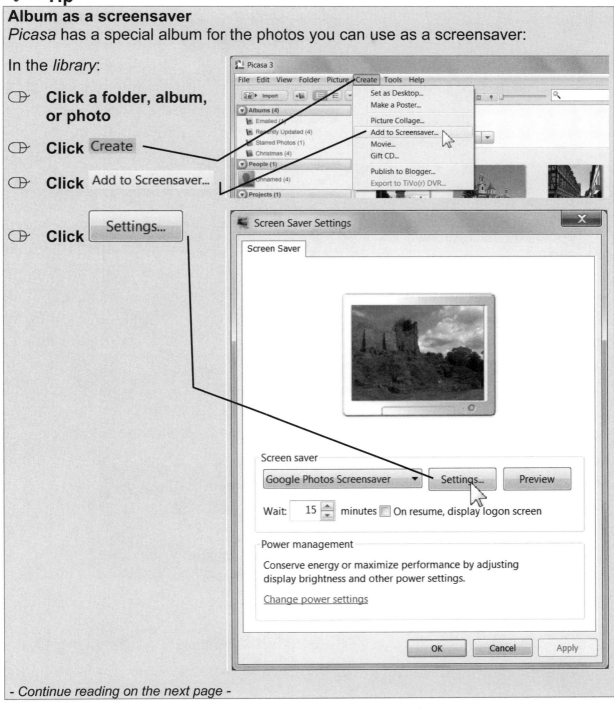

- Continue reading on the next page -

If you only want to use the photos in the 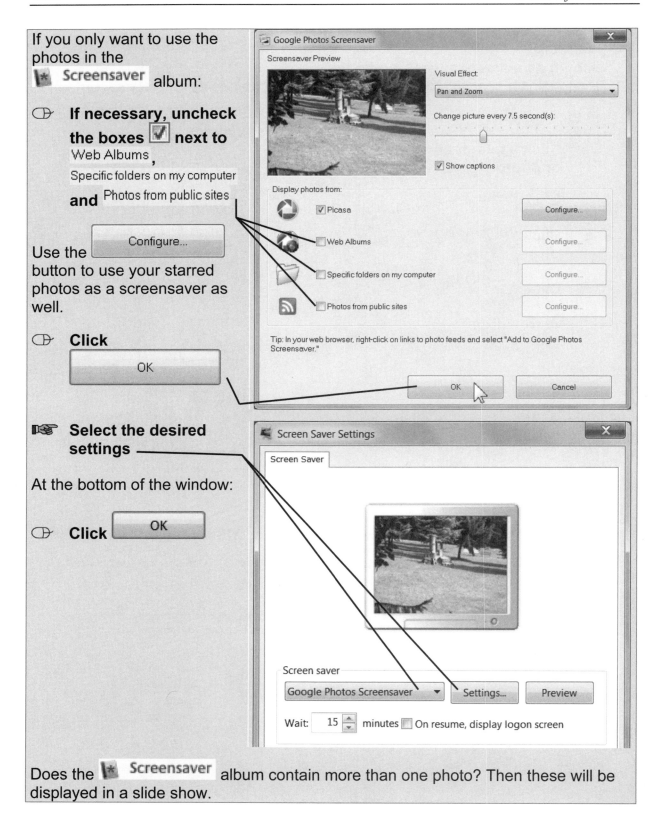 **⁌ Screensaver** album:

☞ **If necessary, uncheck the boxes ☑ next to** Web Albums , Specific folders on my computer **and** Photos from public sites

Use the Configure... button to use your starred photos as a screensaver as well.

☞ **Click** OK

☞ **Select the desired settings**

At the bottom of the window:

☞ **Click** OK

Does the **⁌ Screensaver** album contain more than one photo? Then these will be displayed in a slide show.

6. Slide Shows and Movies

Picasa offers several viewing options for your pictures and videos. You can view them separately, or in a slide show or a movie.

A slide show is a great way to quickly and easily view all of the pictures and videos in a single folder. You can also burn this slide show to a CD or DVD. This makes a wonderful present, too. Anyone who watches this slide show on a computer can select the speed of the slide show and choose how the transitions between the items are displayed.

When you create a movie of your pictures and videos, you can set the display time for each slide, choose the transitions between the slides and add music as well. In this way you can determine the 'look and feel' of your movie. A movie can be exported and viewed with a variety of different media players such as the *Windows Media Player*.

In this chapter you will learn how to:

- play the photos in an album as a slide show;
- add music to a slide show;
- create a gift CD or DVD;
- convert a slide show into a film;
- create and edit title slides;
- set the transitions between the slides;
- set the display time for the slides;
- add music to movies;
- save and play movies;
- shorten videos;
- edit movies;
- upload movies to *YouTube*.

 Please note:

If you want to use the exercises in this chapter, you need to download the *Practice-files-Picasa* folder and save it to the (*My*) *Pictures* folder on your computer. You can read how to do that in *Chapter 1 Installing Picasa*.

6.1 Playing a Slide Show

You can play all the photos in an album as a slide show straightaway. This is how you do it:

☞ **Open** *Picasa* ⠎⠎6

☞ **Open the** 📁 Summer **folder** ⠎⠎4

☞ **Put** [City.jpg] **in the** *Photo Tray* ⠎⠎8

☞ **Put** [Street.jpg] **in the** *Photo Tray* ⠎⠎8

☞ **Open the** 📁 Winter **folder** ⠎⠎4

☞ **Put** [Christmas-trees.jpg] **in the** *Photo Tray* ⠎⠎8

Now you will see three photos in the *Photo Tray*. In this bottom part of the window:

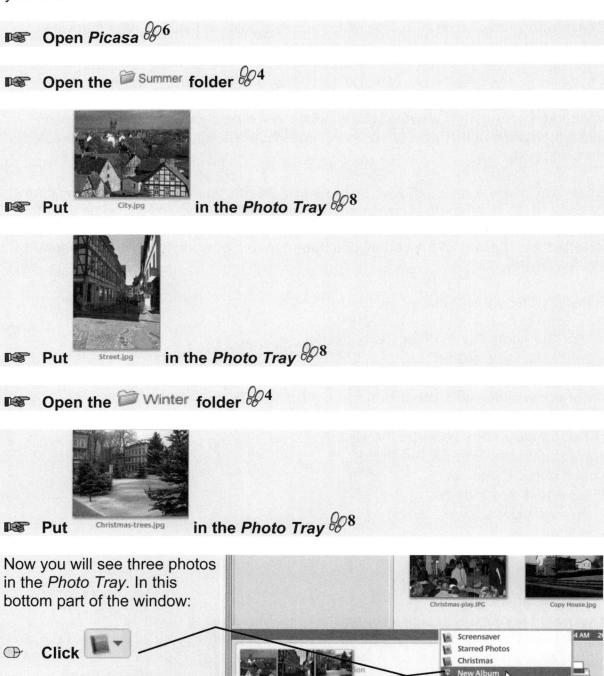

⊕ **Click** [▼]

⊕ **Click** [+ New Album]

Type: Slideshow

At the bottom of the window:

Click OK

Open the Slideshow album ⌐⌐4

Now you are going to play the photos in a slide show:

Click ▶

Please note:

If a particular photo was already selected, the slide show will start playing from that point.

Now you will see the slides on a full screen.

The last slide will remain visible on the screen.
To close the slide show:

Press Esc

In *section 2.7 Viewing Pictures in a Slide Show* you can read more about viewing and setting up a slide show.

You can also add music to the slide show. You will need to save this music in a separate folder, and the music files need to be in the MP3 or WMA file format.

Now you are going to add music:

👆 **Click** Tools

👆 **Click** Options...

👆 **Click the** Slideshow **tab**

👆 **If necessary, check the box** ☑ **next to** Play music tracks during slideshow

👆 **Click** Browse...

Now you will see the *Browse For Folder* window:

👆 **Click your user name**

👆 **Click** 🖼 My Pictures

In *Windows Vista* you need to select the *Pictures* folder.

👆 **Click** 🖿 Practice-files-Picasa

At the bottom of the window:

👆 **Click** OK

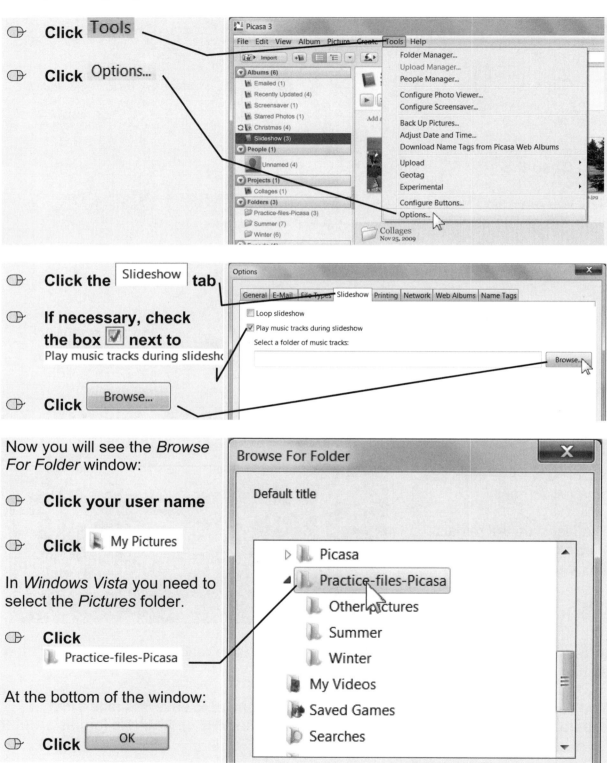

Now you will see that the folder has been selected:

This folder contains a music file.

At the bottom of the window:

⊕ **Click** OK

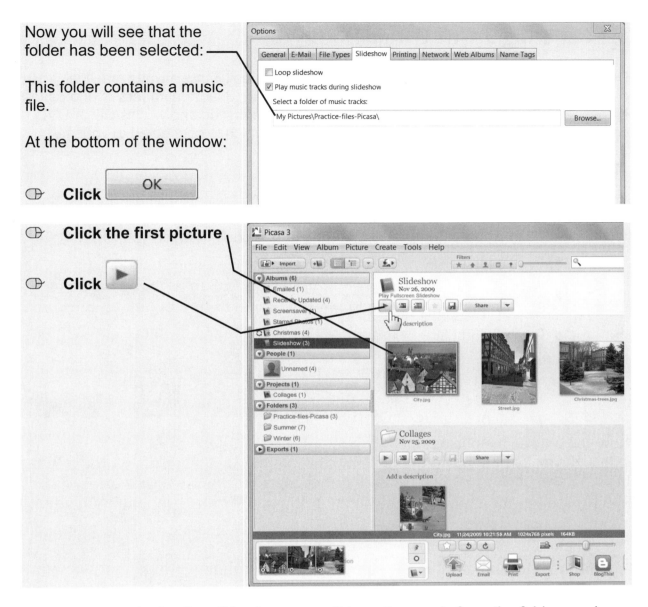

⊕ **Click the first picture**

⊕ **Click** ▶

While you are playing the slide show you will hear the music from the folder you have selected. If the folder contains more music files, they will be played one after the other. In this example the folder contains just one music file. The length of the music file and the length of the slide show are not adapted to each other. In the next section you will learn how to change this.

☞ **Close the slide show after the last slide** 🐾**19**

The automatic slide show option is especially suitable for quickly viewing all of the pictures or videos in a single folder or an album.

6.2 Creating a Gift CD or DVD

Due to the size of the photo files, sending them by e-mail is not always practical. You can only send a few photos at a time. If you want to send large numbers of photos to someone else, you can create a gift CD or DVD of your slide show. This CD or DVD can also be played on a computer or a DVD player which is connected to your TV.

 Please note:

You can only include entire albums or folders in a slide show, not single photos. You will need to copy the photos you want to use to a folder or an album first. It is recommended to create a temporary album for these photos, which you can remove later on, if you like.

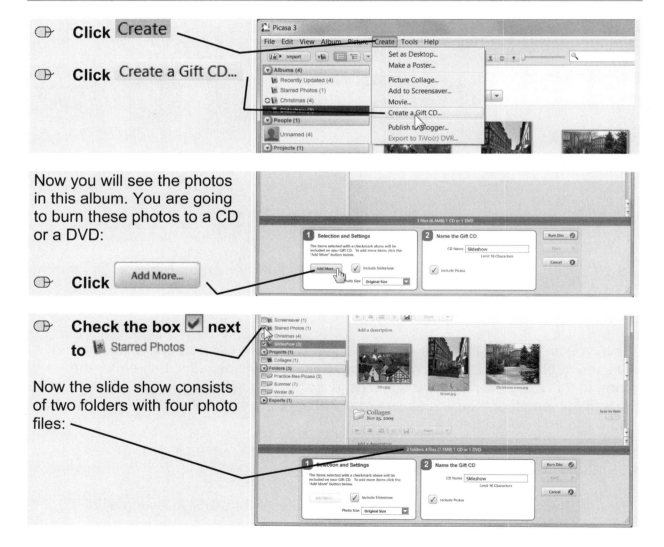

Click **Create**

Click **Create a Gift CD...**

Now you will see the photos in this album. You are going to burn these photos to a CD or a DVD:

Click **Add More...**

Check the box ✔ next to 🌟 Starred Photos

Now the slide show consists of two folders with four photo files:

Tip

Creating a CD for a photo service
If you want to create a CD that can be printed by a photo service, you need to

uncheck the boxes next to `Include Slideshow` and `Include Picasa`. Now the slide show will
not start by itself, and the *Picasa* program will not be included in the CD.
If the photo service is not able to process this CD, you can also try the *Picasa Export*
option to create a CD for the photo service.

 Please note:

If you do not have writable CDs, DVDs, or a CD/DVD burner:

☞ **Click** `Cancel ⊗`

At the bottom of the window:

Next to `CD Name`:

☞ **Double-click the name**

⌨ **Type:** Holiday

☞ **Click** `Burn Disc ✓`

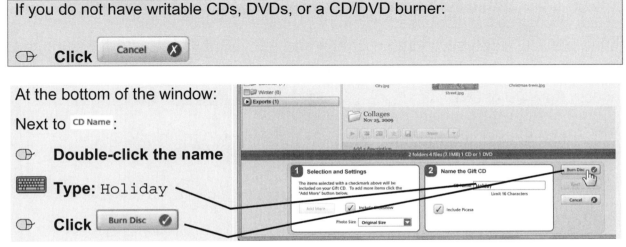

☞ **Insert a disc into your CD/DVD drive**

☞ **Click** `Continue`

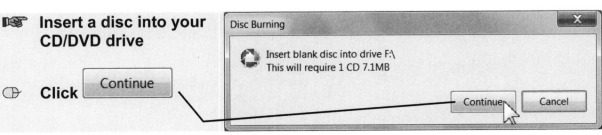

 Please note:

If the disc is rewritable and already contains data, you will see a message asking
you if the disc can be erased. In that case, click `OK`.

To the right of your window
you will see a progress bar:

When the burning process is complete:

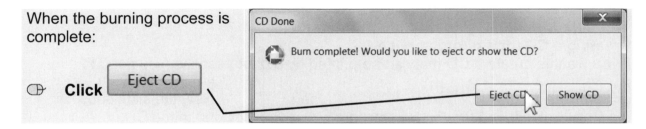

 Click [Eject CD]

Now the CD/DVD drive tray will open to eject the CD:

Please note:
The gift CD or DVD can be played on many DVD players. But not all players are able to recognize the disc. Check the manual that comes with your DVD player to learn which discs your player will recognize.

You can run the slide show directly from CD or DVD:

☞ **Insert the disc into the CD/DVD drive**

Now you will see this window:

 Click
Run PicasaCD.exe
Published by Google Inc.

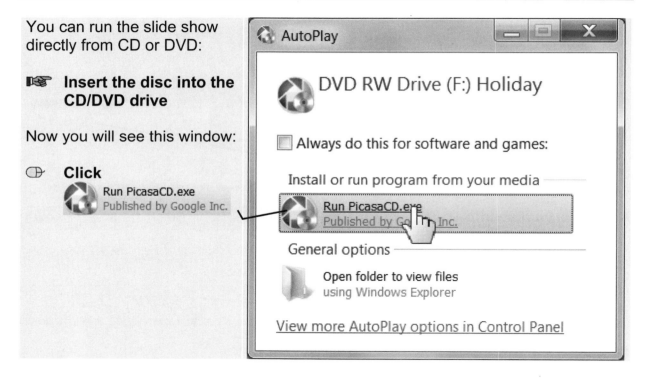

Now you are going to view the photos:

 Click a folder

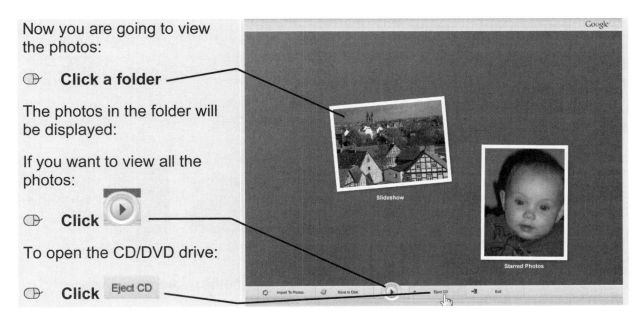

The photos in the folder will be displayed:

If you want to view all the photos:

 Click

To open the CD/DVD drive:

 Click Eject CD

💡 **Tip**

Copy photo files from the gift CD
The receiver of the gift CD can also copy the individual photo files from the CD to their computer's hard drive. After the CD has been inserted into the drive, the

AutoPlay window will be opened. By clicking [Open folder to view files using Windows Explorer] the contents of the CD will be displayed. The photos are stored in the (*My*) *Pictures* folder.

➦ **Please note:**
The music files will not be included on the gift CD. In the next section you will learn how to create a slide show with music files included on the disc.

6.3 Creating a Movie From a Slide Show

The slide show which you have previously made can be played in *Picasa*. But you can also create a movie from this slide show, and play this movie with *Windows Media Player*, or various other programs.

➦ **Please note:**
In *Picasa* the movies you make with your video camera, or have downloaded from the Internet, are called video clips. In *Picasa*, a movie is a combination of photos, video clips and music, which is stored and displayed as a single entity.

This is how you make a movie:

☞ **If necessary, empty the *Photo Tray*** 👣16

☞ **If necessary, open the** 🎞 Slideshow **album** 👣4

🖱 **Click** [image]

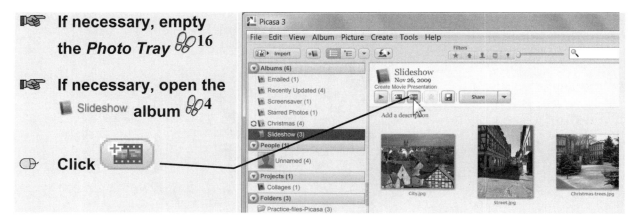

Picasa will automatically create a movie by using the photos in the album, and will add a slide for the title. First, you are going to play the movie:

🖱 **Click** [▶]

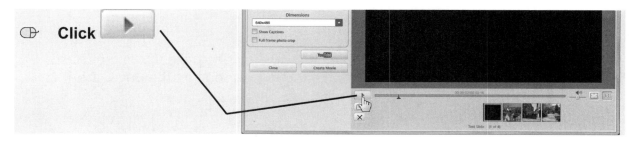

Now the movie will be played. You can pause the movie by clicking the [❚❚]

button. When you want to continue, click [▶].
Afterwards, you can edit the movie. For instance, you can remove photos from the movie without removing them from the album itself:

🖱 **Click** [image]

You will see the photo:

🖱 **Click**

The photo has been removed.

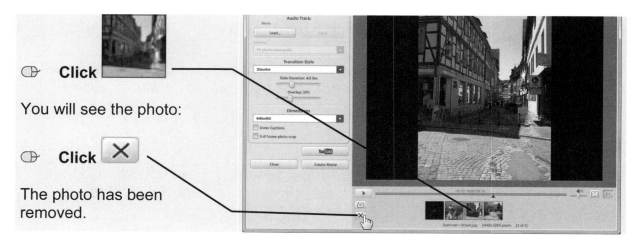

No you are going to add
photos:

⊕ **Click**

⊕ **Click the** Clips (1) **tab**

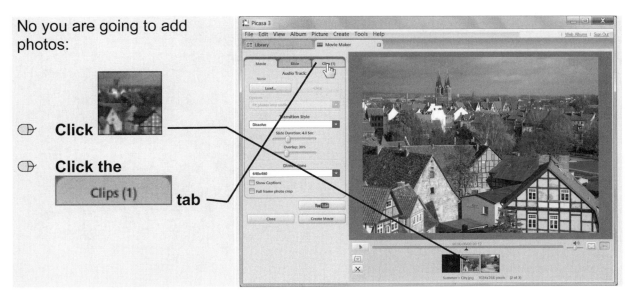

You will see the photo you
have removed:

Now you are going to fetch a
photo from another folder:

⊕ **Click** Get More...

⊕ **Click the** 📁 Summer **folder**

☞ **Put** Cathedral.jpg **in the** *Photo Tray* 👣8

⊕ **Click** Back to Movie Maker

In the row of photos near the bottom of the window, you will now see the photo you just added:

☞ **Drag the photo to the position right after the title slide** ─────

Now the photo has been added: ─────

☞ **Click the**

Movie **tab** ─────

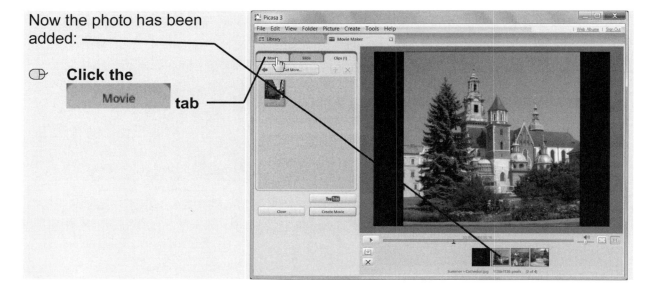

☞ **Check the box ☑ next to** Full frame photo crop ─

Now the photo will be displayed full screen. Due to the cropping operation, part of the top and the bottom of the photo has been cut off.

Tip

Does the photo appear blurred?
Sometimes the photo you have added will appear out of focus when you view it in this window. You can solve this problem by clicking a different photo, and then clicking the previous photo again. The photo will appear sharper.

6.4 Adding and Editing Title Slides

When you create a movie, *Picasa* will automatically insert a title slide. Now you will learn how to edit this slide according to your own preferences:

☞ **Click the Slide tab**

☞ **Click the title slide**

☞ **Select the text**

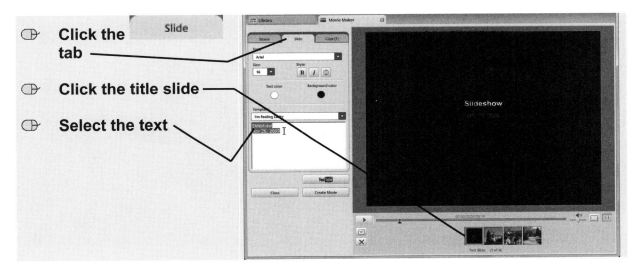

⌨ **Type:** Holiday 2009

⌨ **Press** Enter ↵

⌨ **Type:** Summer and Winter

Now you will see this text on the slide:
Next, you are going to change the background color:

Under Background color :

☞ **Click** ⬤

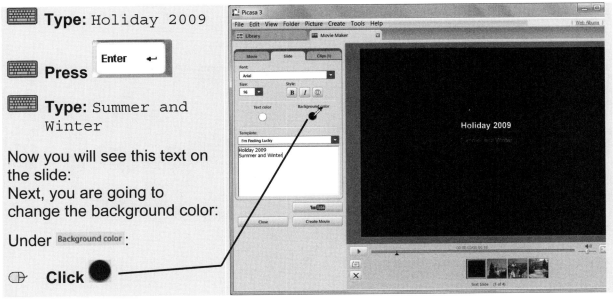

⊕ **Click the desired color**

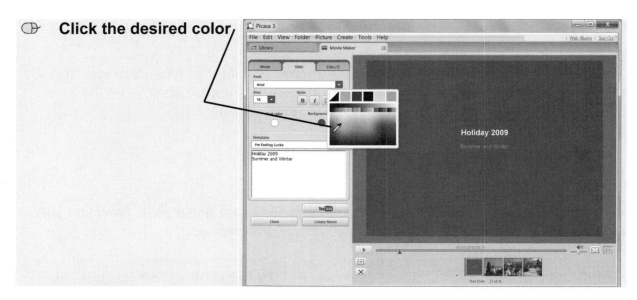

You are also going to change the text color:

Under Text color :

⊕ **Click** ◯

⊕ **Click the desired color**

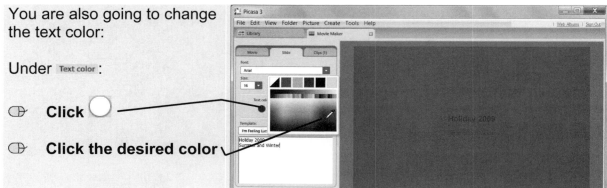

Instead of creating a separate title slide, you can also add text to an existing photo and use this photo as a title slide. If you want to do this, you will need to remove the current title slide first:

At the bottom left of the window:

⊕ **Click** ✕

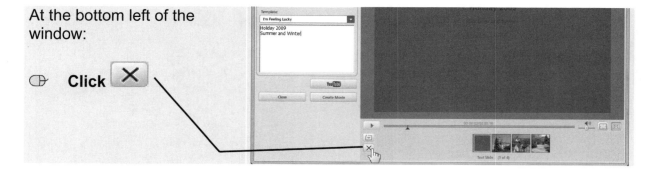

Now you will see the next photo.

⊕ **Click the text box**

⌨ **Type:** Holiday 2009

⌨ **Press** Enter ⏎

⌨ **Type:** Summer and Winter

You will see the text appear in the middle of the photo:

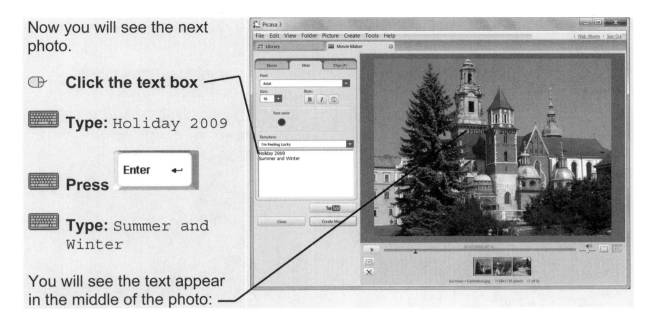

Because photos often consist of a multitude of colors, it will be difficult to find a text color that will be clearly visible. That is why it is better to insert the title in a template. This is how you do it:

Next to **Template:** :

⊕ **Click** ▼

⊕ **Click** Gradient - White

Now you will see the title much more clearly:

♀ Tip

Insert a title slide
If you want to add a separate title slide later on, or if you want to insert a title between some specific photos, you can insert your own text slide:

☞ **Click**

Now you will see a title slide:

☞ **Type the text for this slide and select the color**

☞ **Drag the slide to the correct position**

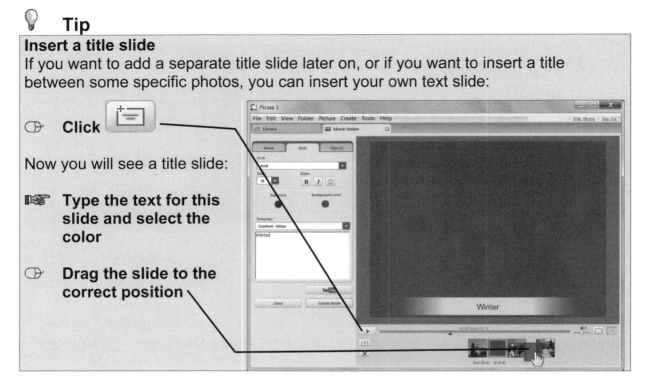

You can edit the text in the same way as you edit text in most text editors:

- By Font: you use ▼ to select a different font.

- By Size: you use ▼ to select a different font size.

- Use **B** to type the title in bold style (or undo the bold style).

- Use *I* to type the title in italic style (or undo the italic style).

- Use this icon ⓪ to display the outline of the letters only (or undo this operation and see the original letters again).

- You can change the text color with the ◯ button under Text color.

6.5 Setting the Dimensions and Transitions

If you want to turn your slide show into a movie, you can also select how the transition between the slides will be displayed. The selected transition style will be applied to all the slides:

☞ **Click the** Movie **tab**

☞ **Play the slide show** 🦶18

Watch closely how you go from one picture to the next one.

After you have played the movie, you can select a different transition style:

Under Transition Style :

☞ **Click** ▼

☞ **Click** Circle

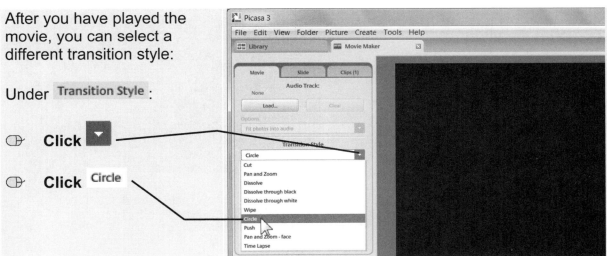

☞ **Play the slide show once more** 🦶18

Now each new slide will appear in a circle that overlaps the previous slide.

You are going to set the
duration for each slide:

☞ **Drag the slider ⬜ at
Slide Duration: 4.0 Sec to the left,
until you see**

Slide Duration: 2.5 Sec

☞ **Play the slide show
🦶18**

Now the amount of time spent
for each slide will be shorter.

You can use Overlap: 30% to set
the duration for the transitions
between the slides:

☞ **Drag the slider ⬜
under Overlap: 30% to the
right, until you see**
Overlap: 80%

☞ **Play the slide show
🦶18**

Because the transition takes
longer, you will see it more
clearly.

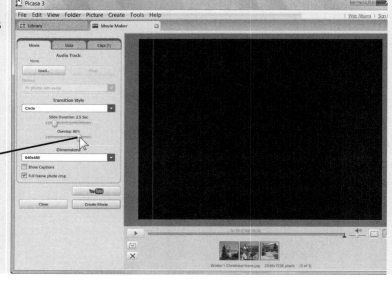

💡 **Tip**

Dimensions

By Dimensions you can select the screen resolution for your movie. If you select a high resolution, the images will be sharper, but the file will be bigger. Furthermore, it will be hard to view the movie on computers with low screen resolutions. This is how you select the dimensions:

Next to Dimensions :

☞ **Click** ▼

☞ **Click the desired resolution**

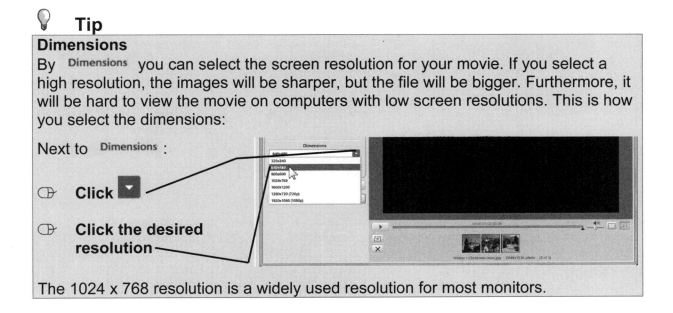

The 1024 x 768 resolution is a widely used resolution for most monitors.

6.6 Adding Music to a Movie

The music you add to a movie will be stored along with the movie. Therefore you will always be able to hear the music whenever you play the movie. You can use MP3 music files, as well as WMA music files. Now you are going to add music to your slide show:

☞ **Click** Load...

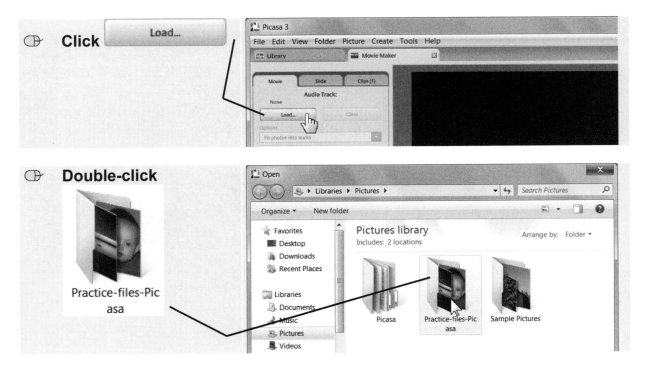

☞ **Double-click**

Practice-files-Pic
asa

Double-click

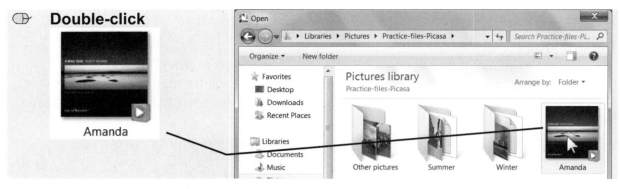

Amanda

You will see the title and the duration of the song:

Click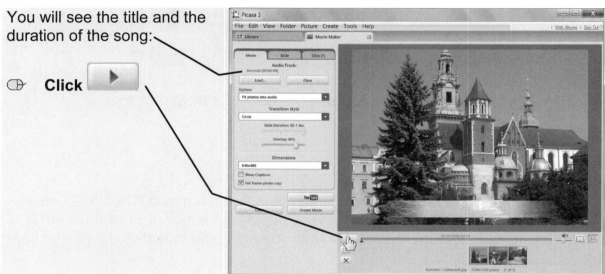

The slide show will be played, but the duration will be adapted to the length of the song. That is why it will take some time before you see the second slide.

When the second slide appears:

Click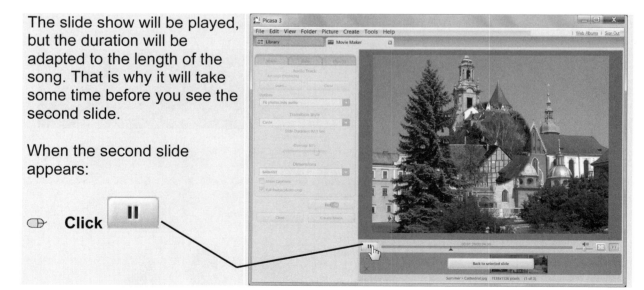

You can display the photos in a loop, until the music has finished:

Under Options :

☞ **Click** ▼

☞ **Click** Loop photos to match audio

☞ **Play the slide show**
👣18

The photos will be displayed in a loop, until the music has finished.

☞ **Stop the slide show**
👣20

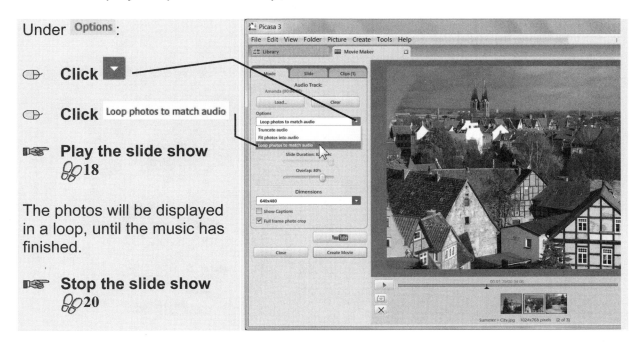

Another possibility is to truncate the audio file. When the slide show has finished, the music will stop as well. Now you are going to explore this option:

Under Options :

☞ **Click** ▼

☞ **Click** Truncate audio

☞ **Play the slide show**
👣18

The music will stop as soon as the slide show has finished.

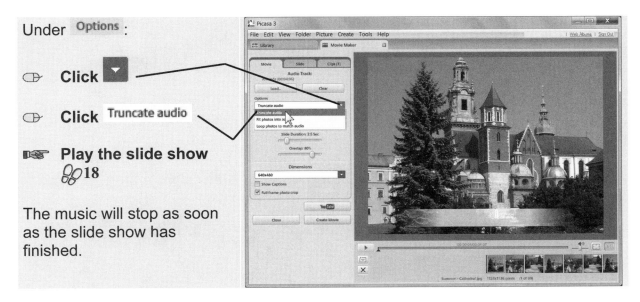

Truncating the audio is especially suitable when you are using neutral background music.

6.7 Saving and Playing Movies

When you have finished the movie, you can save it:

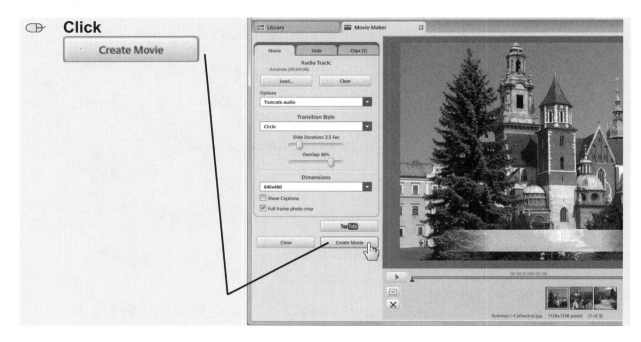

Click

   Create Movie

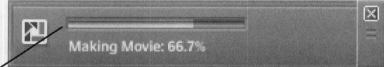

While the movie is being created, you will see a progress bar at the bottom right of your window:

Please note: if your movie is very long, this process may take a while.

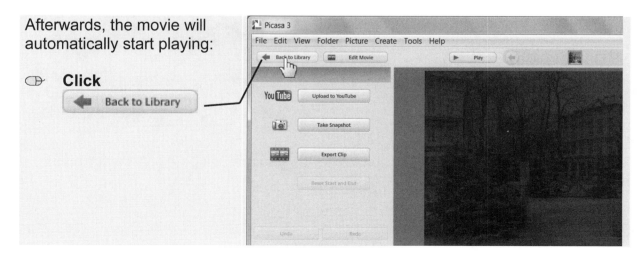

Afterwards, the movie will automatically start playing:

Click

   Back to Library

The film has been stored in the Movies project: ———

⊕ **If necessary, click**
   Movies

Now you are going to play the movie:

⊕ **Click** ▶

☞ **Close the slide show**
   👣19

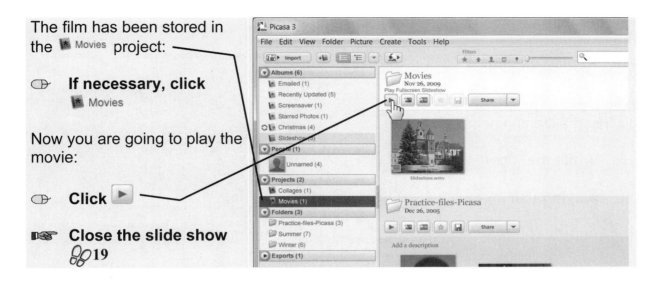

6.8 Truncating Video Clips

Although you cannot edit video clips in *Picasa*, you do have the option to shorten them. If you have a video clip that is too long, you can truncate it in the following way:

☞ **Open the** 📁 Practice-files-Picasa **folder** 👣4

⊕ **Double-click**

Lake.MPG

You will see the video clip:

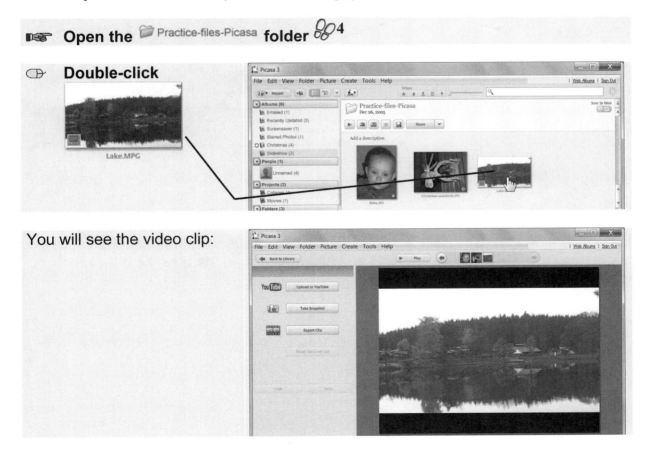

Now you are going to create starting and ending points:

☞ **Replay the movie**
👣21

To insert a starting point:

👉 **While the movie is**

   playing, click 🔺

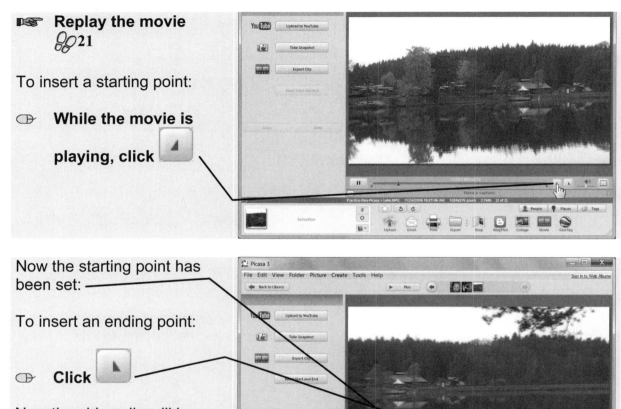

Now the starting point has been set: ──────

To insert an ending point:

👉 **Click** 🔺

Now the video clip will be played once more, beginning from the starting point you have inserted.

 HELP! It is going too fast.

> If the movie is playing too fast, you can play the movie until the end and then start it again. You can also drag the starting and ending points in the timeline bar shown under the movie to different positions.

Now the ending point has
been created: ⎯⎯⎯

☞ **Click**

   ⬅ Back to Library

If you play the video clip once
more, only the truncated part
will be played:

☞ **Double-click**

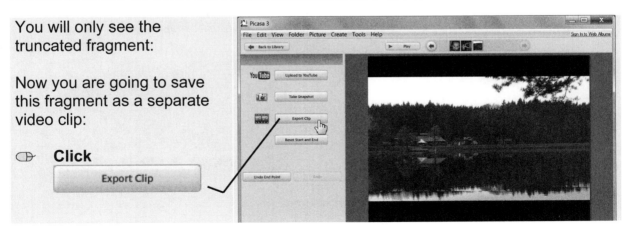

You will only see the
truncated fragment:

Now you are going to save
this fragment as a separate
video clip:

☞ **Click**

   Export Clip

The truncated fragment will be saved as a new video clip:

After the fragment has been
saved, you will see:

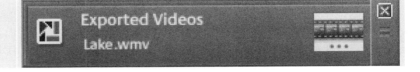

After this you can remove the starting and ending points from the original video clip, and play the entire clip again. This is how you do it:

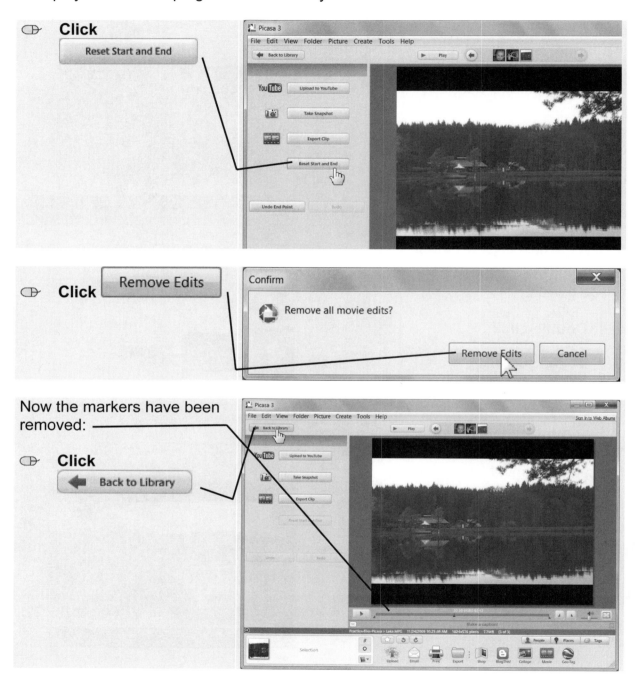

☞ Click `Reset Start and End`

☞ Click `Remove Edits`

Now the markers have been removed:

☞ Click `← Back to Library`

The truncated video clip will be visible in the
 Exported Videos project:

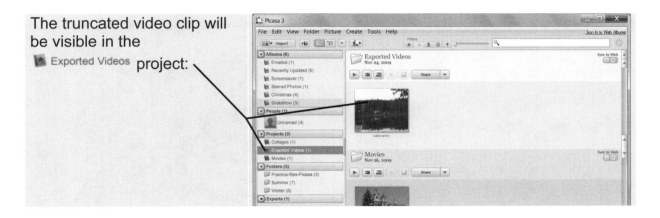

6.9 Editing Movies

Even if you have already finished a movie, you will still be able to edit it afterwards. You can add or remove photos, or even video clips.

Please note:

Currently you will only be able to edit the movies which are created in *Picasa*, but you cannot edit video clips.

☞ **Open the** 📽 Movies **project** 👣4

↪ **Double-click**

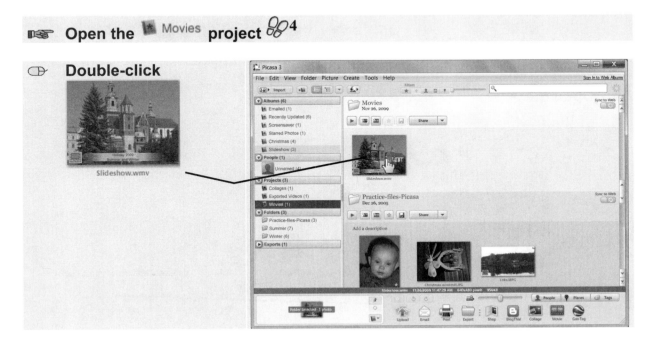

Now the movie will be played. If it takes too long to play the entire movie, click the ⏸ button.

After the movie has finished:

☞ **Click**

🎬 Edit Movie

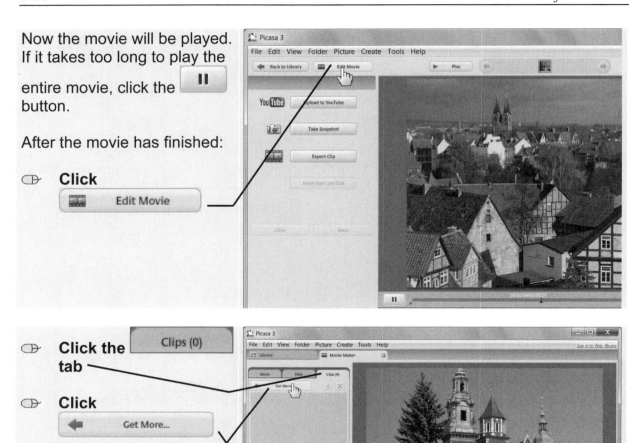

☞ **Click the Clips (0) tab**

☞ **Click**

⬅ Get More...

👉 **Open the ★ Exported Videos project 👣4**

☞ **Click** Lake.wmv

☞ **Click** Back to Movie Maker

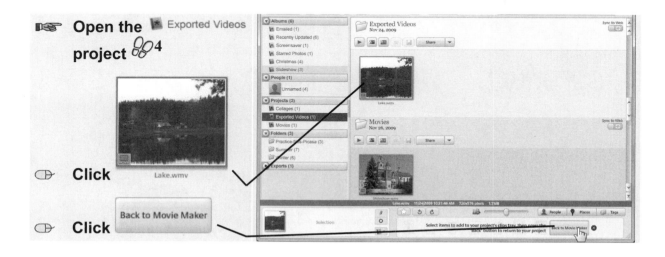

⊖ **Drag the clip to the position between the second and third photo**

Now you will see a temporary pattern of squares:

⊖ **Click the first picture**

⊖ **Click**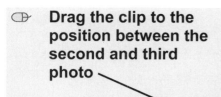

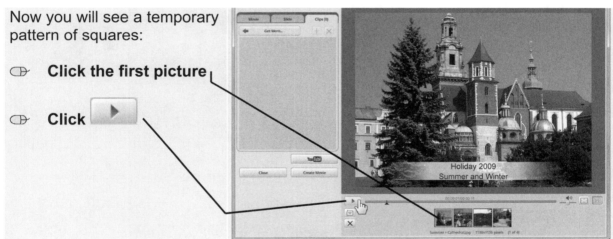

The movie will be played, including the video clip you have inserted.

You are going to create a new movie which includes all the edits:

⊖ **Click**

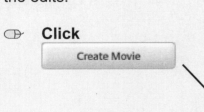

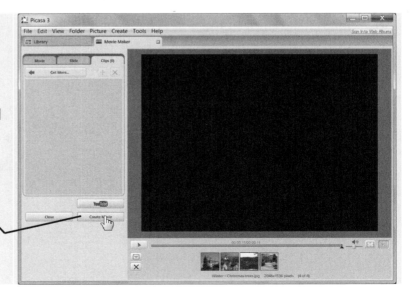

☞ **Click**

Replace Existing

If you want to save the
previous version as well, click

Create New .

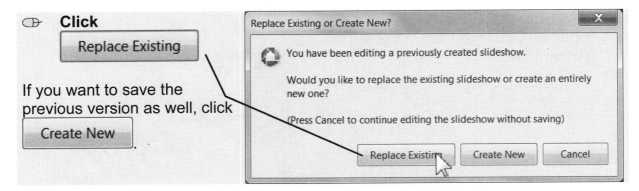

Replace Existing or Create New?

You have been editing a previously created slideshow.

Would you like to replace the existing slideshow or create an entirely new one?

(Press Cancel to continue editing the slideshow without saving)

Replace Existing   Create New   Cancel

Picasa will create the movie.

If the movie is long, this may
take a while.

When the movie is ready, it
will be played.

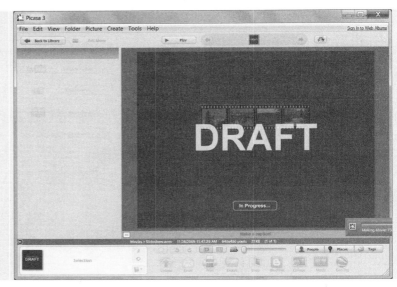

🏹 **Please note:**

> If you have created a gift CD or DVD of this movie, this will not automatically play in *Picasa*. You can only play the movie by opening the *Movies* folder on the CD or DVD, which is located in the (*My*) *Pictures* folder.

If you want to watch the movie in other programs, such as *Windows Media Player*, you will need to export the movie first. In the *Tips* at the end of this chapter you can read how to do this.

You can also burn an exported movie to a CD or DVD and play it on other computers.

6.10 Uploading To YouTube

YouTube is a popular website where you can find a lot of free movies. If you have your own account at *YouTube*, you can upload your own movies as well. This way, family and friends can view your project on the Internet.

**Please note:**

If you do not have a *YouTube* account, click [⬅ Back to Library] and just read the following section. Afterwards you can continue on with the next section.

👆 **Click**

[Upload to YouTube]

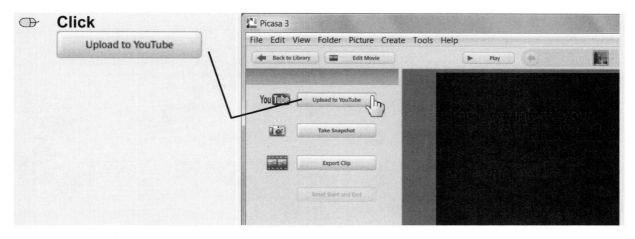

By Title::

⌨ **Type:** Holiday 2009

By Description::

⌨ **Type:** Summer and Winter

👆 **Click**

[--- ▼]

👆 **Click** Travel & Events

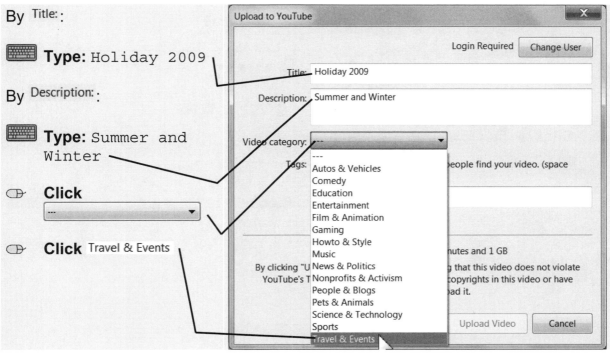

Under Tags: :

⌨ **Type:** Germany

🖱 **Click** Change User

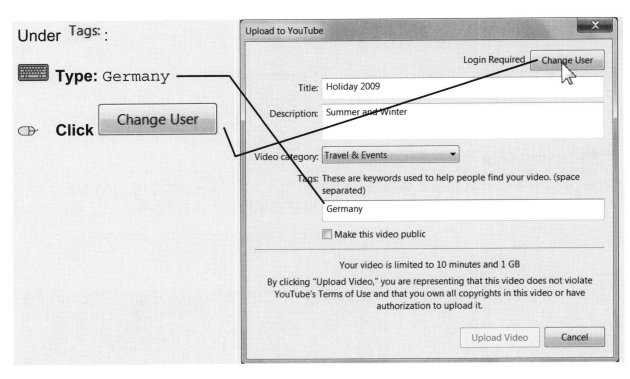

Next to User name: :

⌨ **Type your *YouTube* user name**

Next to Password: :

⌨ **Type your password**

🖱 **Click** Log in

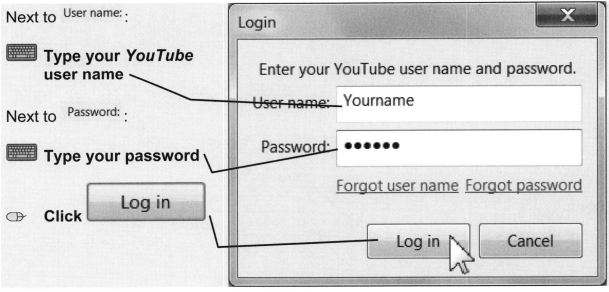

At the bottom of the window:

⬭ **Click** [Upload Video]

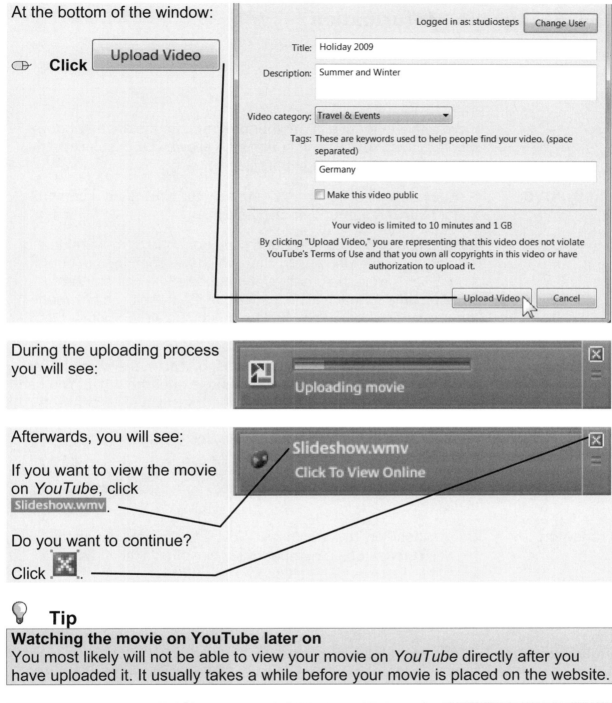

Logged in as: studiosteps [Change User]

Title: Holiday 2009

Description: Summer and Winter

Video category: Travel & Events ▾

Tags: These are keywords used to help people find your video. (space separated)

Germany

☐ Make this video public

Your video is limited to 10 minutes and 1 GB

By clicking "Upload Video," you are representing that this video does not violate YouTube's Terms of Use and that you own all copyrights in this video or have authorization to upload it.

[Upload Video] [Cancel]

During the uploading process you will see:

Uploading movie

Afterwards, you will see:

Slideshow.wmv
Click To View Online

If you want to view the movie on *YouTube*, click `Slideshow.wmv`.

Do you want to continue?

Click ✖.

💡 **Tip**

Watching the movie on YouTube later on
You most likely will not be able to view your movie on *YouTube* directly after you have uploaded it. It usually takes a while before your movie is placed on the website.

☞ **Open the *library* 👣11**

☞ **Close *Picasa* 👣3**

6.11 Background Information

Dictionary	
Export	Save a movie for use in another program, for instance *Windows Media Player*. The *Export* option also allows you to select a different location for the export file.
Gift CD/DVD	A slide show on a CD or DVD, suitable for playing on a computer or TV (with the appropriate DVD player).
Movie	A collection of photos and video clips from one or more folders or albums, possibly also music files, which are combined in one single file. During the creation of the movie you can set the duration time for each slide, as well as the transitions between the slides. Changes in the folders or albums will not affect the movie.
Slide show	A collection of photos and video clips, placed in the same folder or album, which displays the images one after the other. You can set the duration for each slide and the transition style between the slides while the show is playing. If the contents of the folder or album change, the slide show will also change.
Title slide	Usually the first slide in a slide show, displaying the title and date of the show. You can also use a photo as a background to your title slide.
Transition	Determines how to go from one picture to the next during the movie. You can use a number of special effects, such as wipe from left, dissolve, pan and zoom.
Upload	Copy a file from your computer to the Internet, or to another computer.
Video clip	A file that contains animated images and sometimes even sound. Video clips are usually made with a video camera, mobile phone, or webcam, or are downloaded from the Internet.
YouTube	Public website where you need to register first. Afterwards, you can upload your own video clips and display them to others.

Source: Picasa Help

6.12 Tips

 Tip

Taking a snapshot from a video clip
When viewing your video, you can take a snapshot of any individual frame:

To copy the image:

⊕ **Click**

    Take Snapshot

Now the image will be copied:

☞ **Open the** *library* 11

The image has now been stored in the *library*, in the 🖿 Captured Videos project:

⊕ **Click the** 🖿 Captured Videos **project**

Now you will see the captured image:

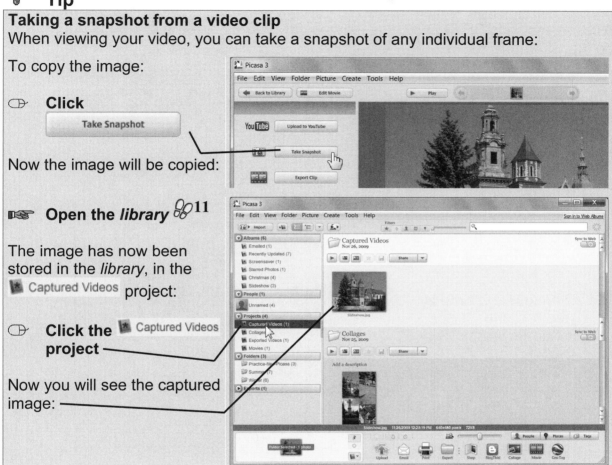

 Tip

Making a movie with a webcam
If you have a webcam, you can directly copy its images to *Picasa*. Here is how you do that:

⊕ **Click**

The webcam images will be stored in the 🖿 Captured Videos project:

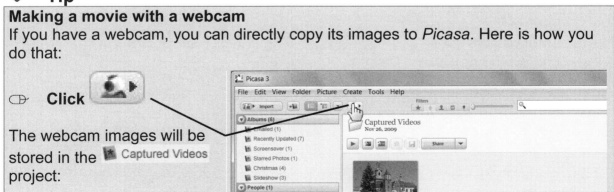

Tip

Exporting a movie
Movies made in *Picasa* can only be viewed in *Picasa*. If you want to view such a movie in other programs, for instance in *Windows Media Player*, or if you want to burn the movie to CD or DVD, you will need to export the movie first. This is how you do that:

☞ **Click the movie**

☞ **Click** File

☞ **Click**
Export Picture to Folder...

⌨ **If necessary, type a folder name**

☞ **Click**
Full movie (no resizing)

At the bottom of the window:

☞ **Click** Export

Now you will see the folder which contains the movie:

☞ **Click** X

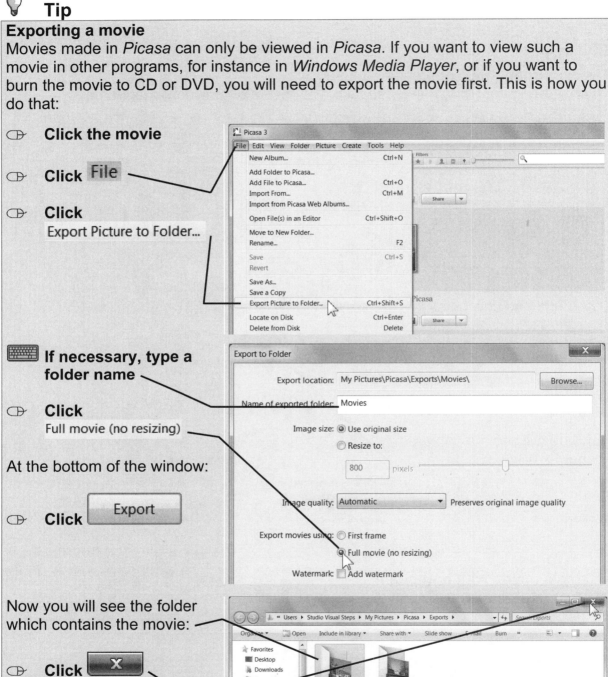

Please note: If you want to burn a *Picasa* movie to a CD or DVD, you need to use a specific burning program, for instance *DVD Maker* or *Nero*.

7. Displaying Your Photos on a Blog

A blog is a special kind of website on the Internet, comparable to a kind of diary. The word 'blog' is a contraction of 'website' and 'log'. A blog is sometimes also called a *blog*. Somebody who maintains a blog is called a *blogger*.

A blog will be updated on a regular basis. Some bloggers add new messages several times a day. Apart from text, you can also add photos, videos, and music to a blog.

In this chapter you will learn how to create a new blog, and how to upload your *Picasa* photos and videos to your blog.

In this chapter you will learn how to:

- create your own blog;
- choose a template for your blog;
- upload photos to your blog.

Please note:

If you want to use the exercises in this chapter, you need to download the *Practice-files-Picasa* folder and save it to the (*My*) *Pictures* folder on your computer. You can read how to do that in *Chapter 1 Installing Picasa*.

Please note:

In this chapter you will only learn the basic operations which will help you publish your *Picasa* photos into your blog. If you want to learn more about using a blog, check out the online Help section of your blog program.
If you want to read more about blogs, you can also read this book: **Google for SENIORS**.

Google for SENIORS
Author: Studio Visual Steps
Nr of pages: 320
Book type: Paperback
ISBN: 978 90 5905 236 9
Website for this book: www.visualsteps.com/google

7.1 Creating a Blog

A blog is a digital diary that you maintain on the Internet. You can also publish your *Picasa* photos and videos to your blog, and thereby share them with others.

First, you need to create a blog, for instance with *Google*. In this section you will learn how to create a *Google* blog. To do this, you need to use the *Blogger* program. If you already have your own *Google* blog, you can continue with *section 7.2 Publishing Photos to a Blog*.

☞ **Open *Picasa* ⁶**

At the bottom of the window:

☞ **Click** BlogThis!

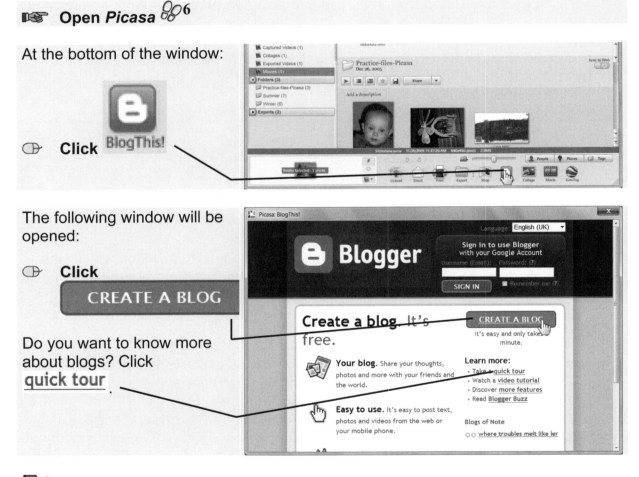

The following window will be opened:

☞ **Click**

   CREATE A BLOG

Do you want to know more about blogs? Click  .

Please note:

To create a blog in *Picasa*, you will need to have a *Google* account. If you do not yet have one, then read *Appendix A Creating a Google account* and learn how to get your own account.

Click <u>sign in first</u>

⌨ **Type your *Google* user name**

⌨ **Type your password**

Click Sign in

⌨ **Type a display name**

☞ **Uncheck the box ☑ next to**
Send me feature announcement

☞ **Check the box ☑ next to**
I accept the **Terms of Service**

☞ **Click** CONTINUE

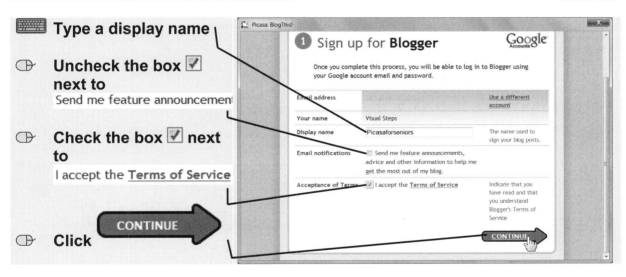

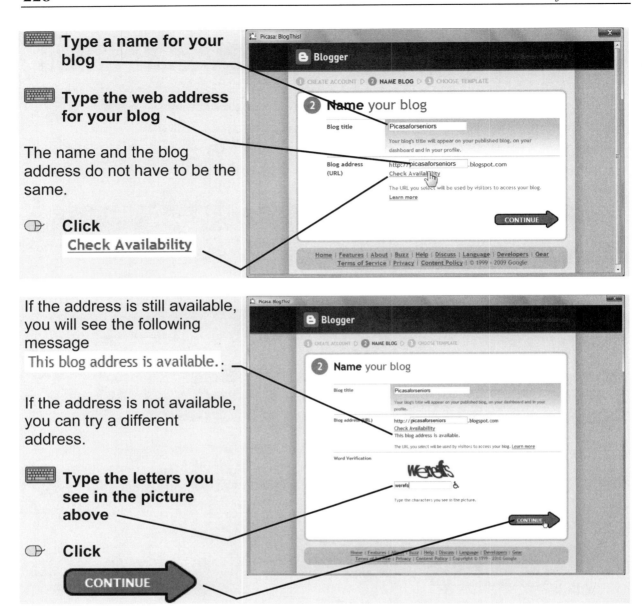

⌨ **Type a name for your blog**

⌨ **Type the web address for your blog**

The name and the blog address do not have to be the same.

☞ **Click**
   Check Availability

If the address is still available, you will see the following message
This blog address is available.

If the address is not available, you can try a different address.

⌨ **Type the letters you see in the picture above**

☞ **Click**
   CONTINUE

☞ **Write down the address of your blog**

In this example the address is: http://picasaforseniors.blogspot.com

You will see various templates that you can use for your blog.

You are now going to take a look at one of these templates:

☞ **Click** *preview template*

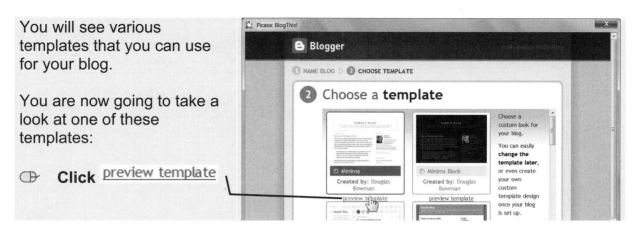

Now a new preview window will open:

☞ **Click** ✖

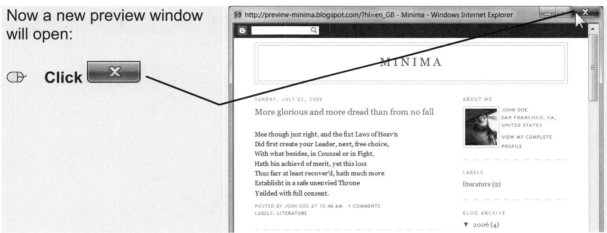

☞ **Click the radio button** ⊙ **next to a template**

☞ **Click**

CONTINUE

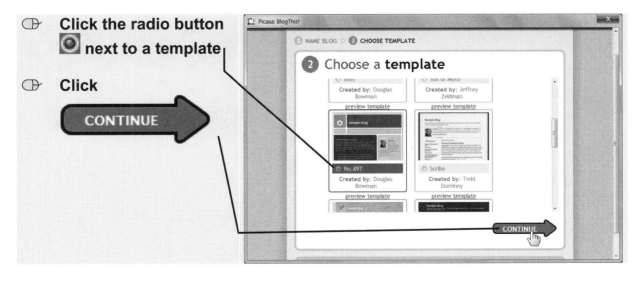

Now you will see a notification that your blog has been created:

⊕ **Click**

START BLOGGING

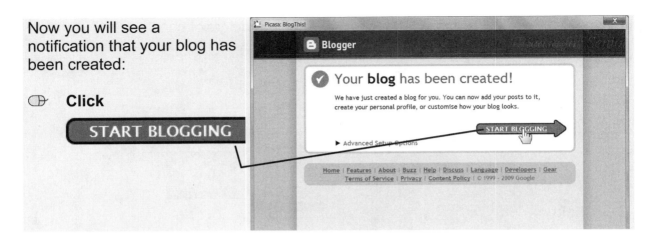

You can now type a message, if you want

⊕ **Click**

PUBLISH POST

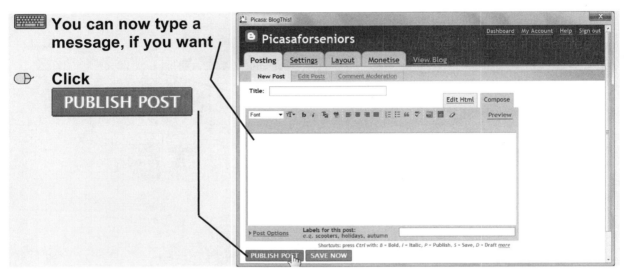

Your message has been published:

⊕ **Click** Sign out

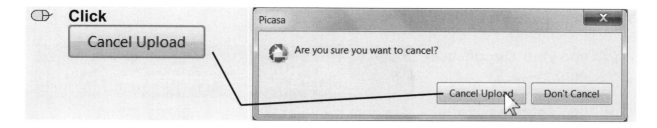

Click Cancel Upload

7.2 Publishing Photos to a Blog

Now your blog is ready to publish your photos. This is how to place your photos on your blog:

☞ **Open the** 📁 Summer **folder** 👣⁴

☞ **Put** City.jpg **in the *Photo Tray*** 👣⁸

☞ **Put** Cathedral.jpg **in the *Photo Tray*** 👣⁸

At the bottom of the window:

☞ **Click** BlogThis!

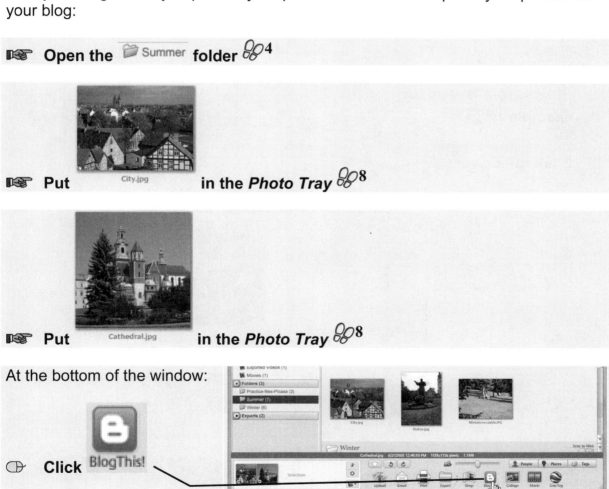

You may need to sign in first. In that case:

Type your *Google* user name

Type your password

Click SIGN IN

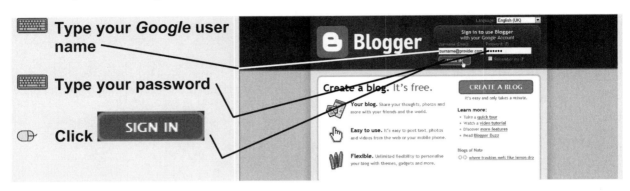

Now you are going to select a layout for your blog:

Click the radio button next to a layout, for example Centre

Click CONTINUE

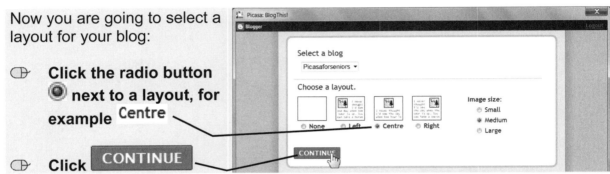

In a little while you will see your photos:

Click PUBLISH POST

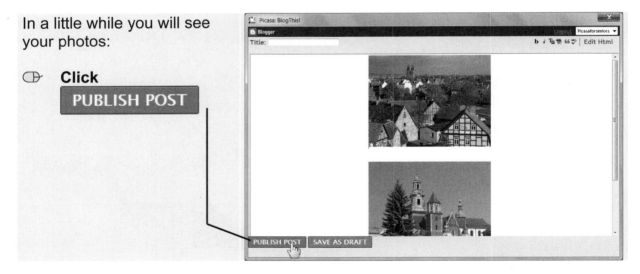

During the publishing process, you will see a progress bar at the bottom right of your window:

Posting...

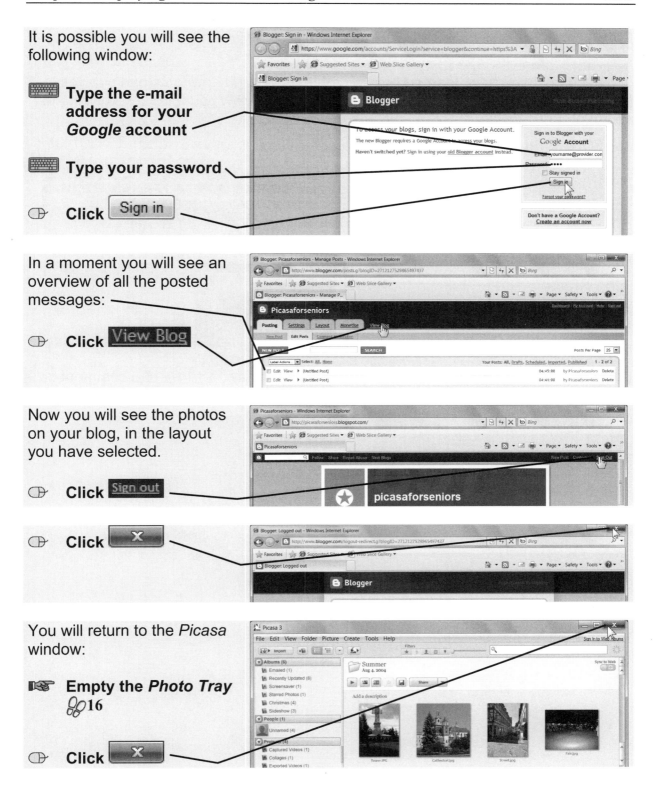

It is possible you will see the following window:

⌨ **Type the e-mail address for your *Google* account**

⌨ **Type your password**

☞ Click `Sign in`

In a moment you will see an overview of all the posted messages:

☞ Click `View Blog`

Now you will see the photos on your blog, in the layout you have selected.

☞ Click `Sign out`

☞ Click `X`

You will return to the *Picasa* window:

☞ **Empty the *Photo Tray* &16**

☞ Click `X`

Tip

Viewing a blog
In this chapter you have learned how to create a blog and how to upload pictures
from *Picasa* to your blog. Other people will be able to view your blog by browsing to
your blog in a browser program such as *Internet Explorer*.

☞ **Open *Internet Explorer***
ᑲᑲ1

⌨ **Type your blog's
address**

Depending on the settings for this blog, your visitors may be allowed to comment on
your stories and photos.

7.3 Background Information

Dictionary

Blog (weblog)	A personal web page that is regularly updated. Blogs are often used to publish personal information in an informal way.
Blogger	Someone who maintains a blog. The *Google* web program is also called *Blogger*. This program allows you to publish your messages on the Internet quickly and easily.
Template	A template is a design which determines the way in which your blog posts will be displayed.
URL	A URL is also called a web address, and designates the location of a web page on the Internet. For example: http://www.visualsteps.com and http://picasa3book.blogspot.com. When you type a URL you do not need to type http:// first. By typing the URL of your blog in their browser, your visitors can view your blog.

Source: Picasa Help

Using Picasa web albums with Blogger

All photos that are uploaded to your blog will automatically be added to a *Picasa* web album with the same name. Each blog that contains photos will have a corresponding online album for these photos. In *Picasa* web albums this will be indicated by a small *Blogger* icon . By default, *Blogger* albums will not be stated, and that is why they cannot be searched on the *Picasa* web albums site. Here are some things you need to keep in mind when you want to integrate the photos on both of these websites:

- All the photos which have been placed on *Blogger*, will be included in the free storage space of 1 GB which is assigned to *Picasa* web albums.
- Remarks and descriptions that are added in one of these programs will only be visible on the related site.
- If you remove photos from your *Blogger* album in *Picasa* web albums, these will be removed from your blog as well.
- If you want to delete a *Blogger* album in *Picasa* web albums, you will need to delete all the photos first.

Please note: if you remove a *Blogger* photo from the *Picasa* web albums, the photo will be removed from your blog as well. If you do it the other way round, the same thing will happen. If you remove a *Blogger* photo, this photo will also be removed from the *Picasa* web albums.

Source: Blogger Help

7.4 Tips

Tip

Publicity for your blog

You do not just maintain a blog for yourself, but for others. If you want to attract visitors, send an e-mail to all your friends, announcing your blog. Make sure to include the web address of your blog page.

8. Getting Started With Your Own Photos

In the previous chapters you have learned how to work with *Picasa*. If you have followed all the steps from the beginning, you will have used the sample photos from the practice files that go with this book. You have created a new *Windows* user account to work with these files.

By now you will be experienced enough to start working with your own photos, in your own *Windows* user account.

When you start editing your own photo collection, it is recommended to follow a standard procedure when adding new photos to your *Picasa* collection, either from your camera or from other sources.

In this chapter you will find:

- a description of the things you can do after you have worked through this book;
- an action plan for working with your own photos in *Picasa*.

8.1 Delete Your New Windows User Account

If you have followed all the steps from the beginning of this book, you will have used the sample photos from the practice files that go with this book. First, you will have created a new *Windows* user account. After you have finished working through this book, you will no longer need to use the new user account, and you can delete it. If you are still logged in to the new *Windows* user account:

☞ **Log off from the *Windows* account and log in with your regular *Windows* user account** $\mathscr{GG}$22

☞ **Delete the new *Windows* user account**

In *Appendix D Creating a New User Account* you can read how to delete an existing user account.

8.2 Getting Started With Your Own Photos

Now you are going to work in your own *Windows* user account, with your own photos.

☞ **Open *Picasa*** $\mathscr{GG}$6

Now you can get *Picasa* to scan your own folders on your computer's hard drive.

☞ **Scan the folders you want to include in *Picasa* (see page 38)**

You will also see the window of the *Picasa Photo Viewer*.

☞ **Adjust the settings for the *Picasa Photo Viewer* (see page 31)**

If you have a lot of photos saved on your computer's hard drive, it will take *Picasa* some time to scan all the photos.
After the scanning process has finished, you can use *Picasa* to organize your photo collection or enhance your photos, if necessary. You can also use the action plan in the next section to process the existing photo collection on your computer, starting with Step 2.

If you have a large photo collection, this may take a while. But once you have organized all your photos, you will be able to you retrieve your pictures much easier and faster later on.

8.3 Action Plan

When you have made a series of photos with your camera and you want to add these photos to *Picasa*, it is recommended to follow a fixed procedure. In this section you will learn which steps you need to follow.

Step 1 Connect the camera to the computer and import the photos in Picasa
On page 71 you can find more information on this operation.
It is advisable to store your photos in the folders according to a standard system. Try to think of a system that is useful for your own collection. For example, you can create a folder for each year. This way, retrieving your photos will be easy.
You can also decide to save your photos according to their subject. For instance, by creating a *Holidays* folder, with various subfolders.
Do not forget to clear your camera's memory card after you have imported the photos. **Please note:** make sure that the date and time settings of your digital camera are correct. Otherwise the chronological order of the photos in *Picasa* will be wrong as well.

Step 2 Assess the imported photos
While using your digital camera, you often shoot vast quantities of photos. Now is the time to decide which pictures you want to save. It is best to view the pictures full screen, this way you will get a better look at them.
This is how you do it in a *library* folder:

☞ **Place the mouse pointer on a photo**

⌨ **Press the** `Ctrl` **and** `Alt` **key combination**

Now you will see the photo full screen.
As soon as you release the keys, you will see the small icons again.

Do you dislike a specific photo? Then you can move this photo to a separate folder. This is how you do it:

☞ **Right-click the photo**

Now you will see a menu:

☞ **Click** Move to New Folder...

⌨ **Type a name for the folder, for example:** Delete

☞ **Click** OK

Now the photo will be moved to the new *Delete* subfolder. This subfolder is located in the same folder as the original photo. You will see this subfolder appear in *Picasa* as well. All subsequent photos you want to move can also be dragged to this subfolder. After you have viewed all the photos, you can take a last look at the photos in the *Delete* subfolder, and restore some of the photos to their original location, if you want.

Afterwards you can delete the entire subfolder. If you have second thoughts about deleting some of the photos, you can always retrieve them from the *Windows Recycle Bin* later on.

Step 3 Edit your photos, if necessary
Now you are going to enhance the photos you want to keep. For instance, by cropping them, adjusting the colors, straightening, etcetera. In this stage you can also add descriptions and stars to the photos (see *Chapter 3 Basic Operations*).

Step 4 Change the order of the photos in the folder and rename the photos
If you want to view the photos in a specific folder as a slide show, you need to organize them in a logical way. Drag the photos in the folder and sort them in the right way. Afterwards you can use the *Batch edit* option to rename all the photos at once, and give them a new number (see page 81).

Step 5 Create albums
In this stage the photos have been selected, edited and renamed. Now you can start creating your albums (see *Chapter 2 The Library*).

Step 6 Saving and making backups
This is the moment to decide if you want to store the edited photos on your computer's hard drive (see *section 4.4 Saving Edited Photos*) and make an additional backup (see *section 4.7 Making Backups*).

It is good practice to make regular backups of your photo collection, and save these backups away from your computer. A good time for making a backup would be right after you have imported and edited a new series of photos.

Step 7 Share your photos
Finally, you can share your photos with others, for instance on your web album or by creating a gift CD or DVD (see *section 5.4 Creating a Web Album* and *section 6.2 Creating a Gift CD or DVD*).

If you consistently follow this action plan, you will maintain a well organized photo collection on your computer. This way, viewing and retrieving your photos will be much easier.

8.4 Visual Steps Website and Newsletter

So you have noticed that the Visual Steps-method is a great method to gather knowledge quickly and efficiently. All the books published by Visual Steps have been written according to this method. There are quite a lot of books available, on different subjects. For instance about *Windows*, photo editing, and about free programs, such as *Google Earth* and *Skype*.

Book + software
One of the Visual Steps books includes a CD with the program that is discussed. The full version of this high quality, easy-to-use software is included. You can recognize this Visual Steps book with enclosed CD by this logo on the book cover:

Website
Use the blue *Catalog* button on the **www.visualsteps.com** website to read an extensive description of all available Visual Steps titles, including the full table of contents and part of a chapter (as a PDF file). In this way you can find out if the book is what you expected.

This instructive website also contains:
• free computer booklets and informative guides (PDF files) on a range of subjects;
• free computer tips, described according to the Visual Steps method;
• a large number of frequently asked questions and their answers;
• information on the free Computer certificate you can obtain on the online test website **www.ccforseniors.com**;
• free 'Notify me' e-mail service: receive an e-mail when book of interest are published.

Visual Steps Newsletter
Do you want to keep yourself informed of all Visual Steps publications? Then subscribe (no strings attached) to the free Visual Steps Newsletter, which is sent by e-mail.

This Newsletter is issued once a month and provides you with information on:
• the latest titles, as well as older books;
• special offers and discounts;
• new, free computer booklets and guides.

As a subscriber to the Visual Steps Newsletter you have direct access to the free booklets and guides, at **www.visualsteps.com/info_downloads**

Notes

Write your notes down here.

Appendix A. Creating a Google Account

To use many of the additional options in *Google* programs you will need to have a *Google* account. A *Google* account is free. Here is how you create a new account:

☞ **Open *Internet Explorer*** 👣¹

☞ **Open the www.google.com webpage** 👣²

Now you will see the *Google* website:

At the top right-hand corner of the window:

⊕ **Click** Sign in

⊕ **Click** **Create an account now**

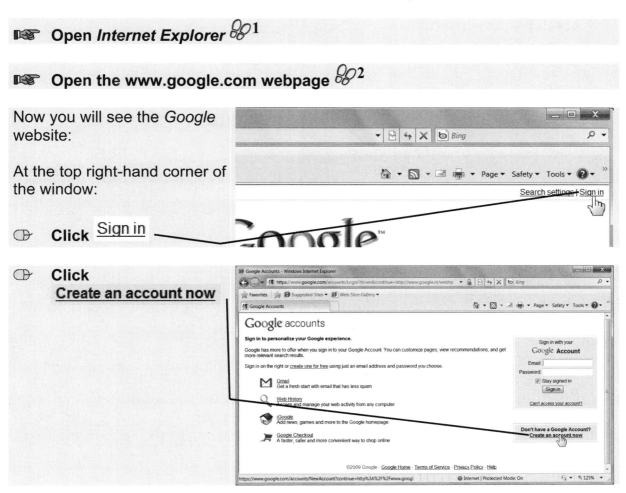

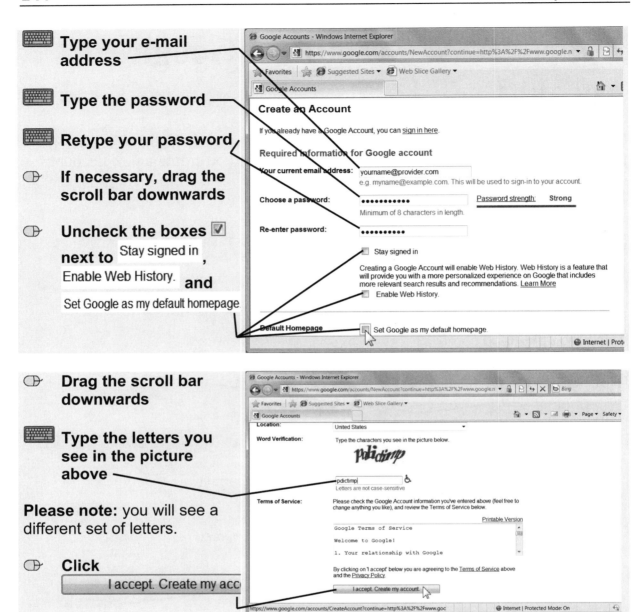

Type your e-mail address

Type the password

Retype your password

If necessary, drag the scroll bar downwards

Uncheck the boxes ☑ **next to** Stay signed in ,
Enable Web History. **and**
Set Google as my default homepage.

Drag the scroll bar downwards

Type the letters you see in the picture above

Please note: you will see a different set of letters.

Click I accept. Create my acc

Now you will see this message:

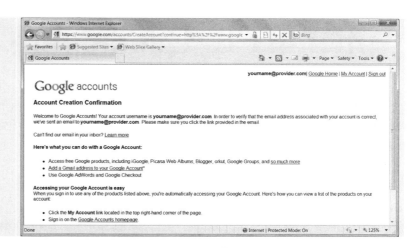

☞ **Open your e-mail program** 🐾²⁴

☞ **Open the** ✉ **accounts-noreply@google.com** .. **message** 🐾²⁵

👆 **Click the**

http://www.google.com/accounts/VE?c=CIaD_dvJ_fKw9QEQqOeFoMmosbvoAQ&hl=en

link in the message

☞ **Close the window** 🐾³

☞ **Close your e-mail program** 🐾³

Your account information has been verified. Now you can use your *Google* account.

☞ **Close** *Internet Explorer* 🐾³

Appendix B. Geotagging Photos

If *Google Earth* is installed on your computer, you can link your photos to the geographical location where the photos were taken (*geotagging*). The GPS location will be included in the photo file, and the photo will be displayed on the *Google Earth* satellite map.

 Tip

Installing and using Google Earth
Do you want to use *Google Earth*, but do not yet have the program installed on your computer? In this book you can learn how to install and use the program:

Interesting Online Applications for SENIORS
Author: Studio Visual Steps
Nr of Pages: 392
Book type: Paperback
ISBN: 978 90 5905 285 7
Website for this book: www.visualsteps.com/online

This is how you geotag a picture:

☞ **Open *Picasa* ⚹⚹6**

☞ **Put the photo(s) you want to geotag in the *Photo Tray* ⚹⚹8**

👆 **Click** Geo-Tag

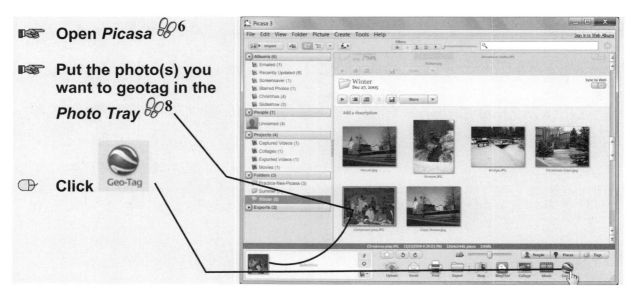

Google Earth will be opened:

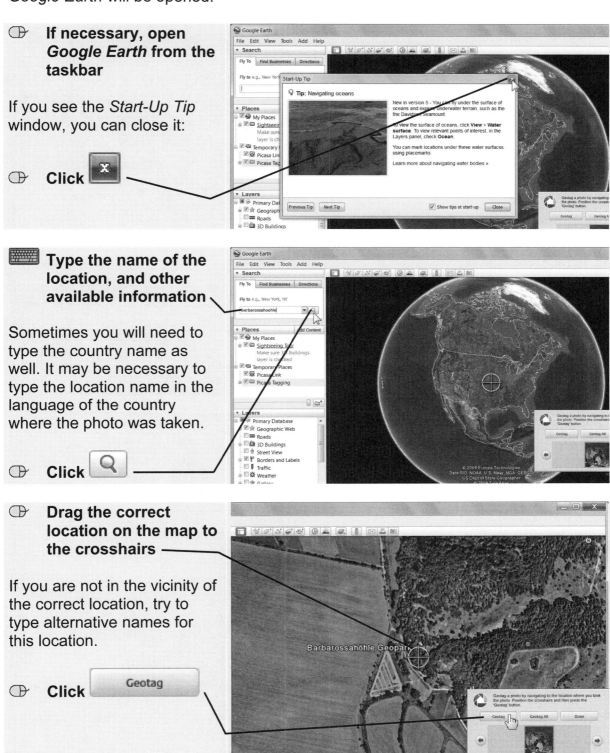

⊕ **If necessary, open *Google Earth* from the taskbar**

If you see the *Start-Up Tip* window, you can close it:

⊕ **Click** [✕]

⌨ **Type the name of the location, and other available information**

Sometimes you will need to type the country name as well. It may be necessary to type the location name in the language of the country where the photo was taken.

⊕ **Click** [🔍]

⊕ **Drag the correct location on the map to the crosshairs**

If you are not in the vicinity of the correct location, try to type alternative names for this location.

⊕ **Click** [Geotag]

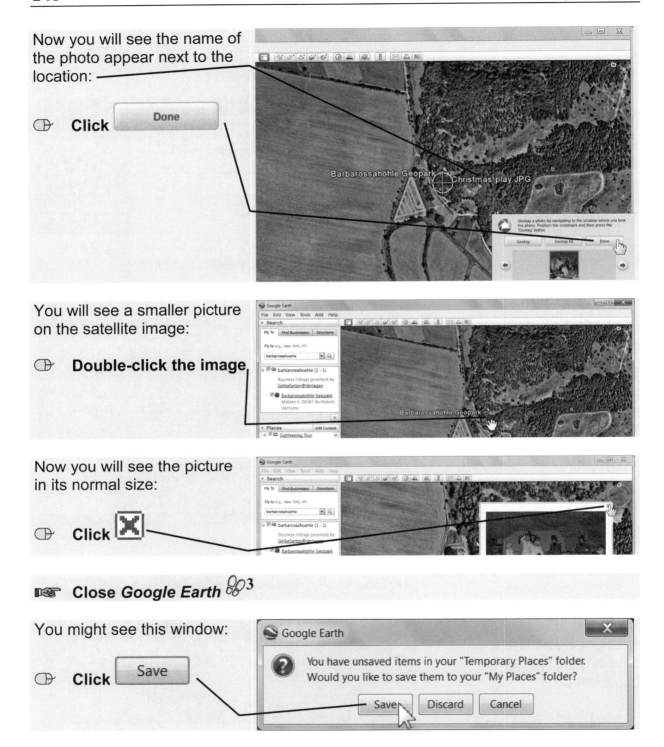

Now you will see the name of the photo appear next to the location: —

Click [Done]

You will see a smaller picture on the satellite image:

Double-click the image

Now you will see the picture in its normal size:

Click ❎

☞ **Close** *Google Earth* 🐾³

You might see this window:

Click [Save]

You have unsaved items in your "Temporary Places" folder. Would you like to save them to your "My Places" folder?

[Save] [Discard] [Cancel]

Now you will again see the *Picasa* window. At the bottom right of the photo you will now see the 🖼 icon.

☞ **Close** *Picasa* 🐾³

Appendix C. Removing Picasa

If you are encountering problems when using *Picasa*, many times the best thing to do is to remove *Picasa* from your computer, and then re-install the program again. If you remove *Picasa*, your photos will remain stored on your computer's hard drive and you can choose what to do with the edited photos.

This is how you remove *Picasa*:

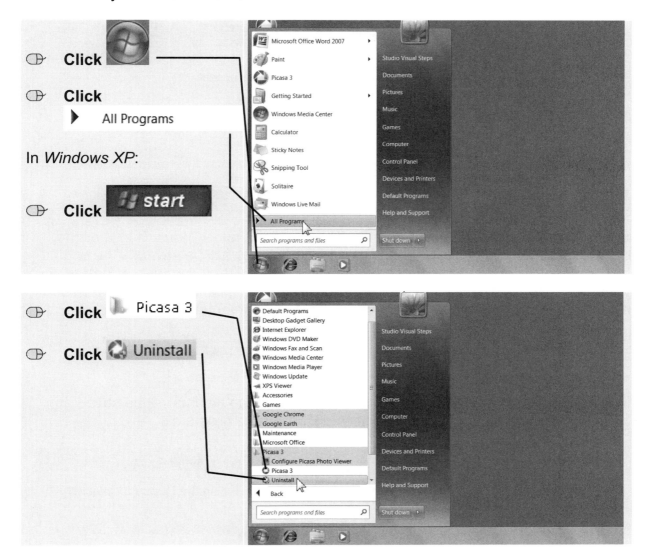

Click

Click
▶ All Programs

In *Windows XP*:

Click start

Click Picasa 3

Click Uninstall

If you are asked to confirm this operation:

Click Yes or Continue

At the bottom of the window:

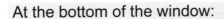

⊕ **Click**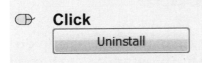

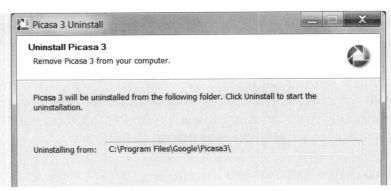

Please note: first read the following information, before you decide what to do.

⊕ **Click** 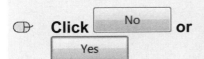 **or**

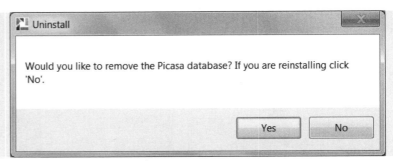

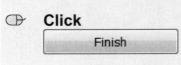 **Please note:**

Select [Yes] if you want to remove *Picasa* permanently. You will lose all the edits, as well as your albums. However, your photos will still be saved in the original location on your computer's hard drive and you can use them in other programs. If your photos are not displayed or located correctly in *Picasa*, it may be necessary to rebuild the *Picasa* database. In that case you need to remove *Picasa* and click

[Yes] as well. If you re-install *Picasa* afterwards, the photo files will be scanned and processed all over again.

If you select [No], the database, the edits, and the albums will be saved. Select this option if you just want to re-install the *Picasa* program.

At the bottom of the window:

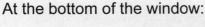

⊕ **Click**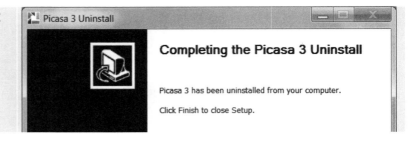

Appendix D. Creating a New User Account

To make sure that you see the same windows and images as in this book, it is recommended that you create a new *Windows* user account. This is how you do it:

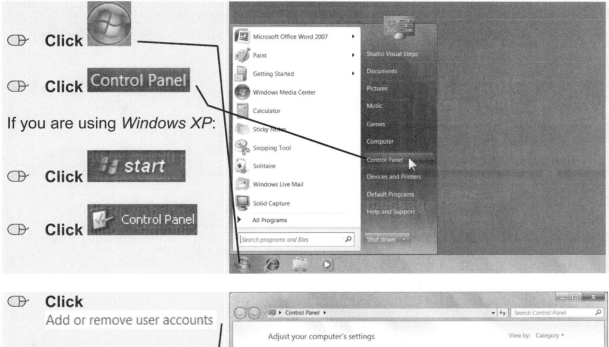

☞ **Click**

☞ **Click** Control Panel

If you are using *Windows XP*:

☞ **Click** start

☞ **Click** Control Panel

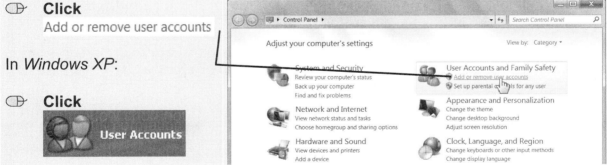

☞ **Click**
Add or remove user accounts

In *Windows XP*:

☞ **Click** User Accounts

If you are using *Windows Vista* or *Windows 7*, your screen will now turn dark and you will see the *User Account Control* window. Here you will be asked to give permission to continue.

☞ **Click** Yes **or** Continue

At the bottom left of the window:

⊕ **Click** Create a new account

In *Windows XP*:

⊕ **Click** → Create a new account

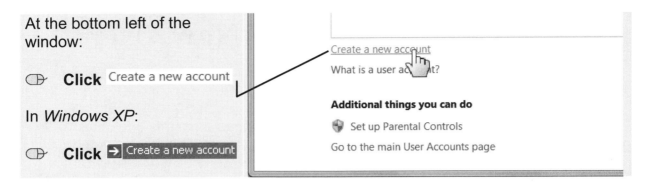

In the next window you can enter a user name and select an account type for the new user account. You are going to select an Administrator account:

⌨ **Type a name in this box, for example:**
Laura

⊕ **Click** Administrator

In *Windows XP*:

⊕ **Click** Next >

⊕ **Click the radio button**
⊙ **next to**
Computer administrator

⊕ **Click** Create Account

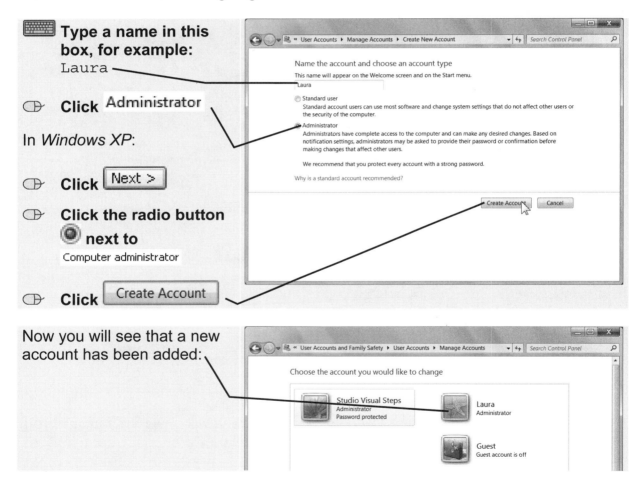

Now you will see that a new account has been added:

You can use this new user account to work through the exercises in this book.

Delete the New User Account

When you have finished reading this book, you can start working with your own photo collection, in your own *Windows* account. Then you can remove the new *Windows* user account. This is how you do it:

☞ **If necessary, log off first and log in again with your regular *Windows* user account** ℘*22*

 Please note:

You can only remove the new account from your regular *Windows* user account.

☞ **Open the *Manage Accounts* window** ℘*23*

☞ **Click the new user account**

☞ **Click** Delete the account

Windows will now ask you what to do with the files this user has created. You can choose to save all the files in the (*My*) *Documents*, *Favorites*, *Music*, *Pictures*, and *Videos* folders, and the files on the desktop as well. Or you can decide to delete them all. If you decide to save these files, they will be placed on your desktop. Here you will find a folder which is named after the deleted user. This folder will contain all the user's files.

In this case you are going to delete the files:

☞ **Click** Delete Files

☞ **Click** Delete Account

Now the new *Windows* user account has been deleted.

Appendix E. How Do I Do That Again?

In this book you will find many exercises that are marked with footsteps. 🐾x
Find the corresponding number in the appendix below to see how to do something.

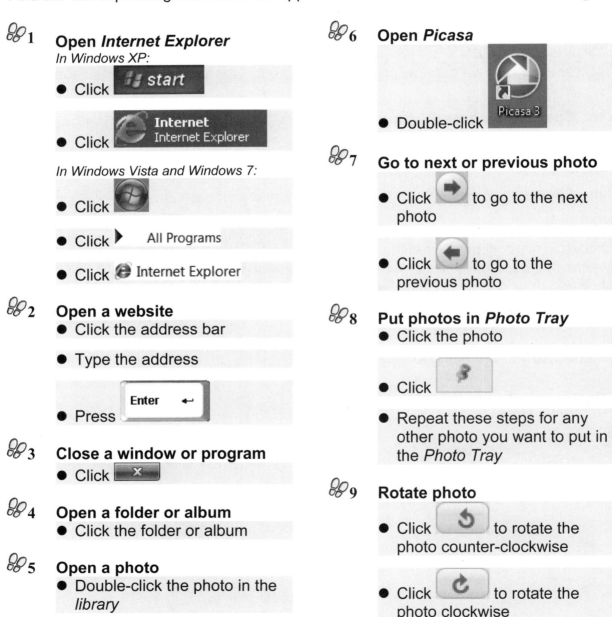

🐾1 **Open *Internet Explorer***
In Windows XP:
- Click start
- Click **Internet** Internet Explorer

In Windows Vista and Windows 7:
- Click
- Click ▶ All Programs
- Click Internet Explorer

🐾2 **Open a website**
- Click the address bar
- Type the address
- Press Enter ↵

🐾3 **Close a window or program**
- Click X

🐾4 **Open a folder or album**
- Click the folder or album

🐾5 **Open a photo**
- Double-click the photo in the *library*

🐾6 **Open *Picasa***
- Double-click Picasa 3

🐾7 **Go to next or previous photo**
- Click ➡ to go to the next photo
- Click ⬅ to go to the previous photo

🐾8 **Put photos in *Photo Tray***
- Click the photo
- Click
- Repeat these steps for any other photo you want to put in the *Photo Tray*

🐾9 **Rotate photo**
- Click ↺ to rotate the photo counter-clockwise
- Click ↻ to rotate the photo clockwise

10 **Set effects**
- Click Effects
- Click the desired effect

11 **Open the *library***
- Click ← Back to Library

12 **Disable scanning of folders**
- Click Tools
- Click Folder Manager...
- Click the desired folder
- Click ✖ Remove from Picasa
- Click OK

13 **Add tag to a photo**
- Click the photo
- Click Tags
- Type a text
- Click +
- Repeat this if you want to add multiple tags to the photo
- Click ⊗

14 **Find photo**
- Click the search box
- Type a keyword.

To view all photos:
- Click ✖

15 **Select multiple photos**
- Click the first photo
- Keep Ctrl pressed down
- Click the next photo
- Repeat this until you have selected all the photos
- Release Ctrl

16 **Empty *Photo Tray***
- Click O
- Click Yes

17 **Place photos in album**
- Put the photos in the *Photo Tray*
- Click ▾
- Click the album

18 **Play slide show**
- Click ▶

19 **Close slide show**
- Press Esc

20 **Stop playing movie**
- Click ‖

21 **Replay movie**
- Click ▶

22 Log off and log on to your regular user account

In Windows XP:

- Click

- Click

- Click

- Click your regular *Windows* account

In Windows Vista:

- Click

- Next to  click

- Click

- Click your regular *Windows* account

In Windows 7:

- Click

- Next to  click

- Click Log off

- Click your regular *Windows* account

23 Open the *User Accounts* window

In Windows XP:

- Click

- Click

- Click

In Windows Vista:

- Click

- Click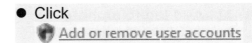

- Click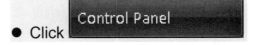
  Add or remove user accounts

Your screen goes dark:

- Click Continue

In Windows 7:

- Click

- Click  Control Panel

- Click
  Add or remove user accounts

24 Open e-mail program

In Windows XP:

- Click

- Click

- Click

In Windows Vista:

- Click

- Click **E-mail** Windows Mail

In Windows 7:

- Click

- Click All Programs

- Click  Windows Live

- Click Windows Live Mail

25 Open e-mail message

- Double-click the message

Appendix F. Index

Microsoft Office 2007 for Independent Contractors and Freelancers

Microsoft Office 2007 for Independent Contractors and Freelancers
Practical Office Solutions for the self-employed and freelancer

Author: Studio Visual Steps
ISBN: 978 90 5905 295 6
Book type: Paperback
Nr of pages: 408 pages
Accompanying website:
www.visualsteps.com/office2007freelance

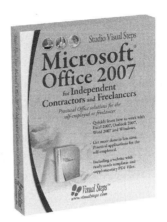

A practical guide for the fast-growing segment of freelancers and independent contractors. Written especially for those who are looking for efficient solutions for everyday tasks such as creating estimates, offers, invoices or budgets and for the easy creation of business cards, brochures, newsletters and company presentations. No time to take a course in business administration? Work instead through this Visual Steps book at home and in your own tempo! Do the chapters that specifically apply to your business. As you follow each step, the results appear directly on your computer screen. In a few short hours you can complete an entire course. You will end up with a series of useful documents that can be directly applied to your business.

Characteristics of this book:
- practical, useful topics
- geared towards the needs of the self-employed, independent contractor or freelancer
- clear instructions that anyone can follow
- handy, ready-made templates available on this website

Topics covered in this book:
- **Excel 2007:** estimates, quotes, invoices, projects, schedules, mileage tracking
- **Word 2007:** letterhead, newsletters and mailing labels
- **Publisher 2007:** business cards, brochures, websites
- **PowerPoint 2007:** company presentations
- **Outlook 2007:** customer, vendor and contact information, organize and archive mail
- **Business Contact Manager 2007:** project administration, manage leads and prospects
- **Windows Vista and XP:** computer maintenance, back-ups and security

Windows Vista and Internet for CHILDREN

Windows Vista and Internet for children
For anyone 9 years old and up

Author: Studio Visual Steps
ISBN: 978 90 5905 056 3
Book type: Paperback
Nr of pages: 208 pages
Accompanying website:
www.studiovisualsteps.com/vista

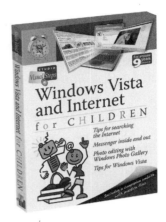

Do your (grand)children chat or mail with friends? Do they know how to use a chat program inside and out? This book will not only show them how to safely use Messenger but lots of other things too. Such as how to best find information on the Internet for their homework assignments. How to make their own e-mail address and do a video chat. How to organize files and folders and how to keep the desktop tidy. And what is really fun, is learning how to use Windows Photo Gallery to edit their own photos.
All of the exercises in this book can be done on their own computer. Everything is clearly explained step by step and each step includes a full color picture. You can get started right away!

In this book children will learn how to:
- mail with Windows Mail and Windows Live Hotmail
- chat with Windows Live Messenger
- do a video chat
- edit photos in Windows Photo Gallery
- search for information on the Internet
- create and open folders
- move, search and delete files
- customize your desktop
- change the color of your windows
- add a gadget to Windows Sidebar

For parents, teachers and caregivers
All Visual Steps books are written following a step by step method. They are designed as self-study guides for individual use. They are also well-suited for use in a group or classroom setting. More information for parent, teachers and caregivers can be found at the companion website for this book: www.studiovisualsteps.com/vista